SERIES

Work Out

Computer Studies

'O' Level and GCSE

The titles
in this
series

MACMILLAN
MASTER
SERIES

Work Out

Computer Studies

'O' Level and GCSE

G. Taylor

MACMILLAN

First published 1986

Published by
MACMILLAN EDUCATION LTD
Houndmills, Basingstoke, Hampshire RG21 2XS
and London
Companies and representatives
throughout the world

Typeset and Illustrated by TecSet Ltd
Sutton, Surrey
Printed at The Bath Press, Avon

British Library Cataloguing in Publication Data
Taylor, G.
Work out computer studies. — (Macmillan work
out series) – (Macmillan master series)
1. Electronic data processing — Examinations,
questions, etc.
I. Title
001.64'076   QA76.28
ISBN 0-333-39660-X

To Naomi

Contents

Acknowledgements

The author and publishers wish to thank the following who have kindly given permission for the use of copyright material:

The Associated Examining Board, the Southern Universities' Joint Board, the University of London School Examinations Board and the University of Oxford Delegacy of Local Examinations for questions from past examination papers.

The Economist Newspaper Limited for extract from *The Economist Science Brief*, 22 August 1981 issue.

The Trustee Savings Bank (TSB England & Wales) for reproduction of a TSB cheque.

Every effort has been made to trace all the copyright holders but if any have been inadvertently overlooked the publishers will be pleased to make the necessary arrangement at the first opportunity.

Thanks to John Muir and Ray Webster, lecturers at Ealing College of Higher Education, for letting me use their exercises and hand-outs.

Help on business computer systems was given by Malcolm Moran (Wang Systems), Alan Weaver (*The Economist*) and Mike Crane (Nixdorf Computers).

I am also indebted to Jane Coton, Pam Bancroft, Anne Spinoza and Shirley Hunt for the word processing.

The University of London Entrance and School Examinations Council accepts no responsibility whatsoever for the accuracy or method in the answers given in this book to actual questions set by the London Board.

Acknowledgement is made to the Southern Universities' Joint Board for School Examinations for permission to use questions taken from their past papers but the Board is in no way responsible for answers that may be provided and they are solely the responsibility of the authors.

The Associated Examining Board, the University of Oxford Delegacy of Local Examinations, the Northern Ireland Schools Examination Council and the Scottish Examination Board wish to point out that worked examples included in the text are entirely the responsibility of the author and have neither been provided nor approved by the Board.

Groups Responsible for Examinations at 16+

In the United Kingdom, GCSE examinations are administered by six groups of examination boards. Syllabuses and examination papers for each group can be ordered from the addresses given here.

Northern Examining Association

Joint Matriculation Board
   Publications available from:
John Sherratt and Son Ltd
78 Park Road, Altrincham
Cheshire WA14 5QQ   (JMB)
**Yorkshire and Humberside
   Regional Exam Board**
Scarsdale House
136 Derbyside Lane
Sheffield S8 8SE
North West Regional Exam Board
Orbit House, Albert Street
Eccles, Manchester M30 0WL

Northern Regional Exam Board
Wheatfield Road, Westerhope
Newcastle upon Tyne NE5 5JZ

**Associated Lancashire School Exam
   Board**
12 Harter Street
Manchester M1 6HL

Midland Examining Group

**University of Cambridge Local
   Examinations Syndicate**
Syndicate Buildings, Hills Road
Cambridge CB1 2EU   (UCLES)
Southern Universities Joint Board
Cotham Road
Bristol BS6 6DD   (SUJB)

West Midlands Regional Exam Board
Norfolk House, Smallbrook
Queensway, Birmingham B5 4NJ

**Oxford and Cambridge Schools
   Examination Board**
10 Trumpington Street
Cambridge CB2 1QB
East Midlands Regional Exam Board
Robins Wood House,
Robins Wood Road, Aspley
Nottingham NG8 3NR

London and East Anglian Group

**University of London School
   Examination Board**
University of London Publication Office
52 Gordon Square, London
WC1E 6EE   (L)
East Anglian Regional Exam Board
The Lindens, Lexden Road
Colchester, Essex CO3 3RL

London Regional Exam Board
Lyon House
104 Wandsworth High Street
London SW18 4LF

Southern Examining Group

The Associated Examining Board
Stag Hill House
Guildford, Surrey GU2 5XJ   (AEB)

Southern Regional Examining Board
Avondale House, 33 Carlton Crescent
Southampton, Hants SO9 4YL

University of Oxford Delegacy of
**   Local Examinations**
Ewert Place
Summertown, Oxford
OX2 7BZ   (OLE)
South-Western Regional Examining
**   Board**
23–29 Marsh Street
Bristol BS1 4BP

Scottish Examination Board

    Publications available from:
Robert Gibson & Sons (Glasgow) Ltd
17 Fitzroy Place, Glasgow G3 7SF   (SEB)

Welsh Joint Education Committee
245 Western Avenue
Cardiff CF5 2YX   (WJEC)

Northern Ireland Schools Examination
**   Council**
Examinations Office
Beechill House, Beechill Road
Belfast BT8 4RS   (NISEC)

10/9/86

Introduction

How to Use this Book

The overall purpose of the book is to help you pass the Computer Studies examination at the GCSE/O level.

Each chapter contains:

- A brief review of the key points for a given topic.
- Worked examples of typical examination questions.
- Questions for you to work out.
- Answers and hints on solutions.

The book is not intended to replace completely a 'solid' textook, although the essential material is reviewed at the beginning of each chapter.

Recent developments in the subject and areas where existing textbooks are inadequate are dealt with in more detail so that the reader has a solid foundation on which to build.

The worked examples are intended to show you how to answer actual or typical exam questions. Where appropriate, the fully fledged answers will be supported by hints and guidelines to show how to tackle the problem and how to avoid pitfalls.

Questions are also provided for you to work out for yourself and answers are given at the end of each chapter. Answers are in outline only where it is obvious what the question demands or where a worked example can be found in the text. It is important that you should try out these exercises for yourself before looking up the answers.

Revision

The following hints will help you to organize your revision in such a way that it becomes enjoyable and highly productive:

1. Obtain an examination syllabus and recent past examination papers. These can usually be ordered from the examination boards whose addresses are given on page viii. Be aware of any recent changes in the structure and syllabus of the examination.
2. Make sure that all your course notes are complete and then gradually summarize them until you have headlines of the main points, which should act as prompts to trigger off your memory.
3. Work out a programme of revision and stick to it.
4. Revise the course topic by topic. The chapter headings and their order given in the contents of this book will be helpful.
5. Work through past examination papers under exam conditions by giving yourself a time limit and not looking at your notes.

The Examination

1. Get to the examination venue in good time.
2. Read the instructions at the top of the examination paper carefully. You should be aware of the format of the exam paper from having worked through previous ones. Where you have a choice of questions tick the ones you will attempt.
3. Follow any advice given on how long to spend on each section.
4. Read the questions carefully, and where you have a choice, tick the ones you will attempt.
5. As a general rule, begin by answering any compulsory question(s) and then answer the questions in the order you find easiest.
6. If you do run out of time towards the end of the examination, answer questions in note form. You will not be given full marks but you will gain some.

In Computer Studies you must cope with the following types of question.

(a) Short-Answer Questions

Questions (usually compulsory) on a wide variety of topics which require short note answers. This demands a comprehensive, if fairly basic, knowledge of most topics. Together these questions can make up about 50% of the total.

(b) Exercises

Exercises on specific areas – for example software or computer applications – make up the other half of the marks. Clearly your knowledge should be more detailed here as each question can be worth 15–25%.

(c) Case Studies

Some examination boards issue a case study (usually about one page long) in advance of the examination. Study it thoroughly and predict what questions might be asked about it.

Practical Assessment

During your course you will be assessed according to your mastery of a number of skills and most examination boards also require you to submit project or coursework which accounts for up to 30% of the marks that go towards your final grade. Chapter 14 gives you plenty of practical help in planning and doing your coursework.

1 Introduction to Computers

1.1 Introduction

Computers are essential tools in most walks of life. This chapter is designed to cover some of the basic questions in computer studies. It is divided into the following sections:

- What is a computer?
- The elements of a computer system — the general nature and functions of each component.
- Types of computer.
- Analog and digital data.
- An example program and flowchart which help to show how a computer 'works'.
- Some advantages and disadvantages of computers.

1.2 Worked Examples — Some Basic Concepts

Example 1.1

Q. What is a computer?

Solution 1.1

A. A computer is a device or set of devices which work under the control of a stored program (which can be changed), automatically accepting and processing data to produce information.

So a computer is:

- *Automatic*   — It carries out instructions with minimum human intervention.
- *Reprogrammable* — It stores instructions (the program). These can be changed and another task performed.
- *A data processor* — It carries out operations on data (numbers or words) made up of a combination of digits to produce information.

Example 1.2

Distinguish between information and data.

Solution 1.2

Data is the name given to facts which must be in the special form, often in code, whilst being used by the computer.

Information is meaningful data which is relevant, accurate and up to date and can be used to take actions or make decisions.

Although a computer processes data, it doesn't 'think' for itself or understand it. If the data used by the computer is wrong (garbage in) the result it produces will be wrong (garbage out).

Example 1.3

Q. What are the elements of a computer system?

Solution 1.3

A. The essential elements (Fig. 1.1) are:

1. *INPUT*   – To read incoming data.
2. *PROCESS* – To perform arithmetic operations, comparisons, data transfer.
3. *STORE*   – To file data for future use.
4. *OUTPUT*   – To produce outgoing information.

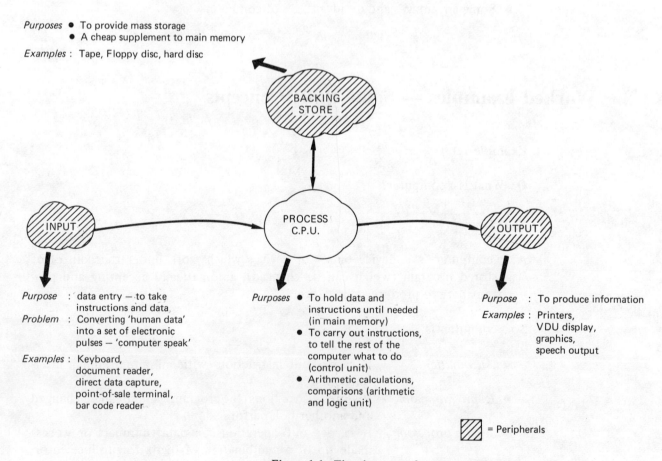

Purposes ● To provide mass storage
          ● A cheap supplement to main memory

Examples : Tape, Floppy disc, hard disc

BACKING STORE

PROCESS C.P.U.

INPUT

OUTPUT

Purpose : data entry – to take instructions and data

Problem : Converting 'human data' into a set of electronic pulses – 'computer speak'

Examples : Keyboard, document reader, direct data capture, point-of-sale terminal, bar code reader

Purposes ● To hold data and instructions until needed (in main memory)
● To carry out instructions, to tell the rest of the computer what to do (control unit)
● Arithmetic calculations, comparisons (arithmetic and logic unit)

Purpose : To produce information

Examples : Printers, VDU display, graphics, speech output

= Peripherals

Figure 1.1 The elements of a computer system.

4

Example 1.4

Define: computer system; hardware; program; software.

Solution 1.4

A computer system is a series of devices which are capable of doing 1–4 above. Collectively this equipment is called *hardware*.

Computers carry out instructions – a set of which is called a *program* which will be written in a *computer language*. A program controls the computer by telling the computer's control unit what to do.

Software is the general term to describe all the programs used in a computer system.

Example 1.5

Outline the basic ways of inputting data to a computer.

Solution 1.5

INPUT (data capture) – The purpose of the INPUT unit is to take in data and instructions. There is a basic problem of entering human data (which can be slow) and then converting it into a coded set of electronic pulses that the machine can understand.

Examples of input devices – There are three basic categories of data capture device: keyboard entry, document reading and direct data capture.

KEYBOARD ENTRY

There are two basic types of keyboard device:

- A *terminal* with visual display unit (screen) and typewriter-style keyboard for on-line (direct) input to the computer.
- A teletype (writer) similar to an electric typewriter (with paper instead of a screen).

DOCUMENT READING

A machine 'reads' source documents (e.g. customer orders), sensing special marks or characters by magnetic/optical reading techniques.

DIRECT DATA CAPTURE

This is an attempt to combine data creation with data entry, i.e. data is captured at source in 'machine-sensible' form; e.g. point-of-sale terminals (POS), voice data entry(VDE).

(a) Store

Many applications, particularly in business, involve storing large amounts of data for future use. Records have to be kept in order to keep accounts, prepare bills, send out reminder notices, etc.

Large stores of information (called databanks) are common: e.g. catalogues, order books, directories, ledgers. These, and similar stores of information, are often kept on computer.

Example 1.6

Q. What are the general considerations of data storage?

Solution 1.6

A. The general considerations are:

- *Storage capacity* – The number of characters stored.
- *Access* – How quickly can you get hold of the data? This depends on: the mode (serial, direct) and speed.
- *Costs* – Relative costs of types of computer storage: tape *versus* floppy disc *versus* hard disc.
- *Robustness* – Durability and susceptibility to corruption/breakdown.

Example 1.7

Distinguish between main memory and backing store.

Solution 1.7

(i) Main storage (or memory)

This holds *current* data and instruction that are being worked upon. This is why it is sometimes called working store. Memory size is measured in k bytes, where K $\simeq$ 1000 and 8 bits = 1 byte;
e.g. 64 K $\simeq$ 64000 bytes of data, 1 Mb $\simeq$ 1 million bytes.

(ii) Backing storage

This is a cheap supplement to main store to meet the mass storage requirements of business. Data and/or programs can be called in when necessary (cf. a filing cabinet in a manual system).

There are basically two types of backing store:

1. *Magnetic disk* – which provides direct access, i.e. you can go directly to the data that you want (cf. placing your record-player needle on your favourite music track).
   Hard disks are more expensive, faster, more reliable and have bigger capacity – typically storing 2–40 Mb.
   Floppy disks are very cheap, not so sobust and can store up to about 1 Mb.
   Discs are popular – 90% of backing store in business is disc.
2. *Tape* provides serial access (cf. finding a track on your music tape cassette). It is often used as 'back-up' for security copies of files, etc. or as an archiving medium – to hold historical records.

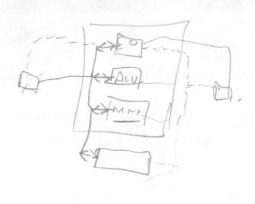

(b) Process

Example 1.8

What does the CPU do?

Solution 1.8

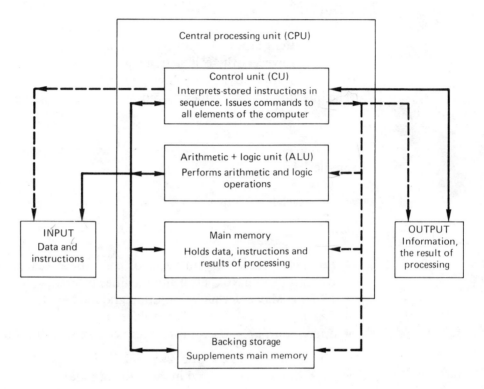

Figure 1.2 The central processing unit (CPU). ↔ = Data/instruction flow (two way); − − → = command/signals (one way), control links. Devices outside the CPU are sometimes known as peripherals.

The purpose of the *Central Processing Unit* (or CPU; Fig. 1.2) is to:

- Carry out instructions and tell the rest of the computer system what to do. This is done by the *control unit* (CU) of the CPU which sends command signals to the other components of the system.
- Perform arithmetic calculations and data manipulation, e.g. comparisons, sorting, combining, etc. The computer's calculator is a part of the CPU known as the *Arithmetic and Logic Unit (ALU)*.
- Hold data and instructions which are in current use. These are kept in the *main store* or *memory*.

Example 1.9

Q. What are semi-conductor processors and memories?

Solution 1.9

A. The basic components of a CPU are very similar. They are made up of complex circuits manufactured on *semi-conductor* materials such as a tiny thin wafer of silicon crystal called a *'silicon chip'*. A semi-conductor allows an electrical current to pass through, but at the same time the current can be precisely controlled.

The main features of semi-conductor devices within the CPU are that they are:

- Wholly electronic and therefore fast and reliable.
- Highly miniaturized and therefore cheap to produce.

(c) Output

At present the output of information is usually on *paper*: as a document, letter or report. However, there is a trend towards the *screen display* of output on a VDU and it is now possible to show pictures and diagrams as well as words.

The question is really: does output have to be *permanent and on paper*?

Example 1.10

Give some examples of output devices.

Solution 1.10

- *Printers* — These vary in terms of cost, speed (character, line, page) quality of print (dot-matrix, etc.) and facilities offered.
- *VDUs* — May offer high-resolution graphic facilities.
- *Graph plotters* — Useful for engineering and design.
- *Speech output* — Useful for announcements, instructions, etc.

It is important to know the use and limitations of input/output and storage devices. These will be covered in more detail in later chapters.

(i) Data Transmission

We can take output one step further because information can be sent from one computer to a completely different place if the need arises.

This data transmission uses *telecommunications* facilities to link computers with terminals or other computers. This link can be two-way.
Systems can be:

- Private, e.g. Rumbelows shop group, where computing equipment is directly connected so that no dialling is necessary.
or
- Public, e.g. British Telecom's (BT's) Gold system, where messages can be sent over the public telephone network.

Example 1.11

Q. What are networks?

Solution 1.11

A. Many systems have computers at both ends of the telecom link and several computers can be interconnected to form a *network*.

These networks may be:

- *Local* – perhaps within one office block. These are called LANs (Local Area Networks).
- *National* – e.g. via Teletext, which provides high-quality text communication via several networks.
- *International* – e.g. via BT's Satstream, the international small-dish satellite service offered by BT International.

Example 1.12

Q. What is information technology (IT)?

Solution 1.12

A. IT is the combination of computing and telecommunications to obtain, process, store, transmit and output information in the form of voice, pictures, words and numbers.

The facility to send and receive data-pictures, words, etc. to and from different locations has important implications.

For example, IT is useful for:

- Message-switching: 'electronic mail'.
- Information retrieval, e.g. BT's Prestel Viewdata system

Example 1.13

Explain what you mean by the term 'Input–process–output procedure'

Solution 1.13

An example of a data-processing system.

Processing of input data to give output information is what computing is all about. Fig. 1.3 shows a data-processing system using a simple payroll example.

(d) Types of Computer (Fig. 1.4)

Example 1.14

Distinguish between mainframe, mini and microcomputers. Give a suitable example of each.

Solution 1.4

   (i) *Mainframes*

These are large, powerful and expensive general-purpose computers with a range of powerful input/output, processing and storage facilities. They usually cost over £100 000.

Examples: IBM 370, ICL 2900.

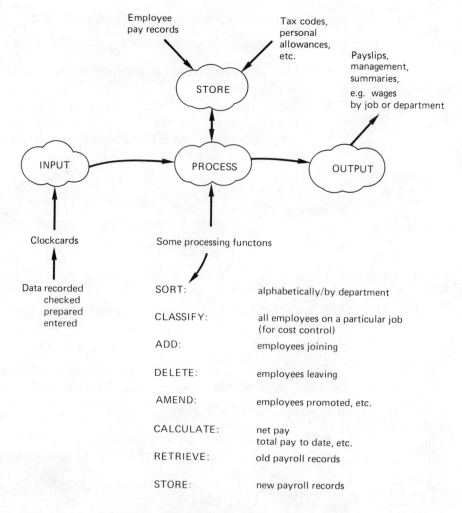

Figure 1.3 Payroll example.

(ii)   *Mini computers (minis)*

These are smaller versions of the mainframes. A typical mini-system might support several terminals with multi-tasking (several different jobs can apparently be done at once), a few printers and a backing store of 10Mb on hard disk. Prices typically range between £20 000 and £1000 000.

Examples: Prime 750, VAX

(iii)   *Microcomputers (micros)*

Microcomputers are small, cheap, relatively slow and have limited memory. A microcomputer's CPU is a microprocessor which is an integrated circuit containing the control unit, the arithmetic and logic unit and usually some memory. Modern large-scale integrated (LSI) technology has allowed all of these components to fit on to a single small chip.

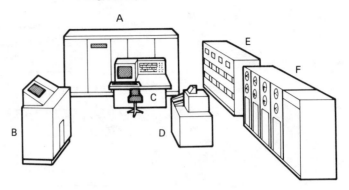

(a)
A . Central processing unit and internal storage
B . High speed printer
C . Operator console
D . Card reader
E . Magnetic disc drives
F . Magnetic tape drives

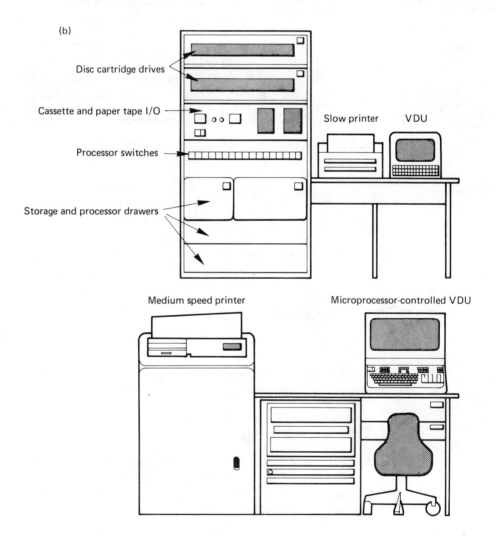

Figure 1.4 Mainframe (*a*), minicomputers (*b*) and microcomputers (*c*). Source: Wright, G. *Mastering Computers.*

(c)

Figure 1.4 (continued)

Microcomputers are, therefore, microprocessor-based systems which are often small enough to be moveable and can be divided into three categories:

(iv) *Small-business Micros*

These are useful for routine business functions and particularly one-off jobs – Visicalc, etc. A typical small-business micro system might include four workstations, a printer and a floppy-disc drive. Prices begin at around £2000.
  Examples: IBM PC, HP 150, Apple Macintosh.

(v) *Personal Micros*

These are usually cheaper (between circa £100–£400) than the small-business ones, tend to be stand-alone and offer limited system software. A cassette tape is the usual form of backing store because the recorder is so cheap.
  Examples: Sinclair QL, BBC Model B.

(vi) *Portable Micros*

Micros are now available which are small and light enough to carry around. They are especially useful to people on the move, e.g. travelling sales people.

There are areas of overlap between the three types of computer. It seems also that computers will continue to get cheaper in real terms and be able to do more as each new 'generation' of computers is developed.

(e) Note

Computers can be bought or leased and computer time can be rented. Thus to use a computer you don't necessarily have to own it.

(f) Analog and Digital

Example 1.15

Explain the differences between analog and digitial data.

Solution 1.15

An analog device measures a *continuous* physical quantity (e.g. your temperature from a thermometer). Numbers are represented by strengths of electric currents (e.g. temperature, pressure). A *digital* device counts individual (separate, discrete) things (e.g. taking a person's pulse) in a binary (two-stage) form, i.e. numbers and letters are represented as digits in some code. Virtually all computers are digital; most of the course (and syllabus) is about them.

When a digital computer is required to process data from an analog device, the data must be *converted* into digital form. This is called an analog-to-digital converter (ADC).Conversion the other way requires a digital-to-analog convertor (DAC).

If a message is sent from one computer to another via analog telephone lines a *modem* is needed at each end of the line to convert the digital data to analog, for transmission, and back again to digital to be read by the receiving computer.

(g) Process Control

Example 1.16

Q. What is Process Control?

Solution 1.16

A.Computers are often designed for *process control* without the need for people. This comprises monitoring the process and taking corrective action when necessary. Applications include chemical and oil refining, parts of steel production and load control at electricity power stations.

Example 1.17

The manufacturing process of a compound chemical is monitored by a computer which constantly measures (samples) the chemical to ensure that it contains the right amounts of each ingredient so that it meets all the health and safety regulations necessary before it is put on the market.

If the difference in the amount required for a particular ingredient exceeds 5% and is less than or equal to 10%, a signal is sent by the computer to increase or decrease its rate of flow. If the variance exceeds 10% it is considered that the process should be halted and the valves, etc. checked.

Draw a flowchart to depict the above process.

Solution 1.17

See Fig. 1.5. For more information on flowchart symbols see section 9.3(c).

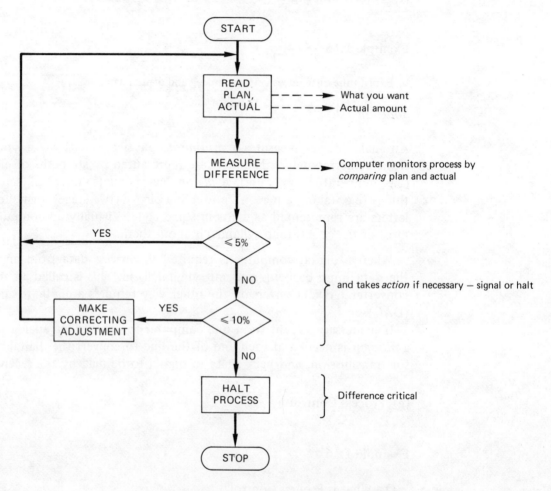

Figure 1.5 Flowchart of a monitoring procedure.

(h) A simple example to show how a computer operates

Example 1.18

(i) *Problem*

Draw up a flowchart and trace table and write a program to find the average of a set of positive numbers.

Solution 1.18

This involves:

- Adding the numbers together (sum).
- Keeping a counter (the number of numbers).
- Dividing the sum by the count.

(ii) *Program*

To find the average of a set of numbers. Write down the solution as a list of instructions.

1. Start with everything at zero.
2. Input a number (terminator (rogue value) is -1).
3. If the number just input is the rogue value, go to instruction 7.
4. Add the number to the sum.
5. Add 1 to the count.
6. Go to instruction 2.
7. Calculate the mean by dividing the sum by the count.
8. Print the mean.
9. Stop.

(iii) *Data*

Here is the data to be used by the program:

   10, 20, 30, -1

This set of instructions has to be expressed in the computer's own language (see BASIC program). The program can be put into the computer and stored in main memory. Once the program is *loaded* the computer can carry out the instructions in sequence when told to do so (usually by the command RUN).

   To develop a program it is useful to draw a flowchart of the problem (see Fig. 1.6).

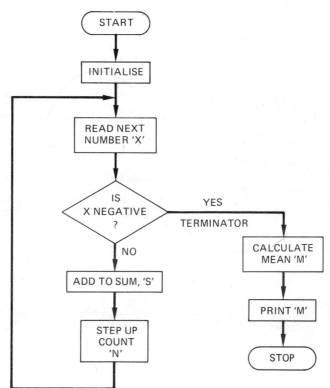

Figure 1.6 Flowchart to find the average of a set of positive numbers.

Program in BASIC:

Program in BASIC :

```
10 REM Calculate mean

20 REM Set values to 0 (clear the decks!)
21 LET X=0          where:X is a number
22 LET S=0                S is the sum
23 LET M=0                M is the mean (average)
24 LET N=0                N is the count

30 REM Read,test,sum,count
31 READ X                 Read a number
32 IF X<0 THEN 40         If the number is negative then goto 40
33 LET S=S+X              Accumulator, adds the number to the sum to
                          give the running total
34 LET N=N+1              Add 1 to the count
35 GOTO 31

40 REM Terminator

50 REM Calculate mean,print
51 LET M=S/N              Divide sum by count
52 PRINT 'THE MEAN =':M Print the result

60 STOP

90 DATA 10,20,30,-1       Data;note that -1 is the rogue value to
                          indicate the end of data (the terminator)
```

(iv) *Trace Table*

Before trying the program on a computer, try to predict what will happen by producing a *trace table* (Table 1.1).

Table 1.1   Trace table

PROGRAM LINE NUMBER		STORES				OUTPUT
		X	S	M	N	
21-24	Initialize	0	0	0	0	
31		10	0	0	0	
33	First Loop	10	10	0	0	
34		10	10	0	1	
	After three Loops	30	60	0	3	
	Final Loop	-1	60	20	3	20
60	Stop					

This table is called a *trace table* because it traces the sequence in which program instructions are carried out and what the data values are at each stage.

Producing a trace table is also part of what is known as a '*dry run*' or *desk check* and can help to check that the program is correct.

Example 1.19

List the advantages and disadvantages of computers.

Solution 1.19

ADVANTAGES

Computers are in demand because they are:

- *Cheap* – Cost effective. Cost – performance ratios are improving all the time, i.e. computers continue to fall in price (at least in real terms) at the same time as their capabilities improve.
- *Reliable* – The computer itself has no moving parts.
- *Accurate* – Computers don't make mistakes. (Humans do!)
- *Quick* – Information can be speedily produced which is up to date and therefore useful.
- *Capable* of processing large volumes of data.
- *Useful* for routine operations, e.g. payroll.
- *Useful* for an enormous range of tasks, given the appropriate programs and terminals.

DISADVANTAGES

- *Dependency* – What happens if the system fails? There is a need for adequate back-up facilities (stand-by equipment, etc.) and contingency plans have to be made to cope with any problems.
- *Security and control* – Another problem is that of ensuring proper control over the use of the computer.
  An organization must protect itself against:
  · the malicious abuse of equipment;
  · fraud;
  · errors and accidental mistakes.
  Security and control procedures must be built into computer systems to ensure accuracy and reliability.
- *Fear and resentment* – People, rightly or wrongly, are worried about computers and their impact on jobs and work practices. Careful planning, consultation and retraining/redeployment will help to promote the need for and introduction of new computer systems.

1.3   Exercises

Question 1.1

(a) Give two advantages and two disadvantages of using a computer.

(b) Define: computer; program; information technology; hardware; software; semiconductor; network.

(c) List any *three*: input devices; output devices.

Question 1.2

Distinguish between main frame, mini- and microcomputer. Give a suitable application for each.

Question 1.3

Explain briefly what you understand by the terms:
Input – process – store – output procedure.
Process control.
Data and information.

Question 1.4

Fig. 1.7 shows the main parts of a computer system. Using – – – for control and ———
for data flow, draw in all the necessary connections, indicating with arrows the direction of
flow.

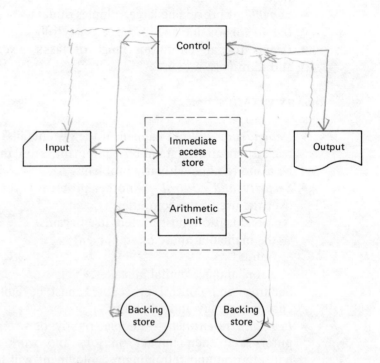

Figure 1.7 Main parts of a computer system.

Question 1.5

(a) Explain how the nature of the information given by a cash register differs from the
information given by a mercury thermometer.

(b) Give a practical application in which an analog-to-digital converter might be used,
explaining why such a device would be chosen.

Question 1.6

Choose two of the following and explain one way in which their work could be assisted by
the use of a computer.

(i) A civil engineer designing a motorway bridge.
(ii) A weather forecaster.
(iii) A bank cashier.
(iv) Police attending an accident involving a lorry carrying a poisonous substance.

Question 1.7

'The advent of chip technology and microprocessor systems has brought the world of computers nearer to the man in the street.'
Discuss this statement with reference to the size, availability and cost of computers, their usage and other relevant information.

Question 1.8

A small business is planning to install a microcomputer system. Give some applications for which the computer might be used. State three advantages to the firm of this computerisation.

1.4 Answers and Hints on Solutions

Answers 1.1–1.4 – see text.
1.5 (a) ● A cash register produces digital information – 1p, 10p etc.
     ● A mercury thermometer produces analog information – temperature is a continuous measurement.

(b) An analog-to-digital converter (ADC) converts data from an analog device into digital form. A practical application is a direct current voltmeter which will have an ADC to convert an unknown voltage into digital form.

1.6 (i) *Civil Engineer*

A computer can be used to provide a model of a situation (e.g. the motorway bridge and various wind speeds or traffic levels) in order to learn, test ideas or predict the effects of introducing changes. *Simulation* can save on real-life tests which are time consuming, expensive and often dangerous.

(ii) *Weather forecaster*

Nowadays weather forecasts are much more accurate than they used to be (in spite of what you might think!). This is due mainly to the use of computers which can process vast amounts of data quickly. Data on temperature, pressure, windspeed and direction, rainfall, cloud cover, etc., is collected from a large number of observation sites and weather satellites. This data is sorted and matched with historic data and is used to make predictions. Computer output forms the basis of the weather forecast.

(iii) *Bank cashier*

A bank cashier could use a VDU terminal linked on-line to a bank's computer to check on account details on a customer's behalf.

(iv) *Police*

Police attending an accident could call the Police National Computer which contains, amongst other things, information on stolen and suspect vehicles, names of vehicles owners, names of people who are banned from driving, etc. This would help them identify vehicle ownership and contact could be made to

find out further details about the poison so that the correct precautionary actions could be taken.
1.7

CHIP TECHNOLOGY

An integrated circuit consists of a number of transistors, and the connections between them, printed on to the surface of a small piece of semi-conductor material, usually silicon, about ¼″ square – the 'chip'. Each integrated circuit is usually encased in a rectangular plastic package with pins to connect it to other circuits. Connections are usually made by soldering the pins into holes on printed circuit boards.

MICROPROCESSOR SYSTEMS

A microprocessor is an integrated circuit which contains a 'computer', i.e. the control unit, the arithmetic and logic unit and usually some memory. Modern large-scale integrated (LSI) technology has allowed all these components to be fitted on to a single chip.

USAGE – 'CHIPS WITH EVERYTHING'

Microprocessor systems can be found in many everyday items such as: digital clocks and watches, calculators, cars, domestic appliances – ovens, washing machines, vacuum cleaners – cameras and microcomputers. They can monitor and control the use of such equipment – e.g. to control wash, rinse and spin in an automatic washing machine. The widespread use of microprocessors is due to several factors. They are:

- Wholly electronic and therefore fast and reliable.
- Cheap – the high-volume production of chips for mass-markets means that each chip costs only a few pence to make (economies of scale).
- Highly miniaturized – so tiny chips can fit easily and inconspicuously into many devices, including computers to control processes, etc.

THE COST, SIZE AND AVAILABILITY OF COMPUTERS

Cost – Microcomputers are now so cheap (starting at about £40.00) that they are affordable for home and leisure use. A typical small business computer system, including a printer and disc drive, only costs the equivalent of a secretary's salary for 6 months.

Size – Within practical limits (keyboard size, etc.) computers are getting smaller. There are now portable micros and hand-held terminals (with limited keyboards) on the market.

Availability – Computers are readily available and now sell direct from the manufacturer, through mail order, specialist stores or general retail outlets. There are a wide range and variety of microcomputers for sale, typical of a highly competitive market.

OTHER RELEVANT INFORMATION

Because of the rapid advances in chip technology it seems that computers will continue to get:

- Cheaper, smaller and more powerful.
- Easier to use (e.g. touch-screen, mouse-control).
- More and better software.
- More applications (e.g. speech/music output).

This means that more people will use computers directly or indirectly.

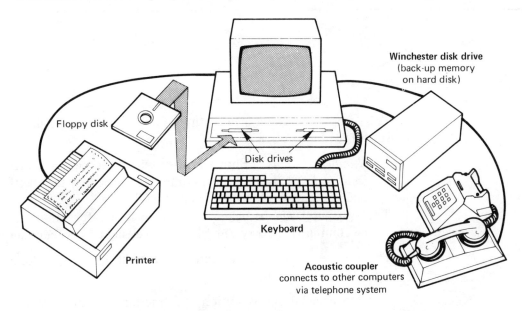

Figure 1.8 A small business microcomputer system.

1.8 A typical microcomputer system in a small business is shown in Fig. 1.8. It consists of:

- A microcomputer.
- A disk drive (or drives) — for direct access backing store. A Winchester disk drive is needed if hard disk is used as well as floppy disks.
- Floppy discs — to store data and programs.
- A printer — for printed output.
- A cheap modem (e.g. acoustic coupler) to link with other computers.

Applications in a small business are typically:

- *Accounting* — Payroll, ledgers-sales, purchasing, invoicing, etc.
- *Financial modelling* — Budgetary forecasting and control; use of 'spread-sheet' packages.
- *Word processing* — The production of business correspondence, e.g. standard letters.
- *Data management* — Keeping up-to-date files on the computer. Facilities to insert/delete/amend/update, e.g. customer records.

Three advantages:

- *Accuracy* — e.g. invoices are correctly calculated.
- *Speed* — e.g. final accounts can be produced very quickly (they may take several days to prepare manually).
- *Cost effective* — A computer-based system should be cheaper than a manual equivalent in terms of labour costs and stationery (that this is not always true is because of poor planning).

2 Representing Data

2.1 Introduction

This chapter is concerned with the representation of data inside a computer. It is divided into three sections:

1. *Number systems* – Shows how numbers can be manipulated by a computer.
2. *Data codes* – Shows how a computer, using just the digits 0 and 1, can store and manipulate characters, including text.
3. *Logic gates and truth tables* – Shows how a few simple logical processes can be combined to carry out all the processing tasks of a computer.

These three sections cover important areas in your examination and you are expected to be able to:

- Do calculations (addition, subtraction and occasionally multiplication) in various bases e.g. binary, hex.
- Understand the need for and nature of data codes.
- Draw up or interpret simple combinations of logic gates and truth tables (not all Examination boards).

2.2 Representing Numbers

The storage and processing elements of a computer are two-state (or *bistable*) electronic devices. They are used in computers because they are quick, reliable and take up only small amounts of space and energy. For this reason the base two or binary number system which uses the two digits 0 and 1 (for off and on) is most suited to computers. The binary digits are known as *BITS*.

We count in the *base* (or *radix*) 10.

Tens	Units
1	3
+	9
2	2

This simple example illustrates the most important feature of a number system: that the *value* of a figure depends on its *position or place*.

For example, the decimal number 267 really means:

$$267 = (2 \times 10^2) + (6 \times 10^1) + (7 \times 10^0)$$

(a) Binary numbers

In contrast, the binary number system has only two digits, 0 or 1, and the place values are units, 2's, 4's, 8's, 16's and so on.

e.g. $0101_2 = 0 \times 2^3 + 1 \times 2^2 + 0 \times 2^1 + 1 \times 2^0$

$= 0 + 4 + 0 + 1$

$= 5_{10}$ (subscript denotes base, i.e. 10)

A decimal number may be represented in a computer by using two-state devices (such as semi-conductors) to represent its binary equivalent. For example, the decimal number 25 could be:

Device	○	●	●	○	○	●
Position	2^5	2^4	2^3	2^2	2^1	2^0
Value	(32)	(16)	(8)	(4)	(2)	(1)

Code: ● device 'on' (1 bit)

○ device 'off' (0 bit)

(i) Conversion from Decimal to Binary

This can be done by successive divisions by 2, recording the remainder of each division.

e.g. 67_{10}

$67 \div 2 = 33$ remainder 1

$33 \div 2 = 16$ remainder 1

$16 \div 2 = 8$ remainder 0

$8 \div 2 = 4$ remainder 0

$4 \div 2 = 2$ remainder 0

$2 \div 2 = 1$ remainder 0

$1 \div 2 = 0$ remainder 1

$\therefore 67_{10} = 1\ 0\ 0\ 0\ 0\ 1\ 1_2$

(b) Octal Numbers

Octal is often used as shorthand for binary. Octal numbers are in base 8. There are eight symbols in this system (0–7) and place values increase in powers of 8.

(i) Conversions

1 *Decimal to Octal*

e.g. 69_{10}

$69 \div 8 = 8$ remainder 5

$8 \div 8 = 1$ remainder 0

$1 \div 8 = 0$ remainder 1

$\therefore 69_{10} = 1\ 0\ 5_8$

2 Octal to Decimal

e.g. 114_8

Place values	8^2 (64)	8^1 (8)	8^0 (1)
Octal number Conversion	1 (1 x 64)	1 + (1 x 8)	4 + (4 x 1) = 76_{10}

3 Conversions between Octal and Binary

This is fairly straightforward because 8 is the cube of 2; just remember the binary equivalents for the eight octal symbols.

Conversion table

Octal	0	1	2	3	4	5	6	7
Binary	000	001	010	011	100	101	110	111

Convert 74_8 to binary

Octal	7	4
Binary (From table)	111	100

Convert 1110011001100_2 to octal
Group the binary digits into 3's, working from right to left. Add extra zeros to the left end if necessary.

Grouped binary digits	001	110	011	001	100
Octal (from table)	1	6	3	1	4

Note conversions between decimal and binary are often quicker via octal.

(c) Hexadecimal Numbers (Hex)

Hex are numbers in base *16*. The symbols are 0–9 and the letters A–F (which are the equivalent to 10–15 in decimal i.e. A = 10, B = 11 etc.) and place values increase in powers of 16. A group of four binary digits can express any value between 0 and 15.

(i) *Conversions*

These follow the same pattern used for binary and octal.

1 Decimal to Hex

Convert 91_{10} to hex

91_{10}

$91 \div 16 = 5 \text{ remainder } 11$ (hex = B)

$5 \div 16 = 0 \text{ remainder } 5$

Thus: $91_{10} = 5 \quad B_{16}$

2 Hex to Decimal

Convert $6D_{16}$ to decimal

Place values	16^2 (256)	16^1 (16)	16^0 (1)	
Hex	0	6	D	
Conversion	(0 × 256)	+ (6 × 16)	+ (13 × 1)	= 109

3 Conversion between Hex and Other Bases

Convert $5B_{16}$ to binary and octal.
A conversion between hex and octal is most easily made via binary.

Hex number	5	B
Binary equivalent	0101	1011

Hex to binary

Binary	001	011	011
Octal	1	3	3

Binary to octal

Note the change from 4-bit to 3-bit binary.
Convert 1111001010_2 to hex
First group the bits into 4s from the right and then convert.

Grouped binary digits	0011	1100	1010
Hex	3	C	A

(d) Binary Fractions

Examples of binary fractions are shown below.

Binary fraction	$2^{-1} = \frac{1}{2}$	$2^{-2} = \frac{1}{4}$	$2^{-3} = \frac{1}{8}$	$2^{-4} = \frac{1}{16}$	Decimal
.1000	$= (1 \times \frac{1}{2})$	$+ (0 \times \frac{1}{4})$	$+ (0 \times \frac{1}{8})$	$+ (0 \times \frac{1}{16})$	$= \frac{1}{2} = 0.5$
.0100	$= (0 \times \frac{1}{2})$	$+ (1 \times \frac{1}{4})$	$+ (0 \times \frac{1}{8})$	$+ (0 \times \frac{1}{16})$	$= \frac{1}{4} = 0.25$
.0010	$= (0 \times \frac{1}{2})$	$+ (0 \times \frac{1}{4})$	$+ (1 \times \frac{1}{8})$	$+ (0 \times \frac{1}{16})$	$= \frac{1}{8} = 0.125$
.0001	$= (0 \times \frac{1}{2})$	$+ (0 \times \frac{1}{4})$	$+ (0 \times \frac{1}{8})$	$+ (1 \times \frac{1}{16})$	$= \frac{1}{16} = 0.0625$

When converting a number which has both a whole-number part and fractional part, remember to do the two parts separately.

(e) Computer Arithmetic

The arithmetic and logic unit of the central processor in a computer performs all its arithmetic by addition and shifting, rather than having different units for subtraction.

(i) Binary Addition

The rules for adding binary numbers are quite simple. There are only four to remember:

$$0 + 0 = 0$$
$$0 + 1 = 1$$
$$1 + 0 = 1$$
$$1 + 1 = 10 \text{ (i.e. 0 carry 1)}$$
$$1 + 1 + 1 = 11 \text{ (i.e. 1 carry 1)}$$

Examples:

$$
\begin{array}{ll}
1100 & = 12_{10} \\
+0111 & = 7_{10} \\
\hline
10011 & = 19_{10} \\
\hline
\end{array}
$$

11 carried numbers

$$
\begin{array}{ll}
1011 & = 11_{10} \\
+1111 & = 15_{10} \\
\hline
11010 & = 26_{10} \\
\hline
\end{array}
$$

1111

(ii) Binary Multiplication

Again this is simple. The four rules are:

$$0 \times 0 = 0$$
$$0 \times 1 = 0$$
$$1 \times 0 = 0$$
$$1 \times 1 = 1$$

Example:
$$101 = 5_{10} \text{ multiplicand}$$
$$\times\ 010 = 2_{10} \text{ multiplier}$$

```
000
 101
  000
```

$$01010 = 10_{10} \text{ product}$$

1 *Steps*

- Start with the most significant digit (the one with the highest place value — on the *left*) of the multiplier.
- If it is a 1 copy down the multiplicand.
- If it is a 0 copy down a row of 0's.
- Then move to the next digit in the multiplier repeating the above but *shifting* one place to the *right*.
- Do this for each digit of the multiplier copying the multiplicand row, or entering 0's and then shifting one place to the right.
- At the end add up all the columns.

(iii) *Binary Division*

Binary division is not examined but is best carried out by long division.

(iv) *Negative Numbers*

There are three common ways of representing negative numbers on computers:

- Sign and magnitude (SM).
- Twos complement (2C).
- Ones complement (1C).

1 *Sign and Magnitude Codes (SM)*

Here one bit represents the sign of the number and the other bits represent the size (i.e. the magnitude) of the number. Conventionally 1 is negative and 0 is positive. The sign bit can be at either end of the binary number.
Examples (the sign bit is underlined):

$$\underline{1}011\ =\ -3$$
$$100110\ =\ +19$$
$$1011\ =\ -5$$

SM *fractions* have the most significant bit as the sign bit also.

2 *Binary Subtraction*

This has more complicated rules:
$$0 - 0 = 0$$
$$1 - 0 = 1$$
$$1 - 1 = 0$$
$$0 - 1 = 0, \text{ borrow } \underline{1}$$

This would be difficult were it not for a simple method of subtracting called *complementation*.

3 Ones and Twos Complements

The reason for using complements is that it enables computers to subtract by using a modified form of addition. Subtraction can be done by adding a negative number, e.g. 15 + (− 6) gives the same result as 15 − 6. Computers work in a similar way.

ONES COMPLEMENT

The ones complement (1C) of a binary number is found by simply reversing the bits (NOT gates in logic circuit terms − see Section 2.4). In 1C the bits have the same place values as binary numbers except that the most significant bit (the leftmost bit) represents a negative.
For example, using six bits:

Place values	−31	16	8	4	2	1
+ 13	0	0	1	1	0	1
− 13	1	1	0	0	1	0

Notice that the most significant bit = − 31

SUBTRACTION USING ONES COMPLEMENT

Example: 26 − 15

	− 31	16	8	4	2	1
Store 15	0	0	1	1	1	1
reverse bits to give −15	1	1	0	0	0	0
store 26	0	1	1	0	1	0
add −15 and 26 add overflow bit	1 0	0	1	0	1	0
						1
= 1 1$_{10}$	0	0	1	0	1	1

The overflow bit must be added to the units column of the sum to give the right answer. This is known as *end-around* or *wrap-around carry*.

TWOS COMPLEMENT

In *twos complement (2C)* coding, the bits again have the same place values as binary numbers except that the most significant bit (the leftmost bit) represents a negative of −32.
For example:

Place values	−32	16	8	4	2	1
Number	1	1	0	1	0	1

$$= -32 + 16 + 0 + 4 + 0 + 1$$
$$= -32 + 21$$
$$= -11$$

The way to convert from a positive to a negative number in 2C form is:

- Reverse the bits (as in 1C).
- Add 1.

SUBTRACTION USING TWOS COMPLEMENT

Example: 25 − 18

	−32	16	8	4	2	1
store 18	0	1	0	0	1	0
reverse bits	1	0	1	1	0	1
add 1, giving −18	1	0	1	1	1	0
store 25	0	1	1	0	0	1
add −18 and 25 (1)	0	0	0	1	1	1

overflow bit

In this case the overflow bit is ignored, the six bit answer 000111 (= 7_{10}) is correct (see next section for errors). *2C fractions* have the most significant bit representing − 1

e.g.

−1	$\frac{1}{2}$	$\frac{1}{4}$	$\frac{1}{8}$	$\frac{1}{16}$	$\frac{1}{32}$
1	0	1	0	0	0

$$= -1 + \tfrac{1}{4} = -\tfrac{3}{4} \text{ or } -0.75$$

(v) *Fixed- and Floating-point Numbers*

1 Fixed-point Numbers

The usual way of representing numbers is to have the decimal point in a fixed position, e.g. where sums of money are concerned, 173.54 would be a typical figure to denote the pence field. Integers, or fractions in sign and magnitude, complement or BCD coding are all fixed-point numbers. However, for very large or small numbers this representation is long and clumsy and so floating-point representation is used.

2 Floating-point Numbers

The name comes about because the binary point always 'floats' to the beginning of the number. It is similar to *standard form*.

There are three parts to floating-point representation:

- The exponent
- The base or radix
- The mantissa (or argument)

$$\text{e.g. } 0.1975 \times 10^3$$

Sometimes computer input and output of floating point numbers is printed as follows:

$1.975 \times 10^3 \quad = \ + 1.975E + 3$

$3.625 \times 10^{-5} \quad = \ + 3.625E - 5$

The E separates the exponent from the mantissa.

A floating-point number is stored as a fraction (the mantissa) multiplied by a power of 2 (the exponent).

Example

		Mantissa					Exponent	
$\pm$	$\frac{1}{2}$	$\frac{1}{4}$	$\frac{1}{8}$		$\pm$	4	2	1
0	1	0	0		0	1	0	0

Thus $= \frac{1}{2} \times 2^4 = \frac{1}{2} \times 16 = \underline{8}$

Sign and magnitude format is used here; complement form can also be employed.

3 Converting a Decimal Number to Binary Floating-point Form

- Change it to a fraction multiplied by a power of 2.
- Convert these to binary.

Note: Always use the next power of 2 larger than the number.

4 Storing Floating-point Numbers

Floating-point numbers take up quite a lot of storage space, typically two or four words. The number of significant figures in a number that can be stored is proportional to the number of bits that the computer allocates to the mantissa. To ensure the maximum use of space, the fraction is always adjusted so that there is a 1 in the $\frac{1}{2}$'s bit, unless the number stored is 0. This is called *normalization*.

The *range* of numbers that can be stored is linked to the number of bits given to the *exponent*.

(vi) **Errors**

It may surprise you to know that computer calculations do not always produce the correct result. This is not because anything has gone wrong, rather it is due to shortcomings in computer arithmetic. The most common errors are *overflow*, *truncation* and *rounding*.

1 Overflow

Overflow occurs when the storage space is too small to store a given number. For example, in 8 bit 2's complement the range is -128 to 127 as follows:

Place value	−128	64	32	16	8	4	2	1
Maximum number	0	1	1	1	1	1	1	1
Minimum number	1	0	0	0	0	0	0	0

If the answer to a calculation is *outside* this range an overflow occurs. The computer usually shows an error message and halts the program.

2 Truncation

Fractions such as $\frac{2}{3}$ cannot be represented exactly as decimals. Likewise, not all fractions can be stored precisely on a computer.

Truncate means to *cut off* and truncation errors happen when a fraction is cut off after a certain number of decimal (or binary) places. For example, in base 10:

$\frac{1}{3} = 0.333$

truncated to three decimal places

in base 2

$\frac{1}{3} =$	$\frac{1}{2}$	$\frac{1}{4}$	$\frac{1}{8}$	$\frac{1}{16}$	$\frac{1}{32}$	$\frac{1}{64}$
0	0	1	0	1	0	1

truncated to six binary places.

Truncation can also occur in division if two numbers don't divide exactly.

Rounding

To reduce truncation errors, fractions in base 10 are rounded by raising the last figure by 1 if the next figure would have been $\geqslant 5$.

e.g. $\frac{2}{3} = 0.6667$

rounded to four decimal places.

In binary, the last figure is raised by 1 if the next figure would have been 1.

e.g. $\frac{2}{3} = 0.101011$

rounded to six places.

Floating-point Numbers

Errors can occur when numbers are converted into their floating point form, or when calculations are done using floating-point numbers.

For example, changing 9 to an 8-bit floating-point number:

$9 = \frac{9}{16} \times 16 = \frac{9}{16} \times 2^4$

$= 0.1001$

which must be truncated to three binary places for storage. Thus 9 is stored as:

	Mantissa			Exponent			
±	$\frac{1}{2}$	$\frac{1}{4}$	$\frac{1}{8}$	±	4	2	1
9 = 0	1	0	0	0	1	0	0

The floating-point form actually stores the number <u>8</u> $(\frac{1}{2} \times 2^4)$

Clearly, computers with larger storage areas for floating-point numbers will be less prone to this type of error.

Rounding, truncation and floating-point errors are not usually detected by the computer.

2.3   Data Codes

Every computer has a *character set* – the set of characters that the computer can recognize and store in memory. Although different computers have different character sets, characters typically include the digits 0 – 9, letters and punctuation marks. They are called numeric, alphabetic (together known as alphanumeric) and special characters, respectively.

(a) Character code

Character code is a type of code where a group of binary digits is used to represent each character. Most data are stored in this form.
Examples of such codes include:

- 4 - bit binary coded decimal (BCD).
- Extended 6 - bit BCD code.
- The ASCII code.
- The EBCDIC code.

(i)   *4-bit Binary Coded Decimal (BCD)*

This was an early code for numbers. With this code a group of four binary digits is used to code each digit of a decimal number. For example, this is how the decimal number 326 would be represented:

3	2	6	Decimal number
0011	0010	0110	Four - bit BCD Code

It is important that you understand the difference between the straight binary representation of a number and its BCD equivalent.

101000110   Binary representation ⎱ Decimal
011 0010 0110 4-bit BCD   ⎰ 326

Notice that the 4-bit BCD representation requires more bit positions; why use it?
  BCD code keeps track of each decimal digit (including fractions) and therefore eliminates the possibility of rounding errors, albeit at the expense of slower arithmetic.

(ii)   *Extended 6 - bit BCD Code*

With 6 bits to represent each character, a total of 2^6 or 64 characters can be handled. So 6 - bit BCD is more useful than 4 - bit BCD; it can be used, for example, to encode the 10 decimal digits, 26 alphabetic characters and up to 28 special characters.

The two extra bits are sometimes called zone bits.
Example using 6 - bit BCD:

Zone bits		Numeric bits (place values)				Character
		8	4	2	1	
0	0	0	1	1	1	7
0	0	1	0	0	1	9
1	1	0	0	0	1	A
1	0	1	0	0	1	R

Note how alphabetic (and special) characters are represented by a combination of zone and numeric bits.

In addition to the six-bit positions, a 7th bit called a check or parity bit is often added for checking purposes in this code to check the validity of the data.

This is done automatically by the computer and is known as *parity checking*. The 6-bit BCD code appears as follows:

Check bit	Zone bits		Numeric bits (place values)				Character
			8	4	2	1	
1	0	0	0	1	1	1	7
1	1	1	0	0	0	1	A

Depending on the computer, the parity check may be *odd* or *even*. Assume that the computer uses an *even* parity check. When a character is stored in the computer in 6 - bit BCD code, the number of 1 - bits in the first six positions is counted. If the number is even, a $\emptyset$ - bit is stored in the check-bit position; if it is odd, a 1 - bit is stored in this position. As a result, the 7 - bit positions always have an even number of 1 - bits. For *odd* parity the procedure is just the opposite.

Q. How would the codes above change for a computer that uses an odd parity check?

A. The check bit would be reversed, i.e. $\emptyset$ for both 'A' and '7'.

(iii) *The ASCII Code*

ASCII stands for American Standard Code for Information Exchange. There are two versions, the 7 and 8 bit. The ASCII - 7 code uses three zone bits and four numeric bits to represent characters, with an 8th bit added for parity checking. Here are some examples:

Check bit (even)	Zone bits			Numeric bits (place values)				
				8	4	2	1	
1	0	1	1	0	1	1	1	= 7
1	1	0	0	0	1	0	1	= E
0	1	0	0	1	0	1	1	= K

(iv) *The EBCDIC Code*

The Extended Binary Coded Decimal Interchange Code was developed by IBM. It is an 8-bit code which therefore permits $2^8 = 256$ distinct characters. In computers that use the EBCDIC code, each addressable unit of storage is 8 bits in length and is referred to as a *byte*, i.e. each character can be stored in 1 byte of computer memory. Here are some examples – the parity bit has been omitted for simplicity:

Zone bits				Numeric bits (place values)				
				8	4	2	1	
1	1	1	1	0	1	1	1	= 7
1	0	0	0	0	1	0	1	= e

This format is referred to as zoned decimal, as each character is stored in 1 byte and is represented as a combination of four zone and four numeric bits. Notice that the four zone bits in the code for the decimal number 7 are 1111. This bit combination indicates that the number is unsigned (neither positive or negative) and room has to be found for this if arithmetic operations are to be carried out.

It is wasteful to store one decimal digit per byte and we know (from the 4-bit BCD) that the decimal numbers 0–9 can be represented with only four binary bit positions. So purely numeric data are generally stored in EBCDIC *packed decimal* format, with two decimal digits packed into each 8-bit byte. Here are some examples of this format:

Numeric bits				Numeric bits			
8	4	2	1	8	4	2	1
0	1	1	0	0	0	1	1
	6				3		

The decimal number 63 is stored in one byte, but there is no sign. In EBCDIC packed decimal the sign of a number is stored in the right-hand four-bit position. A bit pattern of 1100 represents a positive number, 1101 a negative number. In the following example the decimal number + 487 is shown in packed decimal form.

Byte		Byte	
0100	1000	0111	1100
4	8	7	+

The storage capacity of memory devices for numerical data is almost doubled when using this format.

Hexadecimal (hex) is often used as a shorthand for binary numbers. Two hex digits can be used to represent each 8-bit EBCDIC character. For example, 'C' is represented by 1100 0011. Dividing this bit string into groups of four and writing down the hex equivalents gives:

1100	0011	EBCDIC code for 'C'
C	3	hex equivalent

(b) Organisation of Computer Storage

Data codes describe *how* data is represented in computer memory. The computer must be able to *store and retrieve* this data and so memory is divided up into *locations* each with its own address. Each location represents a certain number of bit positions, depending on the computer and the type of instructions used. For example, locations in microcomputers usually consist of 8 or 16 bits.

An address is given to each storage location to allow direct reference. This is similar to a pigeon-hole with its label or box number.

There is an important difference between a computer memory location and a pigeon-hole, however. When the contents of a memory location are *read* by the computer, the contents remain – they are *copied*.

On the other hand, when a new letter is inserted in your pigeon-hole, the previous contents remain unharmed. However, when a computer stores (or *writes*) new data to a storage location the previous contents are erased. The *write* operation is therefore said to be destructive.

It is important to remember the difference between the *address* of the storage location and its *contents*.

(c) Word Lengths

We have not yet specified the length of each storage location. This can either be fixed-length or variable-length. A comparison of the two is shown below; assume that each word can store four characters.

(i) *Fixed-Length*

Address of word	Contents of address			
001	L	I	V	E
002	R	P	O	O
003	L			

(ii) *Variable-Length*

Address of characters	001	002	003	004	005	006	007	008	009	
Character	L	I	V	E	R	P	O	O	L	Terminator

Notice that each individual character can be addressed in (ii).

The main advantage of the variable-word-length organization is storage efficiency – note how wasteful the other format is (address 003 is only 25% used). The number of characters is specified in the instruction itself by markers called terminators, e.g. a comma or carriage return which take up storage space. But the fixed-length format is faster for arithmetic (all arithmetic operations are performed in *parallel* on complete words), i.e. all digits to be processed are added at the same time. In contrast, with variable word length, characters are added serially – one at a time.

Fortunately, today's computers can often be operated either as fixed- or variable-word length machines.

2.4 Logic Gates and Truth Tables

(a) Introduction

Data and control instructions move inside a computer by means of pulses of electricity.

Certain components of computers combine these pulses as if they were following a set of rules. The components are called logic elements. Computer logic is the combination of inputs and outputs produced by logic elements.

Like most computer components, logic elements are *bistable* (on–off switches, 1 or 0) devices.

(b) Logic Hardware

The processing of data is done by lots of complex electrical circuits in the CPU of the computer. The hardware devices which do this are transistors or integrated circuits.

(i) *Transistors*

These can function as amplifiers or logic elements.
All types of transistor are made from semi-conductor material, usually silicon, which is carefully 'doped' with impurities, e.g. phosphorus and boron, so that the electrical current can be controlled.

(ii) *Integrated Circuits*

These are also known as chips and are small circuits consisting of a number of transistors. Large-scale integrated (LSI) circuits and Very large-scale integrated (VLSI) circuits represent thousands of transistors on a chip. Advances in chip-making technology have allowed this miniaturization.

(c) Gates

The commonest use of logic elements is to act as switches, although they have no moving parts. They *open* to pass on a pulse of electricity or *close* to shut it off. This is why they are known as gates.

There are five types of gate: AND, NAND, OR, NOR, NOT which can be described diagrammatically, by truth tables or by expressions (often called Boolean expressions, after their creator George Boole).

The next section introduces these gates and then shows how they can be combined – a popular examination question. Some uses of logic elements will then be shown.

(i) *AND Gate*

An AND gate has an output of 1 if *ALL* inputs are 1, otherwise 0 is output. The diagram and truth table for a two-input AND gate are shown in Fig. 2.1(a).

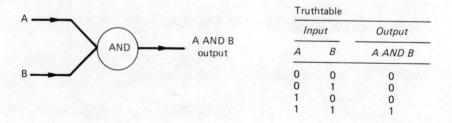

Truthtable

Input		Output
A	B	A AND B
0	0	0
0	1	0
1	0	0
1	1	1

Figure 2.1 (*a*) AND gate. A pulse is output if there is a pulse at both inputs A and B.

Another way of showing this is by means of a switching circuit (see Fig. 2.1(b)).

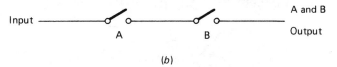

(b)

Figure 2.1 (b) AND switching circuit. Current will flow (i.e. output = 1) if both switch A AND switch B are closed.

(ii) *OR Gate*

An OR gate has an output of 1 if *ANY* of its inputs are 1, otherwise 0 is output. The diagram and truth table for a two-input OR gate are shown in Fig. 2.2. Current will flow throughout the circuit if either switch A or switch B is closed.

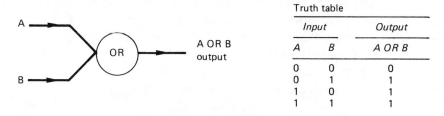

Truth table

Input		Output
A	B	A OR B
0	0	0
0	1	1
1	0	1
1	1	1

Figure 2.2 OR gate. A pulse is output whenever there is an input pulse — at A or B or both.

This is the inclusive *OR* gate, giving a binary 1 if one or more (including all) of the inputs of 1. The exclusive OR gate functions in the same way *except* that when all inputs (2 or more) are 1, a zero output is given.
Unless otherwise stated assume inclusive OR.

(iii) *NOT Gate*

A NOT gate has one input and one output. It has the effect of *reversing* the input signal and is sometimes called an *inverter*. The diagram and truth table for a NOT gate are shown in Fig. 2.3.

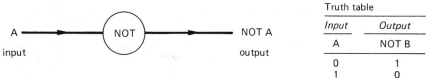

Truth table

Input	Output
A	NOT B
0	1
1	0

Figure 2.3 NOT gate.

(iv) *NAND Gate*

A NAND gate has the same effect as an AND gate followed by a NOT gate. Hence the output will be the opposite of the AND gate. The diagram and truth table for a two-output NAND gate are shown in Fig. 2.4.

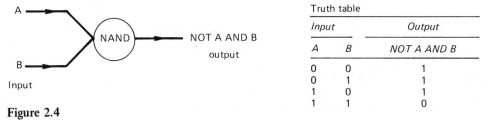

Truth table

Input		Output
A	B	NOT A AND B
0	0	1
0	1	1
1	0	1
1	1	0

Figure 2.4

(v) *NOR Gate*

A NOR gate has the same effect as an OR gate followed by a NOT gate. Hence the output will be the opposite of the OR gate. The diagram and truth table for a two-input NOR gate are shown in Fig. 2.5.

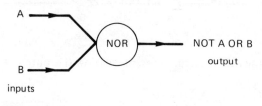

Truth table

Input		Output
A	B	NOT A OR B
0	0	1
0	1	0
1	0	0
1	1	0

Figure 2.5

(d) Combinations of Gates

The five basic logic gates can be used in combination to make up electronic circuits which control data flow, carry out arithmetic and logic functions, help to store information and time operations.

Some examples of these logic circuits now follow.

The truth table for a combination of logic elements is worked out by following all the possible sets of input signals through the logic circuit. NAND and NOR gates are the easiest and cheapest to make from transistors.

Example 2.1 (Fig. 2.6)

The input combination A = 0, B = 1 is followed through the circuit. A similar process will give the other outputs which are shown in the completed truth table below.

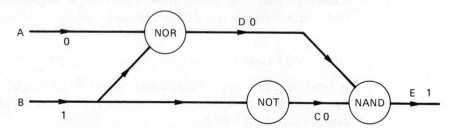

Figure 2.6 Example 2.1.

Input		Intermediate steps		Output
A	B	C	D	E
0	0	1	1	0
0	1	0	0	1
1	0	1	0	1
1	1	0	0	1

Note how it is useful to include the intermediate steps to help your workings.

Example 2.2

Construct the truth table for the logic network in Fig. 2.7.

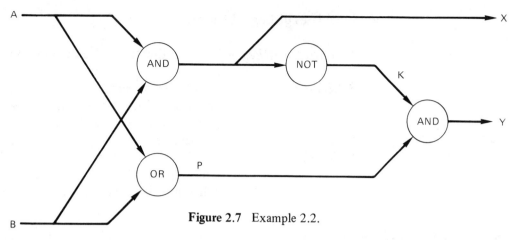

Figure 2.7 Example 2.2.

Inputs		Intermediate steps		Output	
A	B	K	P	X	Y
0	0	1	0	0	0
0	1	1	1	0	1
1	0	1	1	0	1
1	1	0	1	1	0

These examples show how logic elements can be combined for two inputs. Let us try some workings for more complicated networks.

Example 2.3

In Fig. 2.8 there are three inputs and the combination A = 0, B = 0, C = 1 is followed the circuit. The completed truth table below shows the other outputs.

Figure 2.8 Example 2.3.

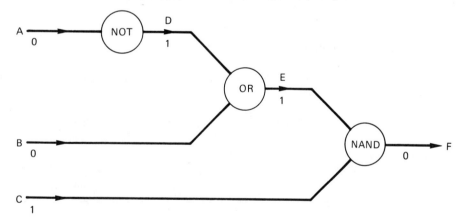

Inputs			Intermediate steps		Output
A	B	C	D	E	F
0	0	0	1	1	1
0	0	1	1	1	0
0	1	0	1	1	1
0	1	1	1	1	0
1	0	0	0	0	1
1	0	1	0	0	1
1	1	0	0	1	1
1	1	1	0	1	0

(e) Some Uses of Logic Elements

- *Control switches* — Control the flow of data and consist of a set of AND gates.
- *Decoders* — Recognize a certain pattern of bits in a word. They are used to locate cells in memory (address decoders) and to respond to different instructions (operation decoders).
- *Flip-flops* — Combine logic elements to store data as a '1' or '0'. One flip-flop stores a single bit. A set of flip-flops, called a register, stores a complete word.

2.5 Exercises

Question 2.1

Convert the following:
(a) 257 to binary and 4-bit BCD.
(b) 18.0625 to binary.
(c) 92 to hexadecimal.
(d) 901 to binary coded decimal.

Question 2.2

(a) Convert the decimal number 259_{10} to binary.
(b) Calculate by binary arithmetic the product $110111_2 \times 11001_2$.
(c) Find the twos complement of the ten-bit positive binary number 0001101111.
(d) Convert the binary answer to decimal.

(OLE)

Question 2.3

Below is the listing of three of the ASCII codes as used in a computer

CHARACTER	DECIMAL	HEXADECIMAL
<	60	3C
=	61	3D
>	62	3E

(a) Why do characters need to be represented by numeric codes?
(b) Why do we use both decimal and hexadecimal codes?

Question 2.4

A computer stores a representation of integers in 4-bit words using *two's complementation*.

(a) What is the largest possible integer represented in a 4-bit word?
(b) What number is represented by 1000?
(c) Show how you would represent the integer −3 in the 4-bit word.

(AEB)

Question 2.5

(a) Using the following example show the steps in the *twos complementation* method of subtraction.
$$01101101_2 - 00110110_2$$

(b) In a computer using a 5-bit *register* to hold positive and negative integers in binary, the arithmetic subtraction, 9 - 2 = 7, is represented by:

Register A   01001
Register B   11110$^+$
Register C   00111   Answer
Explain why the operation shown is addition.

(AEB)

Question 2.6

Define bit, byte, address, absolute address, word, word length.

Question 2.7

A mainframe computer is to be controlled automatically by a logic network. There are three binary signals available which have the following values under the given conditions:

Signal	Binary value	Condition
T	1	Temperature $\geqslant 70°$ C
	0	Temperature $< 70°$ C
H	1	Humidity $> 60\%$
	0	Humidity $\leqslant 60\%$
D	1	Dust/smoke in atmosphere at high level
	0	Dust/smoke in atmosphere at low level

The system outputs an alarm signal (A = 1) whenever either of the following conditions arise:

1. Temperature $\geqslant 70°$ C and dust/smoke in atmosphere is at high level.
2. Humidity $> 60\%$ and dust/smoke is at high level.

 (i) Complete the truth table for this system.
(ii) Draw a logic network which would product the alarm signal A using the inputs T, H and D.

Question 2.8

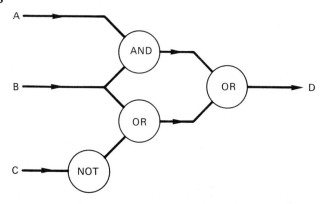

Figure 2.9 Logic network.

(i) Construct the truth table for the following logic network (Fig. 2.9).

(ii) Which one of the inputs to this logic network has no effect on the final output?

(iii) Draw a network with fewer gates which would produce the same output as the network in (i).

2.6 Answers and Hints on Solutions

2.1 (a) $257_{10} = 100000001_2$.

$$\begin{array}{ccc} 2 & 5 & 7 \\ 0010 & 0101 & 0111 \end{array} \text{ in 4-bit BCD}$$

(b) $18.0625 = 10010.0001_2$.

Work out the two parts of the number separately:

$18 \div 2$ remainder 0
$9 \div 2$ remainder 1
$4 \div 2$ remainder 0
$2 \div 2$ remainder 0
$1 \div 2$ remainder 1

$$= 10010$$

$.625 \ (\simeq \frac{1}{16} \text{th}) \qquad = .0001$

$$(0 \times \tfrac{1}{2}) + (0 \times \tfrac{1}{4}) + (0 \times \tfrac{1}{8}) + (1 \times \tfrac{1}{16})$$

Therefore, $18.0625_{10} = 10010.0001_2$.

(c) $92_{10} = 5C_{16}$

$92 \div 16 = 5$ remainder 12 (hex = C)
$5 \div 16 = 0$ remainder 5

Therefore, $92_{10} = \qquad 5 \qquad C_{16}$

(d) $\qquad 9 \qquad 0 \qquad 1$ decimal number

$= 1001 \quad 0000 \quad 0001$ in 4 bit BCD code

2.2 (a) $259_{10} = 100000011_2$ (see question 2.1)

(b)
$$\begin{array}{r} 110111 \\ 11001 \\ \hline 110111 \\ 110111 \\ 00000 \\ 0000 \\ 110111 \\ \hline 10101011111 \end{array} = \text{Product}$$

carry $\left\{ \begin{array}{l} 11111 \\ 1 \end{array} \right.$
numbers

(c) 0001101111
1110010000 reverse the bits
1110010001 add 1 giving 2C form

-512	256	128	64	32	16	8	4	2	1	Place values
1	1	1	0	0	1	0	0	0	1	

(d) Leftmost bit $= -512 + 256 + 128 + 16 + 1$

$\qquad\qquad\qquad = -\underline{111}$

2. (a) Every computer has a character set – the set of characters that the computer can recognize and store in memory. A code is where a group of binary digits is used to represent each character and most data are stored in this form.
3 (b) Hexadecimal is often used as a shorthand for binary numbers (hex is $2^4 = 16$) and can therefore be seen as the computer-code equivalent of the 'human' decimal code.

2.4 In twos complement arithmetic, the most significant bit represents a negative, hence the place values for a 4-bit word are:

	-8	4	2	1

(a) Largest possible integer = $\quad 0 \quad 1 \quad 1 \quad 1_2$ i.e. 7_{10}

(b) 1000_2 represents $\quad 1 \quad 0 \quad 0 \quad 0_2$ i.e. $\underline{-8}$

(c) -3 is represented by $\quad 1 \quad 1 \quad 0 \quad 1_2$ i.e. $\underline{-8 + 5 = -3}$

2.5 (a) Enter number to be subtracted (2nd number)

$$0 \quad 0 \quad 1 \quad 1 \quad 0 \quad 1 \quad 1 \quad 0$$

reverse bits

$$1 \quad 1 \quad 0 \quad 0 \quad 1 \quad 0 \quad 0 \quad 1$$

add 1.

$$1 \quad 1 \quad 0 \quad 0 \quad 1 \quad 0 \quad 1 \quad 0$$

Enter first number

$$0 \quad 1 \quad 1 \quad 0 \quad 1 \quad 1 \quad 0 \quad 1$$

Add the two numbers

$$(1)\, 0 \quad 0 \quad 1 \quad 1 \quad 0 \quad 1 \quad 1 \quad 1 \leftarrow \text{answer}$$
overflow bit

Check: in decimal
$$\begin{array}{r} 109 \\ -54 \\ \hline = \underline{55} \end{array}$$

$55_{10} = 110111_2$ QED

2.5 (b) Subtraction can be done by adding negative numbers, and this is how a computer works.

Hence   01001   represents   9
           00010   represents   2
           11110   represents -2
                  (reverse bits and add 1.)
           00111   result = 7

2.6 A *BIT* is a *BI*nary digi*T* (either Ø or 1).
A *BYTE* is a group of bits (usually 8) which corresponds to a single character. A storage location (or cell) in a computer is identified by its *ADDRESS* and is capable of holding a single item of data.

The actual address of a location in memory, e.g. 34th location gives an *absolute address* of 34.

A *WORD* is a collection of bits which is treated as a single unit by the central processor.

WORD LENGTH is the number of bits in each word in a particular computer.

2.7 (i)

INPUTS			OUTPUTS	
T	H	D	A	
0	0	0	0	
0	0	1	0	
0	1	0	0	
0	1	1	1	*
1	0	0	0	
1	0	1	1	*
1	1	0	0	
1	1	1	1	*

* i.e. the alarm bell will ring (A = 1) in these circumstances.

(ii) See Fig. 2.10.

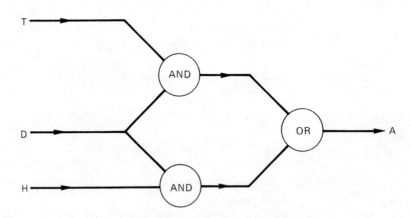

Figure 2.10 Answer 2.7(ii).

2.8

Inputs			Outputs
A	B	C	D
0	0	0	1
0	0	1	0
0	1	0	1
0	1	1	1
1	0	0	1
1	0	1	0
1	1	0	1
1	1	1	1

(ii) A.

(iii) See Fig. 2.11.

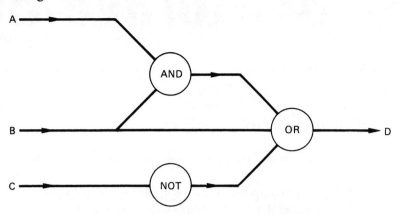

Figure 2.11 Answer 2.8(iii).

3 Storage Systems

3.1   Requirements of a Storage System

Q. What are the requirements of a storage system?

A. All computer-based systems need to keep data and programs for later use. In general, a good storage system should be:

- *Cheap* – Economical and affordable.
- *Accessible* – So that information can be provided quickly enough for any given job.
- *Large enough* – To hold all the data required.
- *Secure and reliable* – So that data can be kept over time without fear of loss, damage or deterioration.

A variety of storage devices and media have been developed to meet these needs.

3.2   Classification of Computer Storage

Q. What is main memory and what is it used for?

A. Every computer has a *main memory* where data and instructions which are currently being processed are stored. Main memory is wholly electric, fast and reliable. Its nearness to the rest of the CPU and the great speed at which it can be accessed mean that it is often called *immediate access storage*.
Main memory has several uses:

- *Input area* – Where the data is stored when it is read in the computer (e.g. data for payroll calculations) awaiting processing.
- *Operating system* – Controls the operation of the computer.
- *Application program area* – Where the user program is held (e.g. a payroll program).
- *Working storage* – Where calculations are performed and data is stored temporarily.
- *Output area* – Where information is stored prior to output (e.g. payroll information used to print pay slips). Both the input and output area are *buffers*.

Q. What is backing store and what is it used for?

A. Although main memory can be expanded within limits, it is expensive and does not provide enough storage for all the data used – especially in business organisations. Backing store is cheaper and has greater storage capacities than main memory, although access times are slower depending on the type of device used. Hence backing storage (also known as secondary or auxiliary storage) is

used for data and programs not currently needed in main memory.
Backing storage is used mainly for:

- Large data files, e.g. personnel or stock records.
- Programs not currently being executed by the computer.
- Temporary storage of input/output data.

Backing storage cannot be directly addressed by the CPU; therefore programs and data in backing storage must be transferred (read into) main memory before they can be processed by the CPU.

For example, floppy disks (see later) hold data and programs. When they are required by the computer, they are inserted into a disk drive and read into main memory.

The manual equivalent of this system would be a filing cabinet (backing store) and the desktop with current work (main memory).

Q. Why is it important to distinguish between main memory and backing store?

A. The distinction between the two is important for three reasons:

- *Cost* — Although the cost per bit of main (semi-conductor) memory is decreasing rapidly, it is still much higher than for backing storage devices such as magnetic disk.
- *Storage capacity* — Backing storage capacities are much greater than main memory.
- *Speed* — The speed of a computer depends largely on the speed of its main memory. Therefore, the fastest devices (semi-conductor chips) are used for main memory.

It is useful to build on the simple division of main and backing store by having levels of storage.

(a) Levels of Storage

For modern computers, particularly large ones, it is useful to see storage divided into four levels:

- *Main memory* — Used, as we have seen, to store programs and data currently being executed/processed.
- *Paging memory* — Used primarily to store segments of program or data which are not being requested by the CPU. Paging memory provides fast access to frequently used program/data which can be read in frames called pages into the computer — hence the name. It is as if the data are 'on-call'.
- *Data base storage* — Used for storing the current data base or files of data used by the organisation.
- *Archive storage* — Used for storing historical data — e.g. for legal or reference purposes. Archive storage should provide adequate access to very large files of historical data.

Table 3.1 shows an overview of the major storage devices used, typical access times and range of storage capacity.

Table 3.1 Types of storage device used in computers

Memory type	Devices used	Typical access time	Typical capacity range (bytes)
Main	Semi-conductors	100 ns or less	4 K to 10 M
Paging	Fixed-head disk	5 ms	10 M to 100 M
	Semi-conductor	0.2 ms	
	Magnetic bubble	0.3 ms	
Database	Moving-head disk	15–30 ms	1 M to 1000 M
	Floppy disk	100 ms	
	Magnetic tape	Seconds or minutes	
Archive	Magnetic cartridge	2–5 s	Up to 1
	Video disk	150 ms	trillion!

s = second, ms = microsecond and ns = nanosecond

Q. Define access time.

A. *Access time* is the time taken to access a stored record, i.e. between asking for data and their being transferred ready for use.

Q. How is storage capacity measured?

A. *Storage capacity* is usually expressed in terms of the number of bytes (or alphanumeric characters that can be stored).

K (kilo, i.e. 1000). Strictly speaking it means 2^{10} or 1024. Therefore, a microcomputer with 256 K main storage actually has 262 144 (256 × 1024) positions. M (mega, i.e. 1 million) actually means 2^{20} or 1 048 576. Thus a mini with 10 MB (10 megabytes) of disk storage has a capacity of 10 485 760 bytes of disk memory.

3.3 Main Memory

Q. What are the types of main memory?

A. There are two main types of main memory:

- *Random access memory (RAM)* is used for temporary storage of data/ programs. It can be changed by a user program. Access time for all locations is the same, i.e. it is not dependent on position. In general RAM is *volatile*, i.e. information is lost when the power is switched off.
- *Read-only memory (ROM)* is used to store data or programs that are permanent or rarely changed. The information is generally put on a storage chip at the manufacturing stage and the contents of the ROM cannot be changed except under special circumstances. Therefore, a computer can read infor-

mation stored in ROM but cannot write to it. Generally ROM is *non-volatile*, i.e. information stored in ROM is not lost when power is removed from the computer. There are Programmable ROMs (PROMS) which can be programmed by the user rather than the manufacturer. Once written they become permanent. However, Erasable PROMS(EPROMs) can, as their name suggests, be erased (by exposure to ultraviolet light) and then written to again. A variant of this is the Electrically Alterable (EA) ROM.

Q. How is data stored or retrieved from main memory?

A. Memory addressing.

A. *Memory addressing.* The computer must be able to locate data before it is stored or retrieved. To achieve this memory is divided up into storage *locations* each with a unique address (see section 2.3(b), Organisation of Computer Storage). There are two ways of addressing main memory:

- *Byte addressing* – Where memory capacity is expressed in terms of the number of 8-bit bytes which can be stored, e.g. an 8 bit microcomputer may have a main memory of 64K. 8 bits = 1 byte; capacity = 64 × 1024 = 65 536 bytes
- *Word addressing* – Which is the number of fixed-length words (usually 16, 32, 36, 48 or 64 bit words), e.g. a 32-bit minicomputer with 256 K words of main memory will have 4 bytes in each word and a capacity of 4 × 256 × 1024 = 1 048 576 bytes.

Q. What is semi-conductory memory?

A. All modern computers are now built with semi-conductor main memory because of its:

- Faster access time.
- Lower cost.
- Reduced space – small physical size.
- Lower power consumption.

A semi-conductor memory chip is made up of thousands of cells organized into a rectangular array of rows and columns (Fig. 3.1).

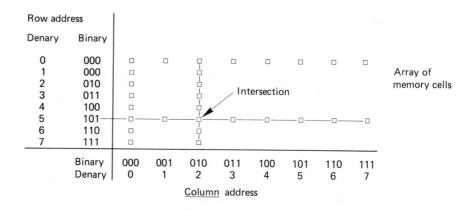

Figure 3.1 64-cell random access memory array.

Each memory cell has two major components:

- The *capacitor* is a two-state device that stores a tiny electrical charge (the '1' bit) or no charge ('0' bit).
- The *transistor* works as a switch to determine whether the capacitor is charged.

Fig. 3.1 shows that a particular cell can be accessed via its row and column number. (Address 52 i.e. row 5 column 2 has been selected in the diagram.) The computer can then read from or write to that cell.

In 1980 the industry standard semi-conductor memory chip was 64K. There are now 256K chips (and larger) which are the same size but store data more densely.

The large-scale integration (LSI) of semi-conductor memory circuits is one of the main reasons why computers have fallen in cost so dramatically. Two types of semi-conductor chip are used in most computers:

- Metal oxide semi-conductors (MOS).
- Bipolar semi-conductors, are faster but more expensive.

Access time:

- MOS,   100 ns to 1 ms.
- Bipolar, 10 ns–100 ns.

Q. Explain 'paging memory' and 'virtual storage'

A. There are many situations where several people want to use a computer at the same time. A multiprogramming operating system can run several programs at once, even though it only executes one at a time. Each user 'takes turns' on the computers and is given a brief 'time-slice' when their program can be brought in and out of the CPU. Processing speeds are so fast relative to input/output operations that each user is not normally aware that other people are using the system simultaneously. (There may be some delay, i.e. slow response times, if the system is very busy, however.)

Another approach is to allocate users a 'slice' of main memory (a partition) for their programs. The size of the partition will depend on:

- The size of main memory.
- The amount of memory needed by the operating system.
- The number of user programs competing for main memory at the same time.

(a) Virtual Storage

Quite often user programs are bigger than the size of the partition allocated. This problem can be overcome by *paging*. A program is divided into sections called *pages* which can fit into a partition, i.e. a page is a block of instructions or data (or both) that can be transferred as a unit between backing storage and main memory (Fig. 3.2).

Fast access to paging memory is essential. Pages must be stored on some form of fast backing storage, so paging memory is usually fixed-head magnetic disk, although semi-conductor memories and magnetic bubbles, etc. are replacing the slower devices. Sets of random access memory chips keep track of where parts of the program actually are and swap segments back and forth when needed. They are sometimes known as **RAM** disks or 'virtual disks'.

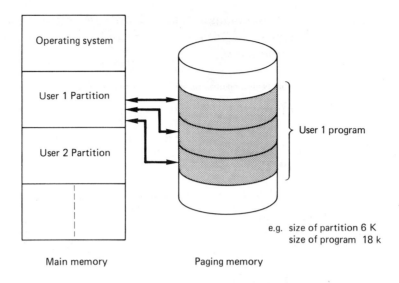

Figure 3.2 Paging memory and virtual storage.

The computer automatically controls the segmentation of programs into pages and the transfer (or paging) of these segments between main and backing store. Programmers can assume that they are no longer limited by the size of main memory. They have an unlimited (or at least very large) partition of main memory — a concept called *virtual storage*. Only part of a program (the page) is active in main memory at any one time and therefore the whole program doesn't have to be in main memory all at once. The concept can be linked to structured programming methods (*see* Chapter 9), where programs are designed and built up in discrete blocks (functions, procedures) of code.

3.4 Backing Storage

Q. Explain the difference between serial access and direct access.

A. There are two main types of backing store device — serial access (tape) and direct access devices (e.g. disk).

(a) Serial Access Devices

- Storage locations cannot be addressed.
- Data records are stored from beginning to end of the storage medium, e.g. magnetic tape. To find a particular record the search must pass all preceding records (like finding a track on a music cassette tape).

(b) Direct Access Storage Devices (DASDs)

DASDs have addressable storage locations. Therefore, if the address of a particular record is known the record can be retrieved directly without searching (cf. finding a track on a music LP). This is an essential feature for when individual records have to be accessed and/or updated e.g. an enquiry system for customers' credit checking, a booking system for airlines.

The most common type of DASD at present is the magnetic disk.

Example. We wish to access record 17 in both cases.

(a) Serial access:

Search from beginning until record 17 is found

| 02 | 05 | 11 | 13 | 17 | 21 | 28 | 34 |

(b) Direct access:

Go directly to location 005, where record 17 is to be found.

| Storage location | 001 | 002 | 003 | 004 | 005 | 006 |
| Record number | 03 | 07 | 10 | 11 | 17 | 19 |

(c) Magnetic Tape

Q. What are the physical characteristics of magnetic tape?

A. *Tape – physical characteristics*:

- Plastic base coated with metal oxide film.
- Data recorded as magnetized spots – each one representing a binary digit.
- Standard width – $\frac{1}{2}''$ – though size varies between $\frac{1}{4}''$ (cassette) and $1''$ (high capacity).
- Standard reel – 2400' in length, but again sizes vary.

Q. How can you read from or write to magnetic tape?

A. *Tape drive (or unit)*:

- Tape drives read from and write to tape.
- Reels are mounted on a tape drive which moves the tape past the read (non-destructive, i.e. copy) and write (destructive, i.e. destroys previous contents) heads (Fig. 3.3).

(i) *Recording on Tape*

- Data are recorded in binary coded decimal (BCD) format.
- The tape width is divided into a series of tracks (or channels) – usually 7 or 9. A character is recorded across the tracks in a row called a *frame*.
- The most common forms of coding are:
  - 7-track ASCII. The American Standard Code for Information Interchange consists of a 7-bit coded character plus a parity bit.
  - 9-track EBCDIC. The Extended Binary Coded Decimal Interchange Code has 8 bits (four zone bits and four numeric bits) plus a parity bit.

Q. What is a parity bit?

A. The *parity* bit is used to check the validity and completeness of the data when they are transferred i.e. read or recorded. The bits in a character or word are added and checked against a parity digit previously calculated. In Fig. 3.4 there is an odd parity bit, i.e. the total number of bits including the parity bit is odd (see Chapter 2 for further details of these codes).

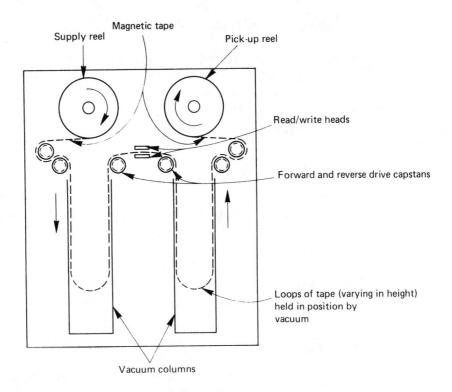

Figure 3.3 Magnetic tape unit.

1 Storage density

Density of storage is measured in bytes (or characters) per inch, bpi. Common storage densities are 800 and 1600 though some high-density tapes can record up to 6250 bpi.

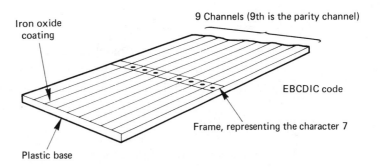

Figure 3.4 Representing data on magnetic tape.

(ii) Tape Records

Data on tape are recorded in *blocks* which are separated by *interblock gaps* (e.g. $\frac{1}{2}'' - \frac{3}{4}''$) to allow the tape to speed up and slow down at the beginning and end of the reading blocks.

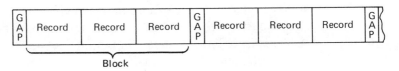

1 Blocking of records on magnetic tape

In the diagram there are three logical records per block, e.g. each one might be a customer record. The number of logical records in each block (or physical record) is called the *blocking factor*. Increasing the blocking factor (i.e. the number of logical records per block) will increase the effective storage density (as the gaps contain no data) and therefore the reading rate.

(iii) *Rate of Reading*

The rate at which data can be read from tape is called the *transfer rate* which depends on the recording density and tape speed. For example,
a tape with 1600 bpi density and a speed of 125 inches per second has a transfer rate of:
$$1600 \times 125 = 200\,000 \text{ bytes per second.}$$
This is known as the instantaneous transfer rate — the actual average transfer rate would be less because of the interblock gaps.

(iv) *Cassette Tape*

This is a smaller version of magnetic tape. Music cassette tapes (C60, C90 etc.) can be used which run on ordinary cassette players. This is an ideal low-cost backing store for microcomputers, particularly in the home, where data transfer speeds are not so critical. Data is usually stored on a single track and two different frequencies of sound are used to represent 0 and 1. Typical transfer rates are 300–1200 baud (30–120 characters per second).

(v) *Advantages and Disadvantages*

Q. What are the advantages and disadvantages of magnetic tape?

A. *Advantages of magnetic tape*:
- *Speed* – The transfer rate of (typically) 50 000 – 100 000 or more characters per second is quite adequate for many applications.
- *Capacity* – A standard reel can hold 10 million or more characters depending on the blocking factor. Thus tapes can be used for large files or for dumping from disk files.
- *Cost* – Magnetic tape is the cheapest magnetic medium.
- *Convenience* – It is light, compact and easy to store in racks. Some organizations have thousands of reels in storage 'libraries' or 'banks'.

Disadvantages of magnetic tape:
- Tape is a serial medium and therefore searching is necessary. This makes it impractical for direct access applications.
- A record on magnetic tape cannot be updated in place ('*in situ*'). Records to be updated have to be read, updated and then written to a second tape. (This does have safety benefits, however, in that the original is preserved (father–son principle).)
- Tape must be stored in a suitable environment where humidity, temperature and dust are tightly controlled; otherwise read errors, etc. occur.
- Tape has a limited shelf life (about 2 years) for reliable results and is therefore not suitable for long-term storage of historical files.

Q. What are the main uses for magnetic tape?

A. *Uses*:

- Off-line storage of large sequential files. Tapes can be conveniently kept in storage racks and are loaded on to tape drives and processed as they are needed.
- Back-up storage for on-line disk files. To prevent loss of data, disk files can be periodically 'dumped' on to tape.
- Medium for key-to-tape data entry (now largely superceded by key-to-disk).

(vi) *Floppy Tape*

Q. Explain what floppy tapes are.

A. *Floppy tapes (or 'stringy floppies')*:

- These are cartridge-based systems which operate much faster than cassette tape (typically 60 times quicker) and are more reliable.
- They contain an endless loop of $\frac{1}{4}''$ tape about 12' long, housed in a drive which is slightly smaller than a standard cassette drive.
- They store about 100 Kbytes (just over 100 000 characters) and can be loaded in 3–4 seconds — the data transfer rate is 10 000 bytes per second.
- Storage cartridges are about the same thickness as a tape cassette and are inserted into the drive rather like a floppy disk. Microdrives are built into the Sinclair QL micrcomputer.
- A drive motor drives the tape past a tiny nine track magnetic read/write head that records a byte of data plus a clockpulse across the width of the tape.

1 Disadvantages

- Non-standard — Sinclair and others.
- Likely to be upstaged by mini floppies ($3\frac{1}{2}''$).

(d) Magnetic Disk

Magnetic disk is the most commonly used form of backing storage, although other media e.g. optical disks, may become become more cost-effective for some applications. However, magnetic disks themselves continue to be improved in terms of cost and performance. Disks are excellent as DASD for large data files and data bases at a reasonable cost.

(i) *Physical Characteristics*

Q. What are the physical characteristics of magnetic disk?

A. *Disk — Physical characteristics*:

- A disk pack is made up of a stack of rotating metal disks (six or more) mounted on a spindle.
- Several disks can be stacked on a spindle and enclosed in a unit called a *disk pack* (or module).

- Each disk is a thin metal rigid platter (similar in size and concept to an LP) coated on both sides with magnetic material, e.g. ferrous oxide.
- Data are recorded on the surface in the form of magnetized spots. Their presence or absence denotes binary 1 or 0.
- The surface of the disk is divided into *tracks*; which in turn may be divided into *sectors*.
- The recording density is greater towards the middle of the disk so that all tracks contain the same amount of data.
- The disk pack can be loaded into a disk drive for reading and writing (Fig. 3.5).
- The capacity of a disk pack is of the order of several million to 200 million characters.

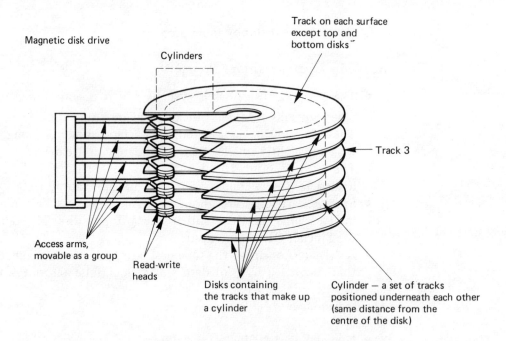

Figure 3.5 Components of a disk pack.

(ii) *Reading and writing to disk*

Q. How can you read from and write to disk?

A. *Reading and writing to disk*

- Data reading and writing is done by read/write heads similar to those used in a tape recorder. There is usually one head for each disk surface.
- Access arms position these heads in the desired locations. The heads do not actually touch the surface of the disk — they 'float' above it.
- When the access arms are moved across *all* the read/write heads are moved together so that each head is positioned over the same track of each recording surface.
- The set of tracks under the heads form a vertical cylinder (see Fig. 3.5) and if related records are all stored on the same cylinder, they can be accessed without moving the access assembly. This is called the *cylinder concept*.
- A record may be accessed directly by specifying the cylinder, track and sector number, as in Fig. 3.6.

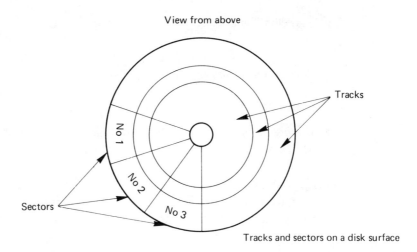

View from above

Tracks

No 1

No 2

No 3

Sectors

Tracks and sectors on a disk surface

Figure 3.6 Addressing on magnetic disk. For example, reading address 040 03 02: 040 = cylinder number; 03 = track number (i.e. the third surface down from the top of the disk pack; 02 = sector number.

(iii) *Disk Capacity*

Q. What does disk capacity depend on?

A. Disk capacity depends on:

- The number of recording surfaces.
- The number of cylinders.
- The recording density (bytes/track).

It is usually stated in terms of megabytes (MB),
e.g. for a disk pack:

    Bytes/track   8500
    Tracks/cylinder   12
    Cylinders/pack   700

giving a total storage capacity of about 70 Mb.

- Several disk drives can be connected to a computer at once so the total on-line backing store can range from around 50 Mb in a mini system to much greater levels.

(iv) *Exchangeable and fixed disks*

Q. What are exchangeable and fixed disks?

A. Disks can be either:

- *Exchangeable disks* — Which can be removed from the disk drive and another pack mounted.
- *Fixed disks* — Which are not removable, and usually store more or less permanent data, e.g. the operating system.

Some disk packs include not only the disks but the spindle and access mechanism in the unit itself. This means that they are reliable and dust free.

In other systems the read/write arms are part of the disk drive. The disk packs for these are consequently much lighter and cheaper.

(v) *Access Time*

Q. Explain '*disk access time*'

A. There are two types of disk access:

- *Moving-head disks* — Where the access mechanism moves in and out to position heads at the required location (NB the cylinder concept saves on movement).
- *Fixed-head disks* — Where the access mechanism is stationary with a head over each track (i.e. 1 read/write head for every track). These are faster as the seek time is eliminated (e.g. useful for paging memory) and are usually more expensive.

Disk drives normally have only a small number of fixed-head tracks; many have none at all.

Access time is the time it takes to access a stored record. The time taken to access data on a disk is made up of:

- *Seek time* — The time taken for the read/write heads to get to the right track (arm movement time).
- *Rotational delay* — The time the disk takes to come round beneath the read/write heads.
- *Data transfer time* — The time it takes to read/write the data to/from main memory, i.e. access time = seek time + rotational delay + data transfer time. Disk performance is usually stated in terms of *average* access time. On average a disk will have to rotate $\frac{1}{2}$ revolution for the selected record to be in the correct position. For example:
  - Rotational speed 3600 r.p.m.
  - Seek time 25 ms.
  - Effective transfer rate (bytes per second).

At 3600 rpm the time for 1 rotation = 16.7 ms and an average rotational delay of $\frac{1}{2} \times$ 16.7 = 8.4 ms.
Thus access time = 33.4 ms plus the data transfer time.

(vi) *Advantages and Disadvantages*

Q. What are the advantages and disadvantages of magnetic disl?

A. *Advantages of magnetic disk*:

- Currently the most popular storage method in business.
- Data can be accessed directly — there is no need to search through other records.
- Sequential processing is possible if needed (as with all DASDs).
- Very high capacity storage at low cost (per character stored).
- Disk packs are convenient to handle and store.

Disadvantages:

- Disk drives and disks are more expensive than tape drives and tapes, respectively.

- Slower than newer 'forms' of storage, e.g. magnetic bubble.
- Can be unreliable — susceptible to dust, static electricity, head crashes, etc.

(vii) *Uses*

- Most business situations
- Particularly useful in on-line enquiry/response systems, where direct access is essential e.g. reservation/booking systems.

(viii) *Winchester disk*

Q. What is a Winchester disk?

A. *Winchester disk* — This is a hard disk for small-business systems (see Fig. 3.7).

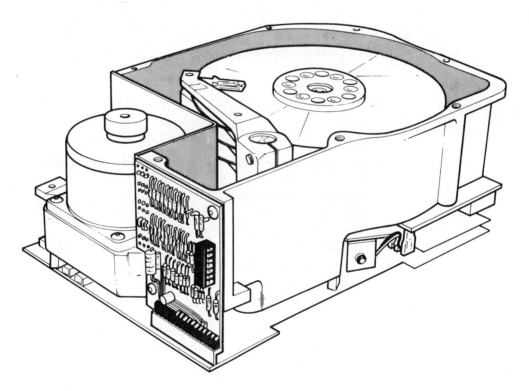

Figure 3.7 A Winchester disk.

- It is made of:
  · Hard, metallic material, aluminium surface.
  · Lightweight read/write head floats just above the surface to such precision that data can be packed very tightly.
  · Sealed in airtight casing.
- Capacity: usually 5–10 times larger than a floppy, typically 25 Mb, but capacities are getting up to 450 Mb.
- Back-up: diskettes, tape streamer.

1 Advantages and Disadvantages

Q. What are the advantages and disadvantages of Winchesters?

A. *Advantages*

- Very reliable (hermetically sealed container).
- Getting smaller in size: 8″, 5¼″, 3½″ (so-called 'mini-winis').
- Doesn't deteriorate as quickly as a floppy.
- Faster than a floppy.

Disadvantages:

- Still relatively expensive.
- Inflexible — disks in sealed container cannot be changed.

2 Uses

- In small-business systems.
- In 'rough' environments where there is dust, etc.

(e) Floppy Disks (or diskettes)

Q. What are floppy disks?

A. These are a simple, low-cost form of disk storage:

- A floppy disk is a single, flexible disk held in a protective jacket (Fig. 3.8).
- It is made of polyester film coated with metal oxide compound and resembles a 45 r.p.m. record.
- They are typically 8″, 5¼″ and 3½″ in diameter with either 40 or 80 tracks.
- They can be hard or soft-sectored. Boundaries between sectors are marked by holes (hard) or recorded by software (soft). Thus soft-sectored disks can have their boundaries changed by re-recording. Because of this they have slightly less space for data.

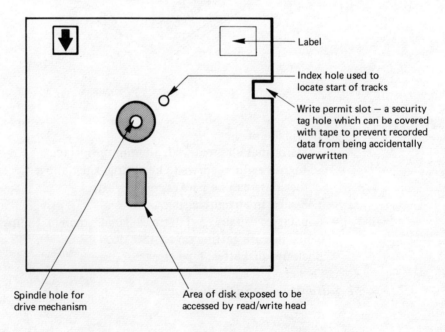

Figure 3.8 A 5¼″ floppy disk in its protective jacket.

- Floppies operate in much the same way as hard disks. The disk is inserted into a floppy disk drive to be read/written to. They are, therefore, interchangeable. There is usually a double disk drive for booting (where one disk holds the operating system, the one in the other drive holds the files and programs) or for security/copying purposes – so that back-ups can be taken when needed.
- *Capacity* – Data are stored in much the same way as on the larger hard disks. Capacity varies according to density and whether the disk has one or two recording sides (now usually two). Typical capacities are between $\frac{1}{2}$ Mb and 1 Mb.

(i) *Advantages and disadvantages*

Q. What are the advantages and disadvantages of floppy disks?

A.*Advantages of floppy disks*

- They are very cheap (a few £s) compared with other disk media.
- Small, lightweight and convenient.
- Exchangeable.

Disadvantages:

- Vulnerable – short shelf life, susceptible to dirt, etc.
- A floppy disk drive is still much more expensive than a cassette tape drive.

(ii) *Uses*

- Ideal backing store for personal computers and microcomputer-based small-business systems.

(f) Mass Cartridge Storage

Q. Explain the term 'mass cartridge storage system'.

A.Some organizations, such as governments, banks and insurance companies, need to keep *very large* data files. An insurance company, for example, may keep records of several million policy holders.

To cope with such massive amounts of data various types of mass storage system have been devised. The most recent consists of small magnetic cartridges, each containing a short strip of tape which can store over 8 million characters. Each strip can be selected (addressed) and the contents read sequentially.

When a computer requires data it selects the appropriate cartridge (from a 'bank' of cartridges which looks like a honeycomb), moves it to a read/write station where the tape is read (or new data recorded) and the tape and cartridge are then returned to the storage cell. Average time to access and read the tape is between 2 and 3 seconds. This is slow compared with CPU speeds so data are often swopped to magnetic disk before entry into the computer.

Cartridges are stored in cells in the storage unit or 'bank'. A unit might hold 2000 cartridges in rectangular cells.

Thus total capacity would be:

2000×8 M $= 16\,000$ Mb of on-line data – the equivalent of about 200 disk packs or several thousand tape reels.

Although relatively slow because of the mechanical movement, mass cartridge systems do represent a cheaper alternative to disk in very large systems.

(g) Optical Storage Systems

Q. What are optical storage systems?

A. Many experts believe that the next big step in storage systems will be using optical methods. The snag is that at present data recorded by lasers cannot be erased or rewritten (but research is going on to overcome this).

(i) *Video tape*

This is useful for mass storage but suffers from the disadvantages of 'ordinary' tape — searching is time consuming.

(ii) *Optical (Video disk)*

- Made up of thin metal film/polymer compound on to which holes/pits are burnt.
- These are read by laser.
- They offer massive capacities, e.g. 2000 Mb and, although expensive, are cheap in terms of cost per byte stored.

In principle a user should be able to use 1 'box' to play pre-recorded audio, video and data storage optical disks which offer video/audio recording and play back with true digital sound and pictures.

Several companies have developed players which can use both video disks (showing films, sports, etc.) and compact audio disks (laser-read versions of ordinary records).

There is available a $4\frac{1}{2}''$ data storage disk (looking just like the audio-disk) storing 55 m bytes of computer information (or up to $\frac{1}{4}$m sheets of A4 size documents) which is more than 500 times as much as today's $3\frac{1}{2}''$ magnetic floppy disks.

However, optical disks will not replace the video-tape recorder and ordinary cassette player or floppies in computers just yet.

The next stage — making optical disks erasable and re-recordable — is still at the experimental stage.

(iii) *Advantages and Disadvantages*

Q. What are the advantages and disadvantages of optical disks?

A. *Advantages of optical disks:*
- They have massive capacity and can store text, moving pictures and audio.
- Information can be retrieved very quickly.
- Reliable. They have long life — no mechanical contact between disk and optical system.
- Exchangeable.
- The disks themselves are fairly inexpensive, especially in terms of the cost per character stored.

Disadvantages

- Costly hardware for reading.
- No standard sizes or formats.
- Temporarily read/record-only. Still problems writing to disk. Even harder is erasing and rewriting (although storage capacity is so great that erasing is not all that important).

(iv) *Uses*

- *Training and education* —
  Self-pacing, optional routes.
- *Financial applications* — e.g. audit trails.
  Auditors can track financial transactions knowing that such records cannot be erased or 'doctored' on optical disk.
- *Large-volume 'image' data bases* —
  e.g. people looking to book a holiday can be shown moving or still pictures of the different locations and accommodation available.
- *Filing documents.*
- *Storing* reference 'books' graphs, maps, still pictures. Such data can be displayed and 'manipulated' on a TV screen, e.g. there is a facility for over-laying text on picture and updating as required. Some councils store ordnance survey maps and planning charts on optical disk and superimpose gas, phone, electricity and water access points so that these essential services can be cross-referenced for repairs and maintenance purposes.
    - The National Air and Space Museum in Washington, D.C., USA, has transferred its collection of a million archive photographs on to disks costing about $30 each, providing a permanent, almost undamageable record. The pictures are photographed onto 35 mm film, then transferred to videotape and then to disk. Apart from the value to enthusiasts and researchers, the original photos do not have to suffer the daily wear and tear of being handled.

(v) *Laser Card*

Q. What is a laser card?

A. A laser card looks like an ordinary credit card except that it has a strip of special film on which data can be recorded by a laser in the form of tiny pits of silver halide particles. Optical detectors can read the data back from the strip very quickly by interpreting reflected light which varies according to the pit pattern. At the moment, laser cards are read-only, i.e. it is not possible to store new information on them. Nevertheless, they still may have uses for storing permanent features such as operating systems. Cards can typically store 5 Mb and are very cheap.

(h) Bubble Memories

Q. What are bubble memories? List their advantages and disadvantages.

A. A store of information in a flat, thin film of garnet. The film is magnetised in such a way that tiny, polarised regions form in the material. Under a microscope these regions look like bubbles, which is how they get their name. The presence or absence of bubbles can be used to represent digital 0's and 1's.

Advantages:

- *Less fragile* – Can withstand extremes of temperature, vibration, dust and humidity.
- *Much smaller* – Higher storage densities can be achieved than with semi-conductor memory.
- *Non-volatile* – Do not lose data during power failure or voltage fluctuation.
- Easier to make than chips.

Disadvantages

- Still too expensive for general use.

Uses

- For paging memory or where fast access is essential.
- In rugged environments.

(i) Future Developments

Storage systems continue to improve rapidly. Very large scale integration, thin-film technology and precision reading have led to increased capacities for the same price, thus reducing cost/performance ratios.

Research is going on into advanced memory systems such as bubble memories and optical systems which may eventually replace magnetic disk and tape media.

3.5 Exercises

Question 3.1

Explain the purpose of each of the following types of storage and the major types of devices or media used:

(a) Main memory. (b) Paging memory. (c) Data base storage. (d) Archival storage.

Question 3.2

Define each of the following terms:

(a) Sequential access. (b) Direct access. (c) Multiprogramming. (d) Virtual storage.

Question 3.3

List the principal advantages of each of the following types of secondary storage:

(a) Magnetic disk. (b) Magnetic tape. (c) Magnetic cartridge. (d) Optical disk.

Question 3.4

Give at least one type of storage device that might be used for each of the following:

(a) Storing programs when not in the main memory.

(b) Storing large sequential data files.

(c) Storing large direct access files.

(d) Storing extremely large direct access files.

Question 3.5

(a) Name two different types of backing storage media and compare the accessibility of data from each of these types.

(b) Define backing storage.

(c) State why backing storage is usually needed.

(d) Give, with reasons, an example of an application of computers which needs direct access storage.

Question 3.6

A doctor may store patients' records either on a microcomputer or on a card index file. Give two advantages of each method of storage.   (L)

Question 3.7

A floppy-disk drive is an auxiliary storage (backing store) device.

(a) With which type of computer would you normally associate this device?

(b) Why does this type of computer commonly have disk drives as well as main memory?

(c) If one character is stored in an 8-bit byte, and a floppy disk is said to store 250 kbytes, calculate the precise number of characters that could be stored on the disk.   (OLE)

Question 3.8

Computers are used in each of the following situations. State which form of backing store is most suitable, irrespective of cost. Give one reason for each answer.

(a) A news room in a national daily newspaper office.

(b) A point-of-sale terminal from which data is obtained for overnight processing.

(c) A laboratory system for checking poisonous substances and their antidotes.   (AEB)

Question 3.9

This microcomputer has 32k bytes of immediate access store.

(a) What is the value of 1k in this context?

(b) What is a byte?

(c) What is immediate access store?   (AEB)

Question 3.10

Part of the specification of a microcomputer reads as follows:
64k RAM, 128k ROM.

(a) Explain what the abbreviations RAM and ROM mean.

(b) Highlight the difference between the two.

(c) How will this difference affect their respective uses?

Question 3.11

Winchester disks, floppy disks and cassette tapes are three backing storage media. For each of the following situations state which one would be used. Give two reasons for each answer.

(a) A microcomputer used in the house for 'fun', e.g. games.

(b) A microcomputer system, with dot-matrix printer, used by a dentist to keep records of his 5000 patients. These records take up about $\frac{1}{2}$ Mb of storage capacity.

(c) A minicomputer system, with 8 on-line terminals, used by an engineering firm for all its accounting and administrative functions. The storage capacity requirement is 20 Mb.

3.6 Answers and Hints on Solutions

3.1

	Memory type	Purpose	Type of device/ media used
(a)	Main memory	For data and instructions which are currently being processed	Semiconductors
(b)	Paging memory	For program or data segments which can be called up quickly by the CPU	Semiconductor, fixed-head disk, magnetic bubble
(c)	Database storage	For database or files	Moving-head disk, floppy disks, magnetic tape
(d)	Archival storage	For historical data	COM, magnetic cartridge, video disk

3.2 (a) *Serial access* – To find a record the search must pass all preceding ones.

(b) *Direct access* – Record can be retrieved directly without searching.

(c) *Multiprogramming* – The operating system can run several programs at once.

(d) *Virtual Storage* – Programs need not be limited by the size of main memory as the 'active' parts of them can be called in rapidly from paging memory. This 'extra' memory is known as virtual storage.

3.3 (a) *Disk* – Direct access, most popular media.

(b) *Tape* – cheap, convenient.

(c) *Cartridge* – Very high storage capacity.

(d) *Optical disk* – Can store moving pictures as well as text and audio.

3.4 (a) Disk drive, tape drive.

(b) Tape drive, cassette.

    (c)   Disk drive, Winchester.

    (d)   Magnetic cartridge.

3.5 (b)   Backing storage is used to store programs and data not currently needed in main memory.

    (c)   Organisations need cheap, large-capacity storage to keep all their files.

    (d)   An on-line enquiry system, e.g. reservations where a user needs a reply immediately. An operator with a VDU linked on-line to a computer with direct access storage can retrieve an individual record straight away. A search on tape would take too long for this application.

3.6 Microcomputer: (1) easy to amend/update; (2) fast information retrieval.

Card index: (1) it is easy to use − more people will understand the system (but confidentiality); (2) hard copy, which can be carried around.

3.7 (a)   Microcomputer.

    (b)   So that floppy disks, which hold programs and data, can be used to provide backing store.

    (c) $250 \times 2^{10} = 256\,000$ characters

3.8 (a)   Magnetic disk, direct access of individual records, e.g. news items.

    (b)   Magnetic tape would be adequate for overnight processing, when there will be time to sort/merge, etc.

    (c)   Searching files for matches and links implies magnetic disk storage, particularly if the laboratory does emergency work.

3.9 (a) $1\,K = 1$ kilobyte $= 2^{10} = 1024$.

    (b)   A byte is a group of 8 bits storing the code for 1 character.

    (c)   Immediate access store is another name for main memory.

3.10 (a)   RAM = Random access memory. ROM = Read only memory.

    (b)   RAM is volatile and is used as temporary store. ROM is non-volatile and is used as 'permanent' store − it is non-destructable.

    (c)   RAM is used for temporary store of data/programs as they are being worked on in main memory. It can be changed by a user program. ROM is used for keeping data or programs that are fixed − e.g. the operating system, word-processing chip.

3.11 (a)   Cassette tapes (with recorder):

- Cheap, reliable.
- Fast loading times are not important in the home.
- Lots of games available in cassette form.

    (b)   Floppy disks (with disk drive):

- Dentist needs fast access to individual patients' records.
- One floppy can easily hold $\frac{1}{2}$ Mb.

(c) Winchester disks (with disk drive):

- Reliable, compact.
- One disk can cope with large storage requirement.

4 Data Input Methods, Media and Devices

The chapter is divided into the following sections:

- Aims of data collection.
- The problems of collecting data.
- The main methods of data input.
- Forms and dialogue design.
- Data verification and validation.
- Coding.
- Input media and devices.

4.1 Aims of Data Collection

The overall aim of any method of data collection is to translate information created by people into a form usable by a computer.

Q. How can you assess an effective data-entry system?

A. An effective data-entry system must be fast, accurate, versatile, efficient, secure and cost-effective. This usually entails:

- Reducing the volume of input to minimum practical levels.
- Reducing the amount of data which needs manual preparation.
- Designing input to ease the task of preparation (using menus and simple boxed forms).
- Using the minimum number of stages from origin of the data to computer input.

4.2 Problems of Collecting Data

Q. What are the problems of collecting data?

A. These are:

- The preparation of source documents is slow, hard work and prone to mistakes.
- Typing speeds are very slow compared with computer speeds. This is known as the 'keyboard bottleneck'.
- It is wasteful to use media e.g. punched cards and paper tape which can be used only once.

- Mistakes can easily be made when copying from one medium to another. Such mistakes are known as transcription errors.
- Transmission delays or losses can occur, particularly if data have to be physically transferred to the computer.
- Data entry can be expensive, often accounting for 40–50% of the total data-handling costs.

So, providing prompt and correct input data is a major problem (remember the adage GIGO—garbage in, garbage out).

4.3 The Main Methods of Data Input

Q. How can the problems of collecting data be overcome?

A. The following methods attempt to overcome some of the problems of data entry. For further details of input devices and media see Section 4.7.

(a) Data Input Methods

The main methods of data input are:

(i) *On-line Data Entry*

Data is entered directly into the computer one transaction at a time (also known as transaction processing) under program control. The main types of on-line data entry device are: VDUs, teletypes, light pens, voice input and shop-floor data collection devices. They can be used off-line also for bulk data collection.

(ii) *Source Document Conversion*

This is where source documents, e.g. order forms and time sheets, are batched and converted into a computer-acceptable medium. The data is entered, verified and validated by computer and then transferred to backing store (tape or disk) for later processing. Such systems are called key-to-storage systems. The keyboard will be part of the VDU type device.

(iii) *Direct Data Capture*

Data is captured directly without a conversion stage. Specially marked or printed documents (e.g. questionnaires, bank cheques) can be read by special input devices. Tags attached to clothing and collected at the point of sale are another example of direct input media. This method eliminates the keyboard, automates transcription, increases speeds and reduces media costs.

Whatever the method of data input chosen one of the aims must be to reduce the number of stages yet still ensure that data is input free of errors. Fig. 4.1 shows the input stages for the main methods of data capture. It should be apparent why on-line is so popular.

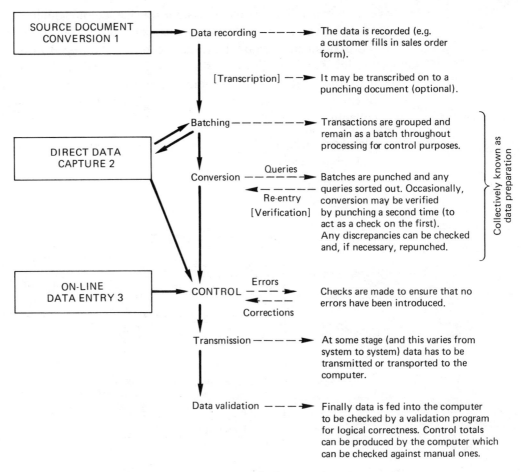

Figure 4.1 Input stages for main data input methods.

Notes: 1. Source document conversion involves tracking through most (or all) of the stages.
2. Direct data capture avoids recording, transcription, conversion and verification.
3. On-line data entry also eliminates the batching requirement as transactions are processed one at a time.

4.4 Forms and Dialogue Design

One general way of easing the problems of collecting data is to design entry forms and dialogues (VDU screen displays) so that they are easy to use and understand. This will help to ensure that data entered from documents at the keyboard is accurate and complete.

Q. What are the principles of form and dialogue design?

A. Forms and dialogues are linked because they follow the same underlying design principles. Formats, whether on paper or on screen, should be attractive and easy to use and this requires careful investigation and analysis before design and testing. It is vital to test forms and dialogues because they are important in getting accurate input data to the computer and meaningful information from it.

Decisions have to be made on content, format, information needed, codes and names, instructions and how the user will complete. Then there are the problems of layout to be overcome. These include such things as space and size (more choice with paper than screen), highlights (e.g. underlinings, type sizes, flashing cursors, inverse video), titles and reference numbers, etc.

For paper (hard copy) decisions on size, colour, quality, printing type, number of copies and make-up (sticky labels, continuous stationery, etc.) have to be made.

For dialogues, more flexibility can be introduced as different screen displays can be shown to different people. For example, a 'dedicated' operator needs less help than the 'casual' or temporary user and should be able to skip detailed instructions designed to guide the beginner. There are basically two types of data collection dialogue:

- *Form-filling* – Where the screen is blocked as if it were a form (Fig. 4.2).
- *Menu-selection* – As in viewdata systems where the user picks from a restricted choice of options.

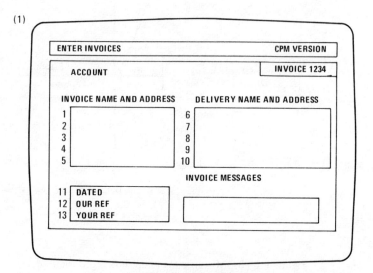

Entry is fast and easy, all account information is generated automatically from sales ledger files.

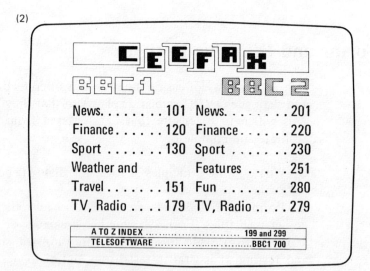

The BBC CEEFAX teletex system.
The user selects the appropriate page number for further details

Figure 4.2 Screen displays helping data input.
(1) Blocks for 'form-filling'; (2) a menu.

When designing a form or screen-display for a particular application remember to:

- Make it clear, concise and easy to complete.
- Leave the user with as little to do as possible:
  - Preprint constant data (e.g. name and address).
  - Include only what is relevant.
  - Use codes and multiple-choice, short answers are much easier to process and analyse than long written replies.
- Keep it neat, tidy and well laid out.
- Account for the physical size of the document (e.g. A4) or screen size (e.g. 80ch × 24 lines).
- Use highlights (e.g. italics, flashing cursor) for important points.

4.5 Data Verification and Validation

Ideally all data entering the computer should be complete and correct. In practice, of course, this cannot always be achieved particularly where data is received from outside sources, such as customer orders, which are not easy to control.

The aim is to minimise the number of errors, and computer-based systems must include extensive checking procedures to guard against incorrect, missing or duplicate data. As a rule of thumb, it is best to trap errors as early as possible to avoid adding to the mistake.

Q. What is data verification?

A. The copying from one medium (e.g. a source document) to another (e.g. punched card) is called transcription. To avoid mistakes in copying (i.e. transcription errors) details are entered *twice* for each transaction. If a difference is detected, the error will be checked and, if necessary, corrected. This process of checking for mistakes in copying is known as verification.

Q. What is data validation?

A. *Checks* — Data validation involves checking input data for errors before the data is passed for computer processing. Data checks can be broadly classified into three types: input validation, feasibility checks and check digits.

(a) Input Validation

(i) *Presence Check*

The computer-based system can check the input data against known values by looking up a record in the files to ensure that the input is valid. Before processing a customer record, for example, a check could be made on customer number and catalogue numbers to make sure that they exist. This is known as a dependency/ presence check. Where applicable, a list of options (e.g. valid quantities of goods ordered) should be displayed so that the user can select from a limited choice, thereby reducing error.

(ii) *Type Check*

It is possible to check if a particular data input is a numeric or a string 'type', e.g. a set of numbers to be totalled can be checked to make sure that:

- All characters are either decimal digits or points.
- There is no more than one decimal point for each number.

By way of confirmation, acceptable numbers could result in the customer name being shown on the VDU screen (known as flashback or echo check). Non-valid numbers can be rejected at this early stage and the fault investigated. The outcome should be a valid set of orders which can be passed forward for further processing.

(b) Feasibility Checking

These checks look for the probability of error as well as for definite mistakes. There are various types of check which are now explained.

(i) *Layout Checks*

Each position within a data item is tested against the item's picture to ensure that only valid values are present. Layout (or picture) checks are commonly applied to code numbers as these often have a complicated layout. For example, if the picture of a national insurance number is AA 99 99 99 A, where A represents a letter and 9 a digit, then the number YT 67 85 C9 A would be rejected as there is a letter in the 7th position instead of a number.

It is also possible that a particular position within a data item must have one of a limited set of values; if this is so a more stringent check can be made. For instance, days in a date field should be no greater than 31.

(ii) *Range (or Limit) Checks*

These are used to check whether data is within a range of possible values. Whether being input, output or processed data items can be given minimum and maximum values which can be set by the width of the data field. For example, 9999 would be the maximum value in a four-character field.

However, IF tests will probably be used to check the feasible limits. For example, the amounts on domestic electricity bills are checked before being sent to customers:

IF $< £1$ THEN

write a message telling consumer to withhold payment until the next bill.

IF $> £300$ THEN

check for error pending possible re-reading of meter.

(iii) *Compatibility Checks*

Data items may pass their own limit checks but fail when checked for compatibility. For example, a customer order for 12 units @ £10 each may be acceptable until it is compared with the customer's credit limit which is found to be only £100. Hence the order would be temporarily withheld.

(c) Check Digits

Q. What is a check digit?

A. *Check digits (self-checking numbers)* – A check digit can be appended to a code number in order to detect errors arising when the number is transcribed manually. A very high percentage of mistakes can be found in this way. The types of error which can arise in the transcription of numeric data are given in Table 4.1.

Table 4.1 Percentage of errors detected by check digit

Error type	Data item	Error	Percentage of errors revealed by check digit
Transposition	45678	54678	100
Transcription	45678	49678	100
Omission	45678	4678	100
Addition	45678	345678	100
Random	45678	9658	91

Average error-finding ratio is 98%.
Assuming that an operator makes one error in 50, the check digit is accurate 99.9% of the time.

In general, check digits are only worthwhile using if the code number is fairly long, say above five digits, and is transcribed fairly frequently.

Q. What are the principles of check digits?

A. The principle behind check digits is that an extra digit is generated from the code number itself by applying an algorithm to it.

A simple but not very efficient algorithm would be to add together the code's digits and use the least significant digit of the sum as the check digit. For example:

    Code number   78435
    Sum   27
    Check digit   7

This method would detect about 80% of the possible errors.

The drawback of such simple methods is that they do not pick up transposition errors. However, these can be detected by dividing the code number by a suitable number and using the remainder as a check digit. An extension of this is to weight each digit before dividing the sum. The larger the dividing number (and hence the remainder) the greater the degree of accuracy, because there is less probability of an incorrect code number happening by chance.

(i) *Modulus – 11 Check Digit System*

This is the most popular check digit method and many systems include it in the validation program which automatically creates and/or verifies the check digit when the code number is input.

Worked example

e.g. International Standard Book Numbers (ISBNs) are based on the Modulus — 11:

- ISBN   0–17–741130   0–17–741130
- Multiply by weight
  (weighting value is   98 765432
  2 for least significant
  digit, 3 for the next,
  and so on)
- Products   9+56+49+24+5+4+9
- Sum the products   156
- Divide sum by 11.   14 remainder 2
  If the remainder is
  0, the check is 0   11 − 2 = 9
  If the remainder is
  not 0, subtract it from
  11 to give the check
  digit. A check digit of 10
  is usually written 'X'

New Code Number: 0–17–741130–9.

4.6 Coding

Q. Why use code numbers?

A. One way of reducing the volume of data input is to use codes. Code numbers are needed in computer-based systems to identify and locate data records. Their design is usually based on existing codes within the organisation, but they must be precisely defined for computer use.

To help the user, code numbers should be easily identifiable and as short and simple as possible to minimise mistakes. The design of coding systems and the assignment of code numbers must be standardised to avoid confusion and duplication.

The best known coding systems are now outlined.

(a) Hierarchical Classification

A good example of this is the Universal Decimal Code as used in libraries. This is based on the notion that everything can be subdivided into smaller groups (sub-classifying); cf. topdown design. For example, suppose we wish to classify the sales regions for a company:

- *Top level* (first digit):
  - 1 = North.
  - 2 = Midlands.
  - 3 = South.
- *Middle level* (second digit):
  - North;
  - 1 = Yorkshire.
  - 2 = Lancashire.
  - 3 = Durham.

Midlands;
    1 = Derbyshire.
    2 = Nottinghamshire.
- *Bottom level* (third digit):
    North-Yorkshire;
    1 = Leeds and Bradford area.
    2 = Wakefield and Doncaster area.
    3 = York, Malton, Scarborough.

Thus the classification code (sales region code) for York would be 113.

(b) Faceted Classification

In this system each position in the code has its own independent meaning, i.e. it does not have to be linked to a higher level as with hierarchical coding. For example, a supermarket classifies soups according to four characteristics: manufacturer, type, size and flavour.

- *Manufacturer* (first digit):
    1 = Heinz.
    2 = Batchelor.
- *Type* (second digit):
    1 = Tinned.
    2 = Condensed.
    3 = Powdered.
- *Size* (third digit):
    1 = $1\frac{1}{2}$ pints equivalent.
    2 = Cup-a-soup.
- *Flavour* (fourth digit):
    1 = Tomato.
    2 = Chicken.
    3 = Minestrone.

Hence a powdered Batchelor's Tomato Cup-a-soup will be coded 2321.

(c) Serial Coding

Serial code numbers are arbitrarily assigned and therefore, give no information about items they represent. Nevertheless, they are simple and may be used to append to classification codes to provide full identification of every item.

(d) Sequential Coding

Items are organised into some natural sequence and then the code numbers assigned are increased each time (incremented), for example, customer account numbers may be assigned in alphabetical order by surname, although care must be taken to leave gaps for later insertions.

(e) Block Coding

This system splits up a set of serial or sequential code numbers into blocks which can be determined by some general characteristic. For example, customer outlets might be block coded as follows:

- Department Stores   1– 99.
- Supermarkets   100–199.
- Off-licences   200–299.
- Other retail outlets 300–

(f) Interpretative Coding

In this system all or some of the digits take the values of the actual quantitative data they represent. For example, 10255 might be the code for 10 fish fingers weighing 255 g. Additional digits can be used to indicate other characteristics.

(g) Mnemonic Coding

Here, all or part of the code number is derived from the real name or description, thus helping recall. Hence in airline reservation systems LDN = London, NYK = New York.

(h) Check Digits

It is common to find an extra digit at the end of a code number which can be used for checking accuracy and control purposes.

4.7 Input Media and Devices

Recall that the physical parts of a computer system are called *hardware* and that any device connected to and under the control of the CPU is called a *peripheral*. The material on which data is stored or printed – e.g. magnetic disk, tape, paper – is called the *medium*. Hence a disk drive is a *device* for reading from or writing to the magnetic disk medium.

Devices can be directly connected to a computer and under its control, in which case they are *on-line*, or else separate from the computer, in which case they are *off-line*. Thus a floppy disk stored in a rack is off-line. When it is placed in a disk drive it is on-line.

Input devices accept data from outside the computer system and transmit it to the CPU. Output devices accept data from the CPU and output it for people to see. The most common input media and devices will now be examined. These are:

- Card.
- Tape.
- Key-to-storage.
- Document readers (e.g. OMR, OCR, MICR).
- Light pens.
- Bar codes.
- Tags.
- Badges.
- Writing pads.
- Speech input.
- Direct input from other instruments.
- Terminals are both input and output devices and will be covered in the next chapter.

Students should be familiar with the characteristics and functions of each, their relative advantages and disadvantages and some typical applications.

Punched Cards and Paper Tapes

Punched cards and paper tapes have been largely replaced by magnetic media. They only remain, for historical reasons, in a few applications. A brief résumé is given, partly to illustrate the stages and problems of data capture.

(i) *Punched Cards*

Q. What is a punched card?

A. Fig. 4.3 shows an example of an 80 column x 12 row punched card. Each character is represented by a pattern of holes punched in a column of the card (1, 2 or more holes depending on whether the character is numeric, alphabetic or special). Therefore, one punched card can store 80 characters.

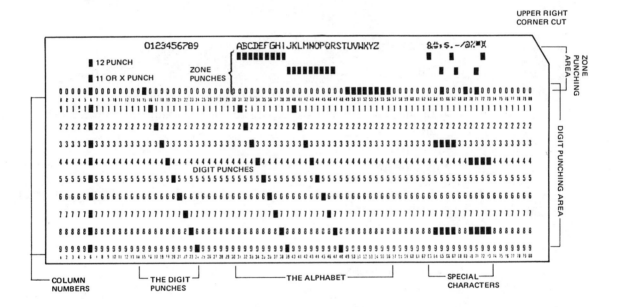

Figure 4.3 The 80-column Hollerith card.

Cards are read by a punched card reader and punched by a punch unit. In most computer systems, the card reader and punch are combined into a single unit.

Sometimes the characters punched are printed out along the top of the card so that people can see what the code is meant to be.

Speeds can be up to 30 cards per second. Cards are read completely so the reading speed could be 80 (columns) x 30 = 2400 characters per second if all the columns were punched. However, this would be unusual and, effectively, typical rates are about 1500 c.p.s.

(ii) *Paper Tape*

Q. What is paper tape?

A. Paper tape varies in width between $\frac{3}{4}''$ and $1''$ depending on the code and is stored in reels up to about $1000'$ in length. Again data is coded in the form of

79

punched holes (a hole represents binary 1, else 0) which is stored in tracks across the tape (see also magnetic tape).

Paper tape can be read at speeds up to 2000 c.p.s. by a reader.

The data entry process for paper tape is very similar to that of punched cards:

- Data is punched on to rolls of tape.
  As paper tape cannot have the coded characters printed on it, punches often produce a hard copy as well.
- Data is verified by either:
  - The call-over method,
    where a copy of the data punched in is visually checked against original documents.
  OR
  - The 2-tape method,
    where a second tape is punched and a verifier compares each character with the equivalent character in the first tape and stops if an error is found.
- Spools of punched paper tape then go as computer input usually via a conversion process for faster input.

(iii) *Punched Card and Paper Tape*

These are:

- Declining in popularity and are now virtually obsolete.
- In need of too much preparation — punching and verification is a lengthy and costly process.
- Not re-usable.
- Read slowly.

For most purposes magnetic media have taken over and more direct input methods have been developed.

(b) **Key-to-storage Systems**

Q. What is a key-to-storage system?

A. Data preparation and input is often the bottle neck of the entire system, e.g. key punching and verifying take a lot of time.

One way of easing this problem is to use key-to-storage systems of which there are two basic types:

- Key-to-tape.
- Key-to-disk.

For details of magnetic tape and disk, see Sections 3.4(c) and 3.4(d).

Such systems typically consist of several key stations (VDUs) connected to a minicomputer (although there may be just a single station in a small low-cost key-to-diskette system using floppy disks). The operators enter data from source documents into the VDUs under the mini's control.

Q. What are the functions of a key-to-storage system?

A. Typical functions provided:

- The minicomputer prompts the operator to enter the correct data at each step.
- The VDU provides sight verification to the operator with backspace/deletion allowing for immediate error correction.
- The data is input to an edit program to filter out most errors, e.g. by using reasonable checks (see Section 4.5) and then stored on disk or tape.
- Verification may then be done by another operator who keys in the same data for a second time. This is compared with the data already stored and differences can be examined and, if necessary, corrected.

  Each key station can be used for keying or verifying.
- Data from all key stations can be stored and merged to produce a disk (or tape) file for further processing.
- The system monitors operator performance and maintains statistics that are useful in improving productivity, e.g. control totals.

Q. What are the advantages of a key-to-storage system?

A. Key-to-storage systems:

- Speed up data input.
- Reduce errors.
- Reduce load on main computer
  (input is handled off-line).

See Figure 4.4.

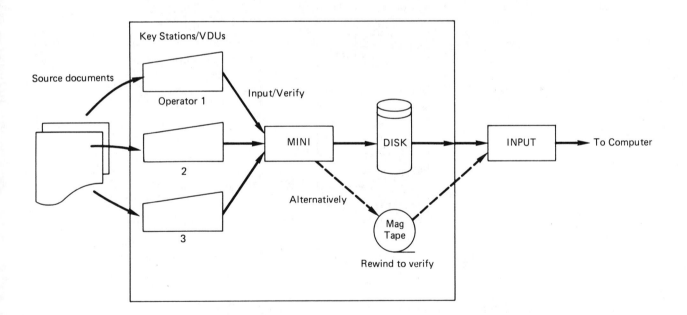

Figure 4.4 Key–to–storage systems.

(c) Document Readers

Q. What is a document reader?

A. A *document reader* is a device which can read data directly from source documents. Documents can come in all shapes and sizes. *Examples* include a bank cheque, a multiple choice question paper, an electricity meter reader form.

(i) *Types of Code on the Documents*

Marks – Short lines are made by hand, usually in pencil, on a preprinted card or document.

Characters – Hand written, e.g. on meter-reading slips; printed, e.g. in magnetic ink on cheques.

Printed lines – The most common of these is the bar code.

(ii) *Optical Mark Read (OMR)*

Q. What is OMR?

A. OMR allows the direct transfer of data from source document to computer. Information is collected on a preprinted OMR form by marking predetermined positions with a pencil or pen to indicate each selected response (Figure 4.5). Large volumes of data can be collected quickly and easily without the need for specially trained staff. A device called an Optical Mark Reader converts the marks into computer-readable data. The Reader detects the presence (or absence) of a mark on a form by sensing reflected infra-red light. The software in the Reader interprets the marks into meaningful characters which can be passed to the computer for storage and analysis.

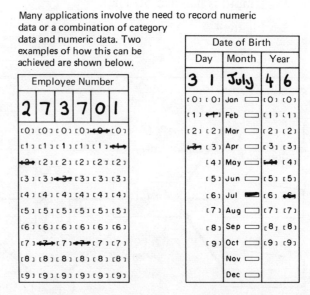

Figure 4.5 An OMR application. Courtesy Data and Research Services Ltd.

Q. What are the advantages and disadvantages of OMR?

A. *Advantages of OMR*:

- Sensitivity can be altered to allow for different surfaces and pencils and inks.
- Has a better recognition rate than OCR.
- Can be prepared where data originates, without machines.
- Errors are easily corrected.

Disadvantages (of marks compared with characters):

- Mark readers are relatively slow.
- Verification of marked data is difficult.

- Document may be difficult to understand and fill in or impractical to design.
- The document reader will have to be reprogrammed for each new document design.

Q. Give some examples of uses for which OMR is suitable.

A. *Uses.* Situations where:

- The data to be input is simple.
- The volume of data is large enough to justify designing documents.
- Turn-around documents are used.
- Preparation equipment would be expensive or impractical.

Examples of uses for:

- Multiple-choice examinations, aptitude tests.
- Insurance premium collection.
- Market research questionnaires – consumer research.
- In supermarkets for stock reordering.
- Traffic surveys.
- Payroll data entry.

1 Character Recognition

Here the document reader recognises *characters* which have been printed by machine or hand, rather than just the presence (or absence) of a mark. The shape of each character is analysed by the scanning device and compared with a set of known shapes. Either the character is recognised or the document is rejected to be checked.

(iii) *Optical Character Recognition (OCR)*

Q. What is OCR?

A. Characters are read by an optical character reader that senses light reflected from the paper and ink (as with OMR) and converts the characters to electric signals. OCR means that the reader has a memory and processing capability so that signals can be matched with internally stored reference patterns for a given character set or *font*. A font is a set of characters of a particular size and style. The most common are OCR-A and B which most Readers recognise. Some can cope with typed or printed fonts and even hand-printed characters, provided they are neatly written like a standard font. Patterns which cannot be read cause the document to be rejected. Data that is accepted can be either read directly into the computer or recorded on magnetic tape or disk for later processing. Some OCR Readers can also sort documents into given categories. Typical OCR Reader *speeds* are between 100 and 1500 documents per minute depending on the type of document and font type used.

Reliability is important and two measures are the reject rate, and the error rate.

The reject rate is the percentage of documents that cannot be read by the reader (usually less than 10%).

The error rate is the percentage of documents read on which one or more characters are incorrectly identified (less than 1%).

Q. Give some examples of uses for which OCR is suitable.

A. *Uses.* OCR is used in billing (e.g. gas and electricity bills, insurance premium renewals) and giro-forms.

Billing often involves a *turnaround* document. For example, electricity bills are prepared in OC by the computer, sent out to customers who return them with payment cheques. The documents are then re-entered via the OC reader into the computer system as evidence of payment. Note that no transcription is needed.

(iv) *Magnetic Ink Character Recognition (MICR)*

Q. What is MICR?

A. Characters are printed in ink containing iron oxide. When the document is passed into the reader the ink is magnetised so that the magnetic pattern formed by the characters can be identified. Usually MICR devices use font E13B which contains only 14 characters (0–9 and 4 special characters). The main applications are in:

- Some local authorities for payment of rates by instalment
- The banking industry (see below).

Q. In Fig. 4.6:

- The cheque has three separate codes printed on it. Write down each code and explain what it could mean.
- Explain the function of the MICR device and say why it is necessary.

A. The three codes at the bottom of the cheque are (from left to right):

- The serial number of the actual cheque.
- The sorting code number of the branch (see also top right corner).
- And the individual customer account number.

The space below the signature line is left so that the amount can be added in MICR after the cheque has been given to the bank. The cheque can then enter the bank's computer system for processing.

The function of the MICR device is, as noted, to read and recognise the characters at the bottom of the cheque. Once the details of the customer, branch and amount are known they can be used by the computer to update the individual bank accounts. The vast number of cheques which a bank has to handle requires the use of some sort of document reading device. MICR devices can read up to 2500 cheques per minute.

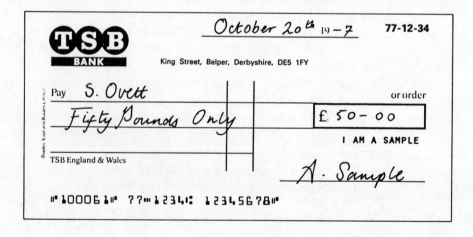

Figure 4.6 Bank cheque.

1 Advantages and Disadvantages

Q. What are the advantages and disadvantages of Character Recognition (CR)?

A. *Advantages of Character Recognition (CR)*:

- As with OMR, *key-entry* is eliminated and data is captured in machine-readable form at the earliest opportunity. This should increase throughput and reduce costs and input errors.
- Characters can be read by people.
- Document design is less complicated and cumbersome than for OMR forms.

Disadvantages of CR:

- Document Readers are relatively expensive.
- Only certain fonts are acceptable.
- The reject rate depends on the quality of the document (e.g. smudges, damaged/torn forms, etc).
- A high standard of printing is needed.
- Hand-printed characters can cause high rejection rates (circa 5%).
- Document design must still follow a rigid format.

Q. Compare OCR with MICR.

A. *Advantages of MICR over OCR*:

- Difficult to forge
- Documents can still be read when folded, written on etc. MICR is more 'robust'.

Advantages of OCR over MICR:

- A wider range of fonts can be used, including some hand printing and normal type; but there is no universal standard-type font.

(d) Light Pens

Light pens are hand-held, pen-shaped devices connected by cable to a terminal which can be used with special software to detect light (Fig. 4.7).

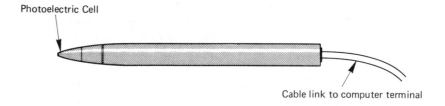

Photoelectric Cell

Cable link to computer terminal

Figure 4.7 Light pen.

(i) *Uses*

They can be used to:

- Read bar codes
- Indicate a point on a screen, e.g. for selecting options for drawings.

The pen is pointed at the screen. The TV screen is 'refreshed' about every 1/50th of a second by a point of light travelling across it. When this light is detected by the pen the computer can work out by timing where the pen's position is on the screen.

(ii) *Advantages*

- No need to type or write.
- Faster input than typing.

(iii) *Disadvantages*

- Can only record the presence (or absence) of light.
- Requires complex software.

(e) Bar Codes

Q. What is a bar code?

A. A bar code is a set of bars and spaces of differing width which represent a number. A space is treated as 0 and a bar unit as 1. The code can be read optically as a bit pattern in which successive groups of bits are treated as BCD or some other numeric code.

Bar codes appear on a variety of items — tags, tickets, plastic cards or on packets/cans in shops.

Fig. 4.8 shows a Bar Code as found on products sold in supermarkets.

Figure 4.8 Bar code.

This is an example of a European Article Number (EAN), known as the Universal Product Code (UPC) in the USA, and is now found on many shop items.

The code itself is an identity tag: its bars correspond to 13 numbers in Europe (12 in America) which in Fig. 4.8 indicate:

- The country of origin — 50.
- The manufacturer — 00136.
- The product — 99970.
- The check digit (modulus 10) — 9.

(i) *How the Data from the Bar Code is Input to the Computer*

The bars can be read by:

- A laser scanning device — which reads the bar code as the product is passed across a window. This is usually part of a point-of-sale (Pos) terminal (Fig. 4.9).

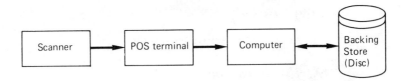

Figure 4.9 POS system.

- A light-pen or 'wand' — which is hand held and attached to a computer terminal or a recording device (Fig. 4.7) and the information passed on to a computer.

The computer can match the information with data in its files (e.g. to tell the check-out counter the current price of the article) and, at the same time, log in its memory a sale of the article.

(ii) *Point-of-Sales (POS) Terminals*

In a typical POS/cash transaction, a cashier passes the bar-coded product over a scanner or hand-held 'wand'. The terminal reads and records the details, looks up the price of the product and displays the price on a lighted panel. It also computes the amount due, including VAT, and prints an itemised receipt. The terminal then sends the data to a central computer where it is used for stock control and sales analysis. Some terminals are also equipped with automatic change dispensers and electronic scales; are capable of reading credit cards; and they also have a keyboard for data entry or messages.

This method of data input is beneficial:

- *To the customer* — It forms the basis for a computerised check-out system. Customers get a quicker and more accurate service (no time wasted or mistakes made entering prices) as well as an itemised receipt.
- *To the supermarket* — The result is that the supermarket management can get instant, or continuous, stock checks and adjust orders precisely to the flow of goods, thus improving efficiency.

(iii) *Advantages and Disadvantages*

Q. What are the advantages and disadvantages of bar codes?

A. *Advantages*:

- The cost of adding a bar code to a label is tiny.
- There is saving on paperwork.

Disadvantages:

- Getting retailers to make use of the codes is a problem.
- The cost of a check-out till that can laser-scan bar codes and link into a centralised computer system is still relatively high.
- Bar code scanners have reliability problems.
- Bar codes cannot be read by people.
- Only numbers can be coded.
- They are relatively fixed — so, for example, they are unsuitable for recording prices which can frequently change. Customers still have to be informed of prices.

(iv) *Uses*

Q. Give some uses of bar codes.

A. *Uses of bar codes*:

- On labels on shelves—used for stocktaking, e.g. in factory stores.
- Printed on shop goods – see supermarket example.
- In libraries—for book and borrower identification.

(f) Tags

Q. What is a tag?

A. A tag is a small card printed or punched in coded form. They are commonly attached to clothes in shops (e.g. Burtons, Lewis's) and removed when the item is sold. The tags are then collected on spikes at the counter, batched and at the end of the day sent to the computer centre for conversion into magnetic form. They can then be input to the computer for stock control and sales analysis purposes.

Many kinds of tag have been used in the past, notably Kimball tags which are small punched cards (Fig. 4.10).

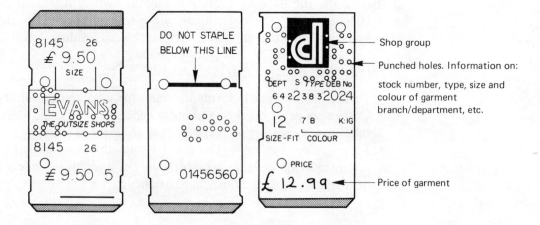

Figure 4.10 Types of Kimball tag.

Currently most tags are printed with optical codes which can be read by a hand-held reader (wand).

(g) Badge Readers

Q. What is a badge reader?

A. Badge readers can read data from small rectangular pieces of plastic. There are several ways of coding data on to these badges by:

- Magnetised marks.
- Optical marks.
- Punched holes.

The badge is inserted into a slot in the reader and the data read off.

(i) *Applications*

Q. Give some applications of badges.

A. Badges have many applications. Typical ones include:

- *Banks* — Credit and service cards. Automated Teller Machines (ATMs) dispense cash automatically when a customer inserts a plastic card and types in a personal identification number (PIN code). These 'holes-in-the-wall' provide a 24-hour service and cut transaction costs to the bank.
- *Transaction telephones* — The telecheck terminal can be used for credit-checking. A shopper's credit card can be 'wiped' over the terminal's reading device and the identity of the credit card company taken from the magnetic stripe. The machine automatically dials up the credit company's computer for authorisation and an LCD display shows the reply. Auto-redialling and storage facilities are also included.
- *Access control* — Access control cards are used for security purposes in many offices to permit access to buildings or rooms. Some even log the time of entry.
- *Car parks* — Badges are used to raise car barriers, allowing entry to or exit from a car park.
- *Production control* — Punched cards can be inserted into data collection terminals on the factory floor. The card can hold data such as employee's number, machine, job etc. and variable data can be entered regarding the number of units completed etc. Data is then transmitted to the central computer and used for production scheduling, stock control and job costing.

(ii) *'Chip-cards'*

Normally a badge holds fixed data, i.e. static data concerning identification, etc. However, some types of badge readers may also *change* the data held on badges. Such a badge or 'chip-card' may be used as a form of electronic money. As the customer purchases an item, the reader can deduct so many units from the card. This process continues until the card has no more currency units left.

One example is British Telecom's phone credit card which can be loaded with a predetermined amount (say £30) and reduced every time it is used to make a call by the appropriate amount. The card is disposed of when the balance drops to zero and the user then buys a new card.

(h) Writing Pads and Tablets

Q. What is a writing pad?

A. These devices consist of a panel display and sensitive pad on which the source document is placed to be filled in neatly by hand using ball-pen or pencil (Fig. 4.11).

As a character is written on to a document, the computer (linked to the pad) works out the X and Y coordinates and builds up a picture of how the character is formed. Having this information on the sequence and direction of pen strokes often gives greater reliability than OCR which can only recognise the character *after* it is printed. An 'S' and a '5' often give problems to OCR devices; but because they are composed in different ways, they present no such difficulties to pad devices.

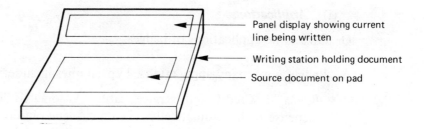

Panel display showing current
line being written

Writing station holding document

Source document on pad

Figure 4.11 Writing pad.

The screen or panel display shows the current characters which have been recognised by the computer and so errors can be corrected before the data is processed.

Although writing pads are slow, they are relatively easy to use and error free. They should appeal to the non-typist but neat hand writing is required.

(i) *Uses*

Q. Give some uses for writing pads.

A. To date they have only limited applications in:

- *Police work* − To record traffic accidents.
- *Banks and insurance companies* − To verify signatures.
  A signature written on a pad can be compared with a digital facsimile of the signature held in the computer. Pads are claimed to be very good at finding forgeries.

(i) Speech Input (Voice Recognition)

Q. What is speech input?

A. Scientists have been seeking ways of 'talking to computers' for years. Special systems can now recognise a limited, standard vocabulary of spoken words via a microphone linked into a small computer system. The system processes the sounds and converts them into binary patterns.

Steps:

Microphone ⟶ filters ⟶ pattern analysis ⟶ convert to digits
                  ↑
               adjust
               volume, etc.

A user must 'train' the system to recognise his or her voice by repeating each word in the vocabulary about 10 times. Each word is analysed and filed for later matching and identification. Once these reference data have been set up, the user can call up the system (by some sort of identification number) and speak into the microphone. The recognition device analyses the spoken commands and matches them against patterns in memory to select the corresponding vocabulary word. The recognised words are usually displayed on screen for checking and it is possible to erase any incorrect word and repeat the right one.

(i) *Problems*

Q. What are the problems of speech input?

A. There are major problems in developing speech recognition systems some of which are:

- *Speaker variability* — The speed, pitch, range, rhythm, intonation, loudness and pronunciation of an individual speaker can vary (especially if they have a cold!).
- *Homophones* — Some words, e.g. see and sea, sound the same.
- *Word separation* — Connected speech has to be segmented. At present input has to be 'clipped' with distinct pauses between words.
- *Background noise* — Can upset voice input without a shielded mouthpiece on the microphone.
- *Recognition is slow* — The number of words in English and the number of words which can be said at a given point (known as the branching factor) mean that response rates are still relatively slow.
- *Context* — The biggest stumbling block of all is context. A computer is 'literal-minded' and cannot *understand* speech. The following dialogue (with acknowledgements to *Airplane*) illustrates how important the *meaning* of speech can be:
  Doctor: 'Your mother is very ill, she'll have to go into hospital.'
  Loving son: 'What is it doctor?'
  Doctor: 'Oh, it's a big building with lots of beds.'

(ii) *Advantages and Disadvantages*

Q. What are the advantages and disadvantages of speech input?

A. *Advantages of speech input*:

- *No keyboard is necessary* — The Japanese are very keen to develop speech input because their language has a very large 'alphabet' (over 3000 characters) which makes keyboard work very difficult.
- *Are useful in situations where*:
  - Hands/eyes are busy handling documents or products.
  - People are moving around, since a wireless microphone can be used.
- *Can be used from remote locations* via the telephone;
  e.g. Unipart stock ordering system, where dealers around the country can re-order parts from the Company's central computer via a voice data entry system over the telephone.

Disadvantages of speech input:

- Still at the early stages of development (see problems) — it is a long way behind speech output.
- Recognition is slow.
- The error rate is relatively high.
- Limited vocabularies —
  most systems are still limited to words in isolation; connected speech is much harder to get right.

(iii) *Uses*

Q. Give some applications of speech input.

A. In spite of these limitations there are many applications, including:

- *Security and access control* — Each person has a unique 'voiceprint' that can be used for identification. This approach could be used in:
  - Electronic funds transfer.
  - House/car security: voice-activated locks.
  - Office security: room access.
- *Data entry in banks* — Some American banks use speaker-dependent data entry devices for transferring funds because they are more secure and less prone to operator error.
- *Quality control and automation in factories* — A checker whose hands are busy does not have to stop work to make entries in log books. He or she can simply give a running commentary on the goods they are examining. In Japan, Hitachi use spoken commands to order robots about.
- *Automated materials handling* — In airports, handlers' spoken commands direct luggage to the appropriate conveyor belt.
- *Computer-aided design (CAD)* — A designer, e.g. of microchips, working at a terminal can call up design patterns which are frequently used, instead of having to punch their catalogue numbers into a keyboard.
- *Voice-activated appliances* — People, particularly the disabled, can use voice-recognition devices to control doors or equipment, e.g. to switch TV channels or turn on the heating.
- *Voice-activated toys and games.*

(j) Direct Input from Instruments

Many measuring devices are both digital and electronic and can be linked to a computer. This usually requires special software and an interface between the device and the computer.

- *Examples of direct input*:
  - Thermostats connected to a computer-controlled central heating system.
  - A pressure pad on a road connected to computer-controlled traffic lights.

4.8   Exercises

Question 4.1

Define each of the following abbreviations:
(a) OCR. (b) OMR. (c) MICR.

Question 4.2

Match each application with the most appropriate input device or medium:

- Low-volume input of data in a small business system.
- Direct input of large volumes of data recorded in a special printing font.
- Capture of sales data in a shop.
- Processing bank cheques.

(a) OCR; (b) MICR; (c) POS terminal; (d) VDU.

Question 4.3

(a) List three advantages of optical character recognition.
(b) Why are OCR devices not more widely used?

Question 4.4

List two examples of each of the following. Input devices which use: optical media; magnetic media; paper media; key-entry.

Question 4.5

Describe the three basic approaches to data entry.

Question 4.6

List five functions of a key-to-disk system.
List three benefits of using such a system.

Question 4.7

What are the problems of voice recognition systems? Give two applications for such systems.

Question 4.8

Below are two pairs of peripherals. Give a circumstance in which the one in italics has an advantage over the other.

(a) *MICR* : OCR.
(b) *Lineprinter*: Teletypewriter. (AEB)

Question 4.9

Explain each of the following terms (and use a diagram if necessary), showing the distinction between them.
Data capture.
Data verification.
Data validation.
Reporting.

Question 4.10

(a) Name two common and contrasting input *media* (not devices).
(b) State a suitable application for each medium, giving your reasons. (OLE)

Question 4.11

Many different forms of input devices are used to enter a variety of data media. Three such devices are magnetic ink character readers (MICR), terminal keyboards, and bar code readers.

(a) (i) For each of these devices, give a suitable application, and suggest reasons for this application.
  (ii) Explain the nature of the medium (if any) each device can accept.
(b) What are the advantages of key-to-disk systems for entering data into a computer system? Name one suitable application for a key-to-disk system. (OLE)

Question 4.12

(a) Compare optical character recognition (OCR), optical mark recognition (OMR) and magnetic ink character recognition (MICR) for the input of data in terms of:

- The need for skilled data preparation staff.
- The means of verification.
- Reliability and environmental factors.

(b) Briefly describe an application of each method of data input in such a way that makes clear why the particular method is suitable for the chosen application. (L)

Question 4.13

(a) Mrs Jones' account number with her mail order Company is 483169. Explain how the last digit could be used to check whether this is a valid account number. (AEB)
(b) Explain how a check digit may be used to detect a transposition error in the following code number:
0–17–741130–9.

Question 4.14

(a) Data prepared for input to the computer in a commercial environment needs to be both verified and validated. Show that you understand the difference between verification and validation by defining each of them.
(b) A record of a weekly payroll transaction file consists of the following fields: employee number, department code, name, hours worked for each day. For each field, state one appropriate test which might be used to validate it.

Question 4.15

Dates are read into a computer as a numeric code, e.g. 010270 means 1 February 1970.
Explain how (i) type and (ii) range checks can be performed on these data. Clearly define any data structure which you use. (L)

Question 4.16

A local Electricity Board uses a computer to process customers' accounts. The manager of this Board has received numerous complaints from customers. These complaints can be summarised as follows:

(i) The Board is sending out bills for ludicrous amounts — either very much too large or much too small.
(ii) The Board is threatening to sue people for very small amounts, e.g. 20p.
(iii) The Board is threatening to sue people who have not paid their bills because they are on holiday, or are in hospital.
(iv) The Board is threatening to sue people who have already paid their bills.

The manager has called a meeting of the chief analyst, the chief programmer, the operations manager and the data preparation supervisor to try to correct these faults. Explain what sort of questions the manager should ask and what precise instructions he should give to reduce the annoyance to customers.

(L)

Question 4.17

For a period of 5 days — Monday to Friday — a survey is made of every 100th passenger using a river ferry crossing. For each passenger the following data is collected and coded into a record on magnetic tape:

- Whether male, female or child (of either sex).
- Whether using season, day return or other type of ticket.
- Whether on business, pleasure, shopping trip or other.

Draw a suitable data capture form for this survey.

(AEB)

Question 4.18

What is a:

(a) Tag.
(b) Badge?

Give one application for each.

Question 4.19

The following is a car paint code:
OC 936 D

(a) Suggest possible meanings for the parts of this code.
(b) Explain why such codes are used. Give one example of another such code and its meanings.

(AEB)

Question 4.20

Postal codes are made up in any of the following formats:
L25 2RB, SH5 7TN, EH5 12RY, SWW6 4BH, NW1X 3QR.

(a) Suggest a way in which the above postal codes could be encoded in binary in an economic manner (use as few bits as possible).
(b) What do you think the post code is trying to represent?

4.9 Answers and Hints on Solutions

4.1 (a) *OCR* — Optical Character Recognition readers can accept either printed or hand-written data directly from documents by measuring the amount of light reflected from the surface and comparing the signals with stored patterns.

(b) *OMR* — Optical Mark Recognition devices can detect the presence or absence of a pencil mark on a predetermined place on a form.

(c) *MICR* — Magnetic Ink Character Recognition devices can read characters which have been formed by ink containing iron oxide. Secure and reliable, readers can often detect characters which are stamped over or smudged.

4.2 The order is: (d), (a), (c), (b).

4.3 (a) • Key entry is eliminated.
 • Data is captured in machine-readable form at the earliest opportunity.
 • Characters can be read by people.
 (b) • Document readers are expensive.
 • Only certain fonts are acceptable.
 • Reject rates are high if the standard of printing or the document quality is poor.
 • Document design must follow a rigid format.

4.4 Optical: (1) OCR.
  (2) Bar code.
 Magnetic: (1) MICR.
  (2) Magnetic tape and disc.
 Paper: (1) Key-to-storage.
  (2) VDU terminals/teletypes.

4.5 Source document conversion:

 • Batch data entry,
  e.g. key-to-disc (Fig. 4.12(a)). Source documents from various departments are batched and sent to a central key-entry section where data prep staff key the data on to cards or more likely magnetic tape or disc for later processing.
 • On-line data entry (Fig. 4.12(b)). Users enter data directly into the computer from terminals. Transactions may be entered as they arrive, rather than batching them.
 • Direct data capture (Fig. 4.12(c)). Batched documents can be read directly by a special reader (e.g. an OCR device). The data from them can then be stored or processed by the computer straight away.

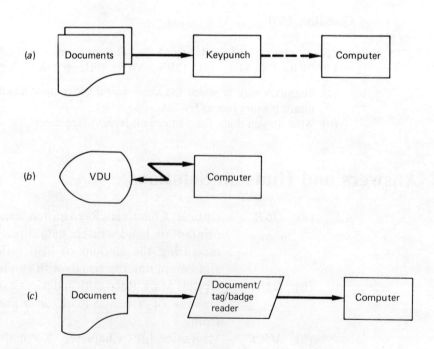

Figure 4.12 Three basic approaches to data entry. (*a*) Batch data entry. (*b*) On-line data entry. (*c*) Direct data capture.

4.6   *Functions*:

- Step-by-step prompts to help the user input the data correctly.
- Sight verification for immediate error correction.
- Editing facilities to check for errors.
- Data can be sorted and merged before storing.
- System provides performance statistics.

Benefits:

- Faster input.
- Reduced errors.
- Reduced load on main computer — input is handled off-line by a micro or mini.

4.7   *Problems*:

- Speaker variability.
- Homophones.
- Continuous speech–word separation.
- Background noise.
- Slow recognition rates.
- Context — a computer is 'literal-minded'.

Applications:

- Security and access control — voice-activated doors and locks.
- Baggage handling — routing of baggage along conveyor belts.

4.8   (a) Reading cheques, MICR devices are more secure and reliable. They can read folded paper or even smudged characters.

(b) Multiple-copies of printed reports — line printers are much quicker than teletypes (character printers) and therefore would be more suitable for running off reports in a reasonable time.

4.9
- Data capture, in this question, is getting the data required for the computer, e.g. filling in a form.
- Data verification is the process of checking for mistakes in copying by entering data *twice* and investigating any differences.
- Data validation is the process of ensuring that data input is accurate and complete. An *edit* program will include a series of *checks* to see if the data falls within certain limits.
- Reporting in this question refers to the output of:
  - Errors, so that they can be checked.
  - Valid data, so that it can be seen what is going forward for processing.
  - The outcome of the processing.

Such reporting will typically include summary information of the data processed, e.g. number of records rejected, accepted; total value of all accounts processed, etc. These are called *control totals*.

4.10 (a) Bar code. Magnetic disk.

(b) As a label on shop goods. For storing data taken from customer orders.

4.11 (a) (i)
- MICR — reading cheques; secure, reliable, robust.
- Terminal keyboards — transaction processing; few errors, quiet.
- Bar code readers — reading product labels; fast, accurate.

(ii)
- Characters printed in ink with ferrous oxide.
- Typed entry, data can be from forms, over the telephone, etc.

- Optical system detects presence (or otherwise) of bars. Printed bar codes can appear on packaging or cards.

(b) Advantages — see 4.6. Application — sales order processing.

4.12

	Best ⟶ worst		
Need for skilled personnel	OMR	MICR	OCR
Means of verification	MICR	OCR	OMR
Reliability and environmental factors	MICR	OMR	OCR

APPLICATIONS

OCR Gas/electricity bills — turn-around documents used as evidence of payments.

OMR Multiple choice exams — marking the appropriate selection.

MICR Banking cheques — difficult to forge.

4.13 (a) 5 digit account numbers often added to them as follows:

(i) Multiply the number by weights 1, 2, 3 etc. starting with the right-hand digit:

```
        4    8    3    1    6
   x    5    4    3    2    1
       20   32    9    2    6
```

(ii) Add the products together;

$$20 + 32 + 9 + 2 + 6 = 69$$

(iii) Use the last digit of the sum as a check and add to the end of the number. Hence the number becomes 4 8 3 1 6 9

Assume that the account number is entered as 4 8 3 6 1. A transcription error has been made. But the check digit would detect this:

```
        4    8    3    6    1
        5    4    3    2    1
       20 + 32    9   12    1  = 74
```

New version of number 4 8 3 6 1 4 which would not be matched with the check digit

(b) ISBNs work using the modulus-11 check digit as follows:

(i) Multiply the number by weights 2, 3, 4 etc. starting with the right-hand digit:

Number	0	1	7	7	4	1	1	3	0
x		9	8	7	6	5	4	3	2
Products		9	56	49	24	5	4	9	0

(ii) Sum the products: $9 + 56 + 49 + 24 + 5 + 4 + 9 + 0 = 156$

(iii) Divide by 11; $156 \div 11$ = remainder 2

(iv) Subtract from 11; $11 - 2 = 9$ which is the check digit. Hence the ISBN will become:

0 1 7 7 4 1 1 3 0 − 9

Any transposition error will be found by reference to the check digit (see 4.13(a)).

4.14 (a) See 4.9.

(b) Sample record 1234,   4,   GALYNSKI S.,   7.5

                              employee   Department   Name   hours
                              number   code   worked

Validation tests:
    Employee number   – append check digit, type check.
    Department code   – presence check, range check.
    Name   – presence check.
    Hours   – range test, e.g. $>0 <10$.

4.15 01   02   70   :   Date field
      day   month   year

A *type* check with test to ensure that all characters are either digits or decimal points (with no more than one decimal point). Anything else will be rejected as a 'string' type field.

A *range* check can be applied to data as follows:
All digits must be whole numbers between:
1st 2 digits 01 and 31 (days)
2nd 2 digits 01 and 12 (months)
Last 2 digits 00 and 99 (years)

4.16 *Questions for the manager to ask*:

- Is there a threshold amount before a bill is sent out?
- Is there a check on very large domestic bills? Are there: time limits, minimum amounts outstanding, or other checks before threatening legal action?
- How is it possible to threaten to sue people who have paid their bills?

Precise instructions from the manager:

A manager would instruct the analyst and programmer as follows (figures are theoretical):

- Set a threshold amount for payment; for example:
  - If the amount owing is under £5, this will be added to the next quarterly charge.
  - If the amount is over £250, contact customer and check the meter readings.
  - Threats to sue should only be issued if *all* of the following conditions are met: the amount owing is over £25 *and* has been outstanding for more than 6 weeks after the final reminder notice was sent. A check should also be made on personal circumstances (e.g. hospitalisation) before taking the customer to court.
- Revise and improve the customer file update procedure so that payments are quickly reflected in the customer accounts. This is to avoid sending out threatening letters.
- Print a disclaimer notice on all reminder notices: 'If you have paid this bill in the last 7 days, please ignore this notice'.

4.17   Data caputre form (not to scale)

Number Ferry Survey

Day of week:	Mon ☐	Tue ☐	Wed ☐	Thur ☐	Fri ☐
Passenger:	Male ☐	Female ☐	Child ☐ (Under 14)		
Ticket type:	Season ☐	Day return ☐	Other ☐		
Purpose of trip:	Business ☐	Pleasure ☐	Shopping ☐ trip	Other ☐	

DRT 3/8/-4

4.18 (a) *Tag* — A small ticket, usually made of cardboard, containing coded data. It is attached to goods in shops (e.g. clothing) to identify them.

(b) *Badge* — A small rectangular piece of plastic on which data is coded by magnetised marks, optical marks or punched holes.

Applications: (a) Kimball tags in shops. Part of the tag is retained for stock-control purposes. (b) Service-till 'ready cash' cards used in banks.

4.19 (a) Paint type (matt finish, etc.)
Colour code.
Batch number for dating, etc.

(b) Codes are used because they are:

• Short and simple.
• Minimise mistakes on input.
• Are used to identify and locate data records.

Another example of a code is with balls of wool which include details of batch and colour or International Standard Book Numbers (ISBNs) which include coded details of the author(s), publisher and book title as well as a check digit on the end.

4.20 (a) Maximum number of characters : 8 spaces
upper case alphabetics A–Z   26
                    numerics 1–99   100
                    space   1
                    ─────
                    127

To encode in binary use $2^7 = 128$
i.e. with 7 bits, 128 distinct characters can be represented, so ASCII-7 would suffice.
e.g. ASCII-7 for   L   2   5   2   R   B

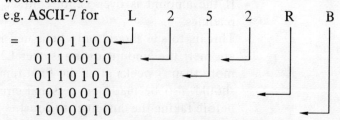

= 1 0 0 1 1 0 0
  0 1 1 0 0 1 0
  0 1 1 0 1 0 1
  1 0 1 0 0 1 0
  1 0 0 0 0 1 0

(b) Geographical location, street and property (or group of properties) within a street.

5 Output Methods, Media and Devices

5.1 Introduction

The overall aim of any output system should be: to provide the right information to the right people at the right time.

Q. How do you assess an effective output system?

A. An effective output system can be assessed in terms of speed, cost, reliability, quality and quietness (for printers).

Q. What are the main types of output?

A. The main types of output are:

- Printed output—printers and plotters.
- Terminals.
- Computer Output on Microfilm (COM).
- Speech output.
- Direct output to other devices.

Examination questions (like those on input and storage) ask for:

- The relative advantages and disadvantages.
- The typical applications of each method, media and device.

Each of these will be considered.

5.2 Printed Output

Q. Why is printed output so popular?

A. At present, printed output – paper documents and reports – is the most common form of output. Printed copy is often called *hard* copy because paper can be taken away and read at any time in any place. It provides a permanent record and is easy to copy and distribute. Familiar computer printed documents include payslips, bank statements, electricity bills, etc.

(a) Printers

Q. What types of printer are available?

A. Printers can be classified in several ways (Fig. 5.1):

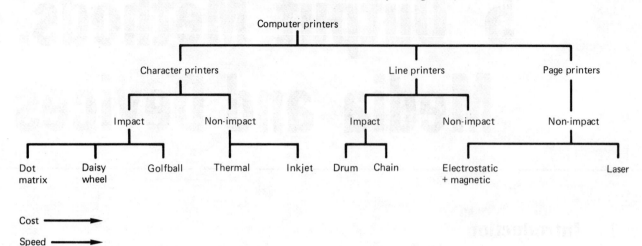

Figure 5.1 Classification of computer printers.

- *Character printers* print serially (one character at a time), much like a typewriter. As a result speeds are quite slow (from 10 to 150 characters per second). They are relatively cheap and are commonly found in small business systems. When a keyboard device has a character printer attached it is called a *teletype* (or teletypewriter). The keyboard acts as the input medium, the printer as the output device.
- *Line printers* are much faster devices which print a line at a time. Some are capable of printing up to 3000 lines per minute. They are accordingly more expensive.
- *Page printers* print a whole page at a time. They are very expensive and are intended to deal with very large volumes of printed computer output in large organisations.

Printers can also be classified as:

- *Impact printers* – Where the type hits an inked ribbon against paper (like an ordinary typewriter).

OR

- *Non-impact printers* – Which use techniques such as ink spray, heat, xerography or laser to form printed copy, i.e. characters are not formed by mechanical impact.

(i) *Advantages and Disadvantages*

Q. What are the advantages and disadvantages of non-impact printers over impact ones?

A. Non-impact printers have two main advantages over impact printers:

- Much quieter – useful in hospitals, etc.
- Much faster printing speeds.

DISADVANTAGES:

- More expensive than impact printers.

- Sometimes require special paper.
- Some do not have multiple copy facilities.

The basic types of printer will now be explained in detail.

(i) *Character Printers*

1 Impact Character Printer

There are two basic types of impact character printer: dot matrix and moving print head (ball or wheel):

- *Dot matrix* printers print a pattern of dots in the shape of the desired character. Speeds of up to around 165 characters per second (c.p.s.) are possible but the print quality is low.
- *A ball printer* uses a rotating and/or pivoting ball as a print head. The printing characters are on the surface of the ball which strikes a ribbon to transfer the character on to paper (e.g. IBM golf-ball electric typewriter).
- *A wheel (or daisywheel) printer* uses a wheel as a print head with the characters forming a band around the circumference of the print wheel (Fig. 5.2).

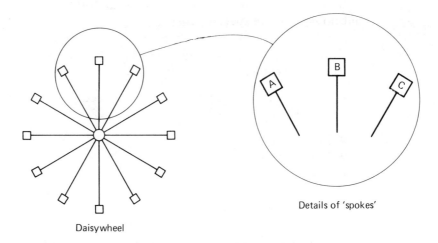

Daisywheel

Details of 'spokes'

Figure 5.2 Daisywheel.

To print a character the wheel is rotated and a hammer strikes the back side of the spoke and presses it against the paper. Some ball and wheel printers can print left to right on one line and then right to left on the next thus increasing the effective print speed. They print at relatively slow speeds (typically 10–50 c.p.s.) but produce good-quality print, i.e. 'full' letter-quality characters.

2 Non-impact Character Printers

- *Thermal printers* create print images on special heat-sensitive paper by heated wires in the print head. They operate at speeds of between 10 and 30 c.p.s.
- *Inkjet printers* fire ink on to paper by using an electrostatic field. No special paper is needed and the print quality can be good, but it is not possible to produce multiple copies and they can be unreliable.

(ii) *Line Printers*

1 Impact Line Printer

There are two main types of *impact line printer*: print characters are mounted on a moving *chain* or belt or engraved on the face of a rotating *drum*. Typical line printer speeds range from 200 to 3000 lines per minute. Multiple copies can easily be produced and characters are of 'letter-quality'.

2 Non-impact Line Printer

The main non-impact line printer is the *electrostatic printer*. This places electrostatic charges in the shape of the required character on to special sensitised paper. They operate up to speeds of 3000 l.p.m. or more. As with thermal printers, the print characters are in dot matrix form. They are not common in business operations.

MAGNETIC PRINTER

A *magnetic printer* operates much like an electrostatic printer except that the magnetic charges are placed on a belt rather than a sensitised paper. Magnetic printers are much slower than electrostatic printers (up to 200 lines per minute) but do not require special paper.

(iii) *Page Printers*

Page printers are non-impact, very high speed printers capable of printing a page at a time. They can be:

- Electrostatic.
- Xerographic.
- Laser.

1 Electrostatic Page Printers

The characters are created using tiny dots (200 to the inch) giving a high quality which doesn't look like matrix printing. The document outlines are coded and stored for printing with the data when ready. Letterheads and logos can be created electrostatically using changeable metal cylinders; preprinted stationery can also be handled.

2 Xerographic Printers

These are an adaptation of the Xerox office copier. (Xerography is the process of electrostatic printing or dry photography in which negatively charged powder is sprinkled on a positively charged surface.)

Xerographic printers produce sharp character images on letter-sized paper. The printer usually has an in-built microcomputer and can produce and collate multiple copies. It operates at about 4000 l.p.m.

3 Laser Printers

These are probably the most advanced printers and use a laser beam to produce character images on the surface of a rotating drum. A toner that adheres to the light images is then transferred to paper. Some laser printers are running at speeds equivalent to 21000 l.p.m. so they are needed only in large-volume applications, e.g. mailing shots, price lists in major companies.

(iv) *Criteria for the Selection of a Printer*

1 Cost

Price is obviously an important consideration. It is often related to printer capability, speed and print quality. As well as the initial cost, paper and other supplies should be taken into account.

2 Speed

The required speed of the printer depends on the types of application and volumes of output.

3 Reliability and Ease of Maintenance

4 Print Quality

Readability and neatness of printer output. Get a rough idea of the print quality provided by some of the main types of printer. Good quality is obviously important where hard copy is sent *outside* the organisation — to customers, creditors, etc. — not least in order to present the correct image. A lower quality output may be acceptable for internal purposes, however, e.g. for interdepartmental correspondence.

5 Range of Capabilities

Some printers offer:
- A range of line-widths,
  say from 72 to 132 characters.
- Various character sets,
  e.g. OCR fonts, italics, etc.
- Built-in guillotines, trimmers, collators.
- Multiple copy facilities: important in invoicing and ordering.

Many printers are capable of printing on to multiple forms, or, when necessary, on to preprinted stationery such as invoice or order forms. Because of the speeds involved, continuous stationery is necessary, with perforations to separate sheets and sprocket holes at the edges to guide the paper through the printer.

6 Compatibility with Computers and/or Main Communications Devices

The printer should be able to interface with the main models of computer and office equipment without needing to buy extra connecting devices.

(b) Plotters

Q. What is a plotter?

A. A plotter (or graph-plotter) is a device for producing graphical output on paper. It converts digital computer output into illustrations such as graphs, bar charts, pie charts, maps or technical drawings. A *digital plotter* works by converting digital coordinates (rather like map references) into pen movements. Alternatively, an *incremental plotter* sends signals to tell the pen how far to move from its present position.

Plotters are not usually directly connected to the computer (they are off-line) because pen output is fairly slow, thus wasting computer time. Rather, a program will produce the graph or design and write the information to, for example, magnetic tape. The tape can then be run later by a small processor (reader) which will control the specialised plotter system.

There are two basic types of plotter:

- *A flatbed plotter* (Fig. 5.3) – This is a fixed, flat table or bed on which the writing pen can move over the paper: up (to move without drawing), down (to draw) and in north, south, west, east directions.

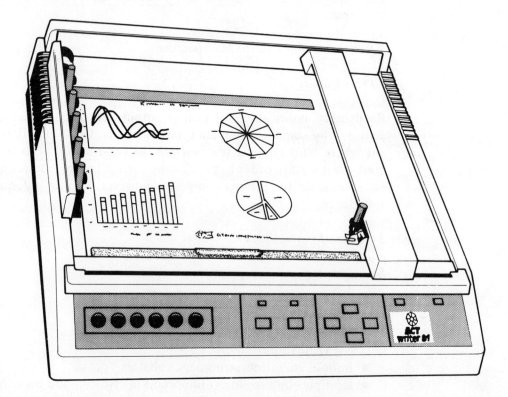

Figure 5.3 A flatbed plotter.

- *A drum plotter* – Here a roll of paper, mounted on a drum, can be moved back and forth whilst the pen moves across the paper. A combination of drum and pen movements allows a line to be drawn anywhere on the paper.

(i) *Applications*

Q. What can plotters be used for?

A. Plotters can be used where paper copy of graphical output is needed. Plotters can produce graphs or designs of varying sizes, using different coloured inks and even imprint designs on to metal or plastic surfaces.

They are useful in Computer Aided Design (CAD). Maps, machine and architectural designs can be created by computer and then output on to graph plotters.

5.3   Terminals

A terminal is a combined input/output device which enables a user to communicate with a computer, often from a distant location. Input is via a keyboard or by one of several 'keyboard-avoiding methods' (e.g. touch-screen) and output is printed or video. They are typically used where small amounts of data is input since, at least until recently, input occurred at typewriter speeds.

(a) Teletypes

Teletypes (or teletypewriters) are keyboard printers; data input is by a typewriter-style keyboard and output is printed on a character printer. They are noisy, slow and waste paper but are necessary where a hard copy record is needed of (say) an interactive conversation or the log of a computer's operations.

(b) Visual Display Units (VDUs)

VDUs are a combination input/output device where data is entered on a typewriter-like keyboard (or variant) and output appears on a television-like screen (usually a cathode ray tube (CRT)). VDUs differ in the information that they can show on screen at any one time. Screen dimensions vary, but a typical size is 24 lines × 80 characters.

There are two basic types of terminal: 'intelligent' and 'dumb'.

'Dumb' terminals are used mainly for enquiry/response and timesharing applications. *'Intelligent'* terminals, are capable of *local processing*, i.e. they have a built-in microprocessor and memory and are therefore programmable. They can be used to display input 'forms' and to edit input data before transmission to a central computer. Cheap microprocessors mean that most terminals are 'intelligent' nowadays.

VDUs are a widespread and increasingly popular method of output.

(i)   *Uses*

Q. Give some general uses of VDUs.

A. Typical uses include:

- Data entry, on-line or keying-in.
- Enquiry/response, e.g. hotel, airline reservations, database queries.
- On-line programming.
- Computer-Assisted Instruction (CAI).
- Operator's console to control the computer.

(ii)   *Advantages and Disadvantages*

1 Advantages

INPUT

- A formatted screen can be provided for data entry applications — the operator just 'fills in the blanks'.
- Immediate sight verification is provided to the user as data is entered.

- Data can easily be edited on-line (by character or by line) using the cursor control before it is transmitted to the computer. Audible alarms or highlights can be used to indicate input data errors.

OUTPUT

- Output is usually much faster than by printer.
- Output can be 'paged' (one block at a time) or 'scrolled' (moving up and down).
- Paper is not wasted.
- Screen displays are compact, reliable, and silent (very important in a busy office).
- Many terminals now offer colour, graphics, split-screen and other 'output-enhancing' attributes.

2 *Disadvantages*

- There is no automatic permanent hard copy although, of course, a printer can be attached to the VDU.
- Some screen formats do not replicate printed documents, i.e. what you see on screen is not always what you get on paper.
- People are still wary of 'electronic, transient output'. They like carrying bits of paper around!

Hand-held Terminals

Q. Comment briefly on the features and uses of a hand-held terminal.

A. These are portable devices which tend to have limited keyboards (cf. the remote control for a TV receiver). Typically the ten digits, a few alphabetic keys and certain function keys such as INPUT, REPEAT, DELETE, etc. are included (Fig. 5.4).

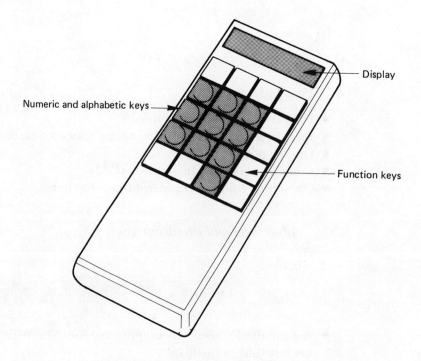

Numeric and alphabetic keys

Display

Function keys

Figure 5.4 Hand-held microcomputer terminal.

They are powered by batteries and have a small memory to hold data keyed-in. Useful to anyone on the move, a typical application is where a travelling salesman takes orders from a number of shops. At the end of the day the teller-terminal can be linked to the company's central computer via a modem (or acoustic coupler) attached to an ordinary telephone line. All the day's information (the orders taken) stored in the terminal's memory can then be transmitted to head-office. In return, the central computer could 'download' the calls for the next day and any messages for the salesman.

(d) Graphics Terminals

Q. What is a graphics terminal? Describe the application for which it might be used.

A. Graphic display units (GDUs) are expensive special terminals used to show graphs and pictures as well as text. They will be equipped with good quality (high-resolution) graphics for detailed display and often feature graphics function keyboards and light pens for input, as well as the usual screen and alphanumeric keyboard.

They can be used in Computer Aided Design (CAD) for producing designs on screen. To 'draw' a design the user:

- Loads the appropriate software.
- Points a light pen to indicate the position of each part of the diagram. A light pen is a hand-held, pen-shaped device connected by cable to the terminal which can be used with special software, to send its position to the CPU.
- Uses the function keys to give the size and shape required.

Amendments can be made 'interactively' until the new design is satisfactory, when it can then be dumped on to a graph-plotter for a hard copy print-out.

(e) Keyboard-Avoiding Devices

Q. List the main types of 'keyboard-avoiding device'. Explain in more detail how one of these devices works.

A. Much time and money has gone into developing terminals to avoid the 'keyboard-bottleneck', i.e. the constraint of typing speed. Such devices include (as well as the conventional facilities):

- Voice recognition facilities (see Section 4.7(i)).
- Light pens.
- Touch-screens, e.g. the HP150. These are similar in concept to the light-pen terminal only here your finger can be used to point and give commands.
- Mouse-control, e.g. the Macintosh. A 'Mouse' is a small box that slides across the desk and moves the cursor to point to easily understood symbols on the screen (Fig. 5.5). User-friendly software turns the screen into a work-top. The 'documents' you are working on look just like sheets of paper on a desk, displayed in screen windows that can be changed in size and shape by the mouse. A document in a window can be brought to the 'top' of a pile on the desk with one mouse command and the keyboard 'forgotten'. Around the 'desk-top screen' are various symbols called 'icons' which represent actions to do with documents, e.g. amend, file, delete. For example, a document can

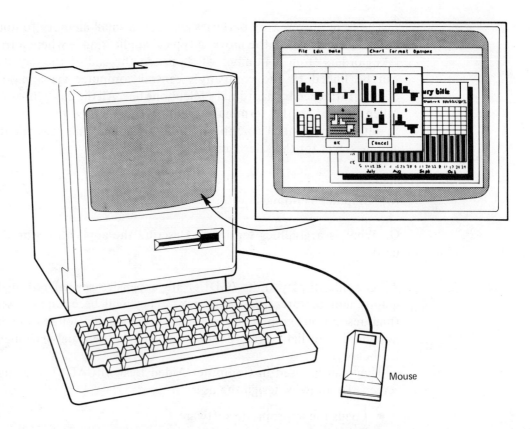

Mouse

Figure 5.5 Mouse control. Apple's Macintosh system with overlapping windows shown on the screen and 'mouse' input.

be discarded by using the mouse to point to a dustbin symbol. The idea is to make data management by computer 'user-friendly' and open to non-typists and people who can't be bothered to learn lists of commands.

5.4 Computer Output on Microfilm (COM)

Q. What is COM?

A. COM devices record computer output (images or text) on to photographic film which can be viewed later by special microfilm readers (Fig. 5.6). Recording

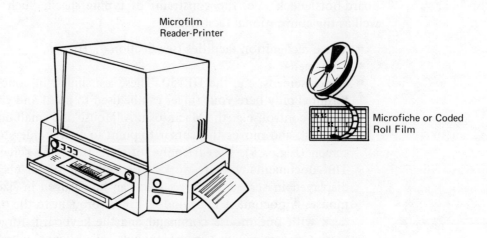

Microfilm
Reader-Printer

Microfiche or Coded
Roll Film

Figure 5.6 Microfilm systems.

can be achieved by either photographing the display of a cathode ray tube screen or, more recently, by writing directly on to microfilm using laser or fibre-optic techniques. The COM device may display data on-line from a computer or, more likely, off-line from magnetic tape. The computer also produces an index to locate the frame for a given output.

Q. What is the difference between microfilm and Microfiche?

A. Microfilm output is usually on a roll of film (e.g. 35 mm) or, more often, on microfiche — a page of film on which data images are arranged in a grid pattern. A microfiche can represent hundreds of A4 pages, depending on the reduction ratio. Microfiche is easily displayed on a microfiche reader and is easy to store. A printer can be attached to the reader to produce a hard copy of any document.

(a) Advantages and Disadvantages

Q. What are the advantages and disadvantages of COM?

A. *Advantages*:

- Can store large volumes of data in a small, compact space.
  Microfilm costs are lower than the paper equivalent.
  Printed output is bulky, slow and costly in comparison.
- Recording on COM can be 25–50 times faster than printing.
- Microfilm reproduces a document in exact facsimile.
- Microfilm lasts longer than magnetic tape or paper output.
- Graphics and/or text data can be accessed easily and quickly. Computer assisted retrieval (CAR) means that, given an identity number, the computer can search and display the frame that is wanted on screen.

DISADVANTAGES:

- COM equipment is expensive compared with printers.
- Microfilm records cannot be read by a computer or easily updated.
  Therefore, COM is not suitable for data that frequently changes.
- Special equipment is needed. A microfilm reader is necessary for people to view the output.
- People are used to paper!

(b) Applications

Q. What is COM used for?

A. In many computer applications large quantities of data must be kept for reference, historical or legal purposes. So where data doesn't get out of date too quickly and storage space is a problem COM may be used. COM applications include:

- *Libraries* — which often microfiche catalogues, periodicals, newspapers, etc. for the 'archives'.
- *Companies* — which may keep old customer records, personnel records or financial accounts (for tax purposes).
- *Local authorities* — which retain town plans, maps, engineers drawings etc. for planning purposes.

5.5 Speech Output

Q. What is speech output?

A. Computer output can now be in the form of the spoken word. At first computers selected words on tape but now the human voice can be 'synthesised' by storing word patterns as bit strings. Digitised speech takes up lots of storage so ways are continually being developed to 'compress' the data. A small LSI microchip can be used to reproduce the human voice via a small loudspeaker amplifier. Its first application was in TI's Speak'n'Spell learning aid for children (ET phone home!).

Q. How does a computer 'talk'?

A. Engineers have found several ways of making computers 'talk'. Fig. 5.7 shows the most important one based on linear predictive coding.

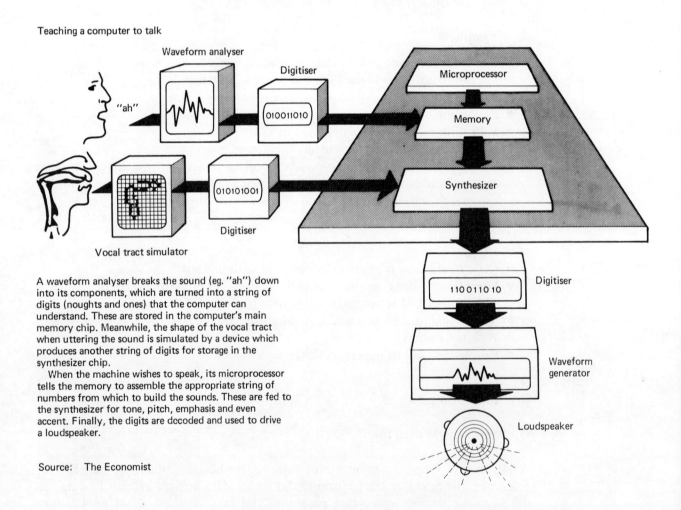

Teaching a computer to talk

A waveform analyser breaks the sound (eg. "ah") down into its components, which are turned into a string of digits (noughts and ones) that the computer can understand. These are stored in the computer's main memory chip. Meanwhile, the shape of the vocal tract when uttering the sound is simulated by a device which produces another string of digits for storage in the synthesizer chip.

When the machine wishes to speak, its microprocessor tells the memory to assemble the appropriate string of numbers from which to build the sounds. These are fed to the synthesizer for tone, pitch, emphasis and even accent. Finally, the digits are decoded and used to drive a loudspeaker.

Source: The Economist

Figure 5.7   Teaching a computer to talk. Courtesy *The Economist*.

(a) Advantages and Disadvantages

Q. What are the advantages and disadvantages of speech output?

A. *Advantages:*

- No reading is necessary.
- Useful in situations where you can't look or where you are busy.
- Fast, natural output.
- People grow fond of 'computer-speak'!

DISADVANTAGES:

- Not suitable for noisy situations.
- Inappropriate for lengthy or permanent information.

(b) Applications

Q. What is speech output used for?

A. The uses are:

- *Learning aids, games and toys* — e.g. hand-held devices for foreign language translation and other Computer-Assisted-Learning (CAL).
- *A talking voltmeter* — Used to test electronic components. This presents the operator with fewer visual tasks, so helping to prevent accidents.
- *Lifts* — Messages can be used in lifts to greet visitors, tell them which floor they are on, etc.
- *Emergency messages:*
  - In Public Address systems.
  - In cars — 'You are running out of petrol', 'Your oil is low'.
  - In household appliances — washing machines, vacuum cleaners — 'the tub is over-loaded. . . .'.
- *Answering services.*
- *Situations where you can't look (or are too busy)* — Spoken dashboard information for a pilot or a car driver.
- *Text-to-speech translations (reading machines)*   — For blind or disabled people an alternative to braille.

5.6   Direct Output to Other Devices

Computers are often used to control devices without transcribing data on to an intermediate medium first. Because of their low cost, microprocessors are particularly suitable for this. If the device being controlled is analogue, a DAC (digital-to-analogue converter) will be needed to convert the digital messages from the computer into analogue movements.

- *Examples of direct output:*
  - Robot.
  - Machine-tool control.

5.7   Exercises

Question 5.1

Define each of the following abbreviations: (a) COM. (b) VDU.

Question 5.2

List five factors to consider when selecting a printer.

Question 5.3

(a) What are the essential differences between character, line and page printers?
(b) Give a typical application for each.

Question 5.4

'We use far too much paper in this office, why don't we use more modern methods to output our information?'

Question 5.5

Describe in brief the difference between:

(a) A flatbed plotter and a drum plotter.
(b) Microfilm and microfiche.
(c) A 'dumb' and an 'intelligent' terminal.

Question 5.6

(a) What are the advantages of computer output on microfilm over printed output?
(b) Give one application of COM, stating two reasons for your choice.
(c) Why isn't microfilm usage more popular?

Question 5.7

What type of terminal could be used by each of the following people to help them in their jobs? Explain the reasons for your choice:

(a) A design engineer in a firm manufacturing engines.
(b) A counter clerk in a branch of a national house-selling agency.
(c) A cashier at a supermarket checkout.

Question 5.8

(a) List four advantages and two disadvantages of speech output.
(b) How might speech output devices help:

- The housewife?
- The disabled?
- The car driver?

Question 5.9

Give two situations where good print quality is essential and two situations where it is not so vital.

Question 5.10

Teletypewriters and Visual Display Units are common Input/Output devices and are often used in school and colleges. Explain, with reasons, which would be the most appropriate device for the following educational applications:

(a) A Computer Assisted Learning program which simulates the problems in motorway construction.
(b) The writing and testing of a typical student program to be submitted as coursework for an Ordinary Level Computer Studies course. (AEB)

Question 5.11

It is now possible to buy cheap hand-held microcomputers intended as aids to learning in areas such as arithmetic, spelling and languages. Discuss the kind of input and output facilities which would be most suitable for these uses. Describe the functions one of these devices offers to the user. (AEB)

Question 5.12

The following are all output devices:
GRAPHICAL DISPLAY UNIT
TELETYPEWRITER
LASER PRINTER

In each of the situations below state which one of the output devices above would be most suitable and give one reason for your choice.

(a) A mail order company producing a very large number of customer statements overnight.
(b) A cartographer (map-maker).
(c) A member of a city transport department who is reorganising the bus routes and time-tables.

5.8   Answers and Hints on Solutions

5.1   (a) COM   – Computer Output on Microfilm. Pages of print can be reduced photographically on to rolls or sheets of film (microfiche).

   (b) VDU   – Visual Display Units. A common, dual-purpose input/output device. A television screen/monitor is used to check data and examine output. A keyboard is used to enter data, programs, etc.

5.2   (1) Cost (2) Quality of print. (3) Speed. (4) Reliability. (5) Range of capabilities.

5.3   (a)   Character printers – characters are printed one by one:

   ● Both impact and non-impact.
   ● Dot matrix, daisywheel and thermal or inkjet.
   ● Speeds–slow, 30–600 c.p.s.
   ● Inexpensive.

      Line printers – print a line at a time. Speeds – 100–3000 lines per minute (l.p.m.).
      Page printers – print a page at a time:

- Non-impact.
- Speeds up to 20 000 c.p.s. (about 150 pages a minute).
- Expensive.

(b) Character printers — used for low-volume input work, e.g. a teletype.

Line printers — can be used with preprinted stationery (address labels, bills). Adequate for most business needs.

Page printers — rapid production of high-volume output of good print quality for very large companies.

5.4 Hard copy, printed output still popular.

- It is the traditional method of reading output.
- Paper can be carried about.
- Hard copy is permanent.
- People are still reluctant to try new methods.
- VDU displays and speech output are transient.
- These methods are inappropriate for lengthy or permanent information.
- COM is useful for archive material but special readers are required to use it.

5.5 (a) Drum plotter—a roll of special paper moves back and forth through the plotter and a pen moves across the paper.
Flat-bed plotter — a fixed, flat table on which paper rests; the pen moves in all directions.

(b) Microfilm is a role of film (e.g. 35 mm) holding e.g. 300 A4 pages.
Microfiche is a page (or sheet) of film, e.g. 105 × 148 mm, and will hold about 100 pages of A4 reduced in size about 25 times.

(c) A 'dumb' terminal is a keyboard and screen connected on-line to a computer. An 'intelligent' terminal is likewise linked to a computer but is also a computer in its own right. It has a built-in microprocessor for control and memory and can therefore be programmed, carrying out 'local processing', e.g. data input editing, local jobs, etc. Microchips are now so cheap that it is usual to find intelligent microcomputers acting as terminals in network systems.

5.6 (a) COM advantages:

- A large amount of data can be stored in a very small space.
- Graphics and text can be recorded very quickly.
- Facsimile documents can be reproduced.
- Microfilm lasts longer than magnetic tape or paper output.

(b) In libraries for archiving newspaper, periodicals, etc. Reasons—compact, no deterioration.

(c) COM readers are necessary and they are expensive:

- Microfilm records cannot easily be updated, therefore microfilm is unsuitable for volatile data.
- People are used to paper.

5.7 (a) Graphics terminal, with built-in graphics software and high-resolution display, giving good-quality definition for the technical drawings of the designer.

(b) VDU — A standard VDU can be used for data entry (e.g. customer payments) and screen output of information (e.g. updated account balance).

(c) Point-of-sale (POS) terminal—used in shops. Terminal reads data from a bar code (or a code number is typed in) and records and prints this, displaying the price (which is looked up in store) on a lighted panel. It also calculates the total bill, prints an itemised receipt and returns change. Data can be sent to a central computer where they are used for stock control and sales analysis.

5.8 (a) 1. No reading is necessary.
2. Fast, natural output.
3 and 4.   Useful in situations where you can't look or where you are busy.

1. Not suitable in noisy places.
2. Inappropriate for lengthy messages or permanent information.

(b) Housewife — in domestic appliances; e.g. oven 'the dinner is cooked', vacuum cleaner 'the dust bag is full'.
Disabled — text-to-speech translators for the blind. Such reading machines are an alternative to braille.
Car driver — warning messages; 'you are low on oil', 'release hand brake'.

5.9 External documents — going to (1) shareholders, (2) customers, etc. — need to project a good image to people outside an organisation. Internal documents — (1) memos, (2) progress reports.

5.10 (a) VDU with graphics facilities — quick, continuous and easy adjustment of data.
(b) Teletype — to give a permanent hard copy of the program's development so that the teacher can monitor progress. (Alternatively frequent screen dumps of VDU work.)

5.11 Cheap, hand-held, special-purpose devices.

- Keyboard for input facilities designed to meet the special needs of the machine.
- Output display is an LCD (Liquid Crystal Display) or LED (Light Emitting Diode) which uses more power but is easier to read.

Other forms of input/output are also possible, e.g. speech output on TI's 'Speak and spell'. A typical maths helper will offer:

- The choice of arithmetic functions (e.g. $+ - \times \div$) to be practised.
- The choice of level of difficulty, ranging from easy to hard.
- The timing of a person's performance over say 10 calculations and a score for the number of correct answers.

5.12 (a) Laser printer — rapid production of thousands of printed statements for postal despatch.
(b) Graphical display unit — offering the definition and colour which a map maker needs.
(c) Teletypewriter — offers hard copy of all simulations (models) of route times so that they can be studied and an optimum solution devised, although a VDU would be more useful at the planning stage. A GDU would be more appropriate for route mapping.

6 Data Structures

6.1 Introduction

Data must be organised in a logical and consistent way if it is to be of use. In computer systems data is organised into the hierarchy shown in Fig. 6.1.

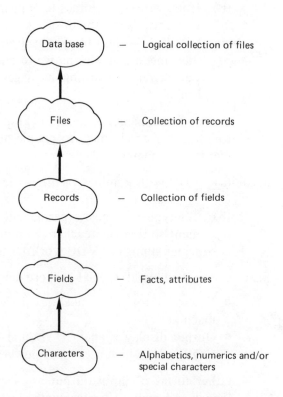

Figure 6.1 Data hierarchy.

6.2 Files, Records and Fields

This is a computer print-out of a section of an employees file for a large company:

NAME	SEX	AGE	DEPARTMENT
TAYLOR B	F	21	ACCOUNTS
TAYLOR G	F	50	PERSONNEL
TAYLOR G J	M	36	COMPUTING
TAYLOR W	M	43	PRODUCTION

Q. Describe this file in terms of fields and records.

A. A *file* is an organised collection of related records — in this case employees.

A *record* is a collection of related data items (or fields). In the extract above there are four employee records each containing four fields: name, sex, age, department. Each data *field* or item describes some attribute of the employee:

- Fields can be fixed length or variable length.
- If the fields are of fixed length then each field has a set number of character positions.
- If the fields are of variable length the number of characters in each is not predetermined.

Each field has three essential properties:

- Name.
- Value.
- Representation, which specifies the length and type.

In our example they are:

Data item:	*name*	*value*	*representation*
	Employee-name	TAYLOR	20 alphabetics
	Sex	M/F	1 alphabetic
	Age	16–65	2 numerics
	department e.g.	ACCOUNTS	10 alphabetics

- Note the use of codes (M/F for Male/Female) to save storage space.
- Note that the fields are of fixed length.

Q. What are the advantages of fixed-length over variable-length fields?

A. *Advantages*:

- Searching is quicker.
- Allocating storage space is easier.
- Updating of files is simpler — if a record is changed it doesn't disturb any of the other records as it will still take up the same amount of space.

DISADVANTAGES:

- There is waste of storage space for the short items in a given field.

Q. In the interrogation of this file, how could confusion between the four surnames be avoided?

A. Each record in a file is usually identified by a data item called an identifier or *Key*.

The Key can be used for locating records in the file and for arranging the records in the file in sequence (e.g. alphabetically or by department).

The Key may be numeric or alphanumeric and will uniquely identify each record. Hence each worker may be given a reference number; the Key will usually be the first field in a record.

6.3 Tables and Arrays

There are two special data structures used in computing, called tables and arrays. These are important, particularly when it comes to programming.

(a) Tables

The simplest table is a set of paired entries. The first entry in each pair is called the *argument*, the second entry the *function* of the argument. The table is searched until the required argument is located, the value read out of the table is its function (see Table 6.1).

Table 6.1   British Rail: return fares from London

Ticket type	Destination		
	Bristol	Hull	Newcastle
Awayday	12	16	20
Midweek	16	18	25
Ordinary	25	35	50

So a midweek return to Hull will cost £18

An *index* (or directory) is a table that is used to locate items stored elsewhere. It is often used in applications to locate records stored in DASDs. For example, an index to locate student records held on magnetic idsc:

Track number	Student number
1	1–25
2	26–50
3	51–75
etc.	etc.
8	176–200

Arrays are a special form of table in which the data is stored by position. For example:

```
1   OVETT   3:52
2   COE     3:55
3   CRAM    3:56
```

Arrays are important because the computer need only store the data, and the location of the first data element. The location of any other item may then be determined by addition.

Rather than a single column of data (as above) an array may also appear as a two-dimensional table with both rows and columns. For example, the students in a particular school may be categorised according to year and subject studied (see Table 6.2).

Table 6.2   Two-dimensional array of students by class and year

Year	Class			
	Computing	History	Geography	Drama
1	24	26	10	7
2	20	19	22	16
3	18	15	9	7

Subscripts are used to reference individual elements within the array. Given that the above array is called STUDENT then the elements in the 3rd row, 2nd column will be referenced as STUDENT (3,2). In the example above this will locate value 15, i.e. the number of students taking history in the 3rd year.

6.4   Databases

(a) Comparison between Database and Conventional File Approaches — An Example

(i)   *Conventional File Approach (Table 6.3).*

Personnel File		
Employer		Data
No.	Name	
1234	A THOMAS	XXX

Payroll File		
Employee		Data
No.	Name	
1234	A THOMAS	XXX

Department File		
Employee		Data
No.	Name	
1234	A THOMAS	XXX

Table 6.3   Conventional file approach

- Data duplication — loss of valuable file space and possible inconsistencies if one file is updated before another.
- Difficult to access or report data that is contained in more than one file, e.g. a manager may wish to know the labour cost for his department and this might entail searching the payroll file to extract the relevant information.
- Data isn't shared between applications so if A. THOMAS changes names (by getting married) this will cause three updates.
- Changes to data structures (files) often require changing many computer programs — which can be expensive and time consuming.

(ii)   *Database Approach (Table 6.4)*

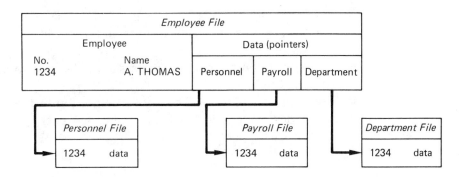

Table 6.4   Database Approach

The database approach is used to overcome the problems in Section 6.4(a)(i). A single employee file is created with one record containing basic data (e.g. on A. THOMAS). Files are also created for each activity and *pointers* or links made to each of them. In this case the employee number becomes the entry point for processing all enquiries about a worker, and data is shared between applications.

(b) Definition

Q. What is a database?

A. A database is a non redundant collection of logically related files, organised in a manner to satisfy the needs of an organisation.

A database is a store of data structured so that access and update can be made by different people in different ways without needing to change its design or contents. For this to happen it is essential that all data items are logically related, otherwise the system will be file based.

(c) Advantages

Q. What are the advantages of a database over a conventional file based system?

A.

- Generally it is only necessary to store a data item once:
  - Shared data leads to lower input costs.
  - Data have only to be entered once.
- Duplicate records are largely eliminated, thereby saving space and ensuring data consistency.
- Validation and security are improved because they are under central control.
- There is easier application development. Fewer application programs need to be written or changed because data will be retrieved using a standard procedure.

(d) Hardware Requirements

Q. What are the hardware requirements necessary to provide an effective database service?

A. The hardware must have, at least, the following:

- *On-line storage* – This permits the CPU to access a given data record by means of a link between storage and the CPU, without operating staff intervention.
- *Multi-access* – A number of users should be able to access the database at the same time.
- *Direct-access storage* – The above points imply the need for direct access storage devices to hold the database, i.e. disk packs.

(e) Management Systems

Q. What is a database management system?

A. The database is separated from the applications programs by special software known as the database management system (DBMS).

The DBMS is a general set of programs designed to interface with the application programs of the various users and departments and the database itself (Fig. 6.2). It controls access, is used for adding, modifying and retrieving data and includes facilities for data independence, integrity and security.

Q. Why is a DBMS necessary?

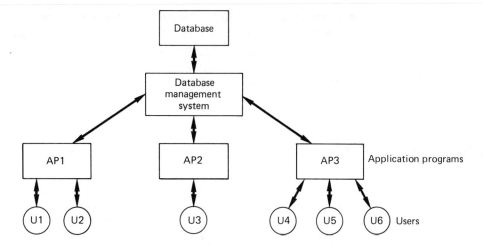

Figure 6.2 Database management system (DBMS).

A. It is needed because in many organisations there are:

- Large amounts of data with many types of record occurring many times.
- Complex data structures including many relationships between data items.
- Many different user requirements.
- Requirements for flexibility to allow changes to be made.

(f) Software

Q. What software is needed for a database?

A. This is supplied by the hardware manufacturer or software house and is of three basic types:

- A *data description language* (DDL, e.g. CODASYL) is the way of telling the **DBMS** about the structure, format and interrelationships of the data and will include details on files, records, data items and keys.
- A *data manipulation language* (DML) is part of the application program (and therefore has the same syntax) and is used to access and manipulate the data.
- A *database interrogation language* allows a person to use the database easily and simply by using simple commands.

If programs are revised, the database is unaffected. Conversely, if the database is restructured, applications programs are unaffected. For the first time there is true separation between the two. This is why a database is referred to as being *data independent*.

(g) DBA Functions

Q. What are the functions of a database administrator (DBA)?

A. The responsibility for the planning, organisation and control of the database lies with the database administrator who will:

- Coordinate database design.
- Load the database.

- Control access to the database and ensure privacy and security.
- Establish back-up and recovery procedures in case of failure or loss of data.
- Control changes to the database.
- Select and maintain database management software.
- Meet with users to resolve problems and determine changing requirements.

6.5 Types of File

Q. *What are the types of file used in computer systems?*

A. Various types of file are used in computer systems: the master file, transaction files, and other files (Table 6.5).

Table 6.5 Types of file

Type	Purpose	Examples
Master file (MF)	Set of relatively permanent records	Student file
Transaction file	Made up from source documents used to update MF	Student attendance records
Other types		
Reference file	Used for reference/look-up purposes	Teacher list
History file	Retained for historical use or back-up	School records for last 10 years
Report file	Set of records extracted from data in MF, used to prepare reports which can be printed at a later date	Truants, 100% attenders, etc.
Dump (or work) file	Used to hold data for security and recovery purposes or for temporary storage whilst other work is being carried out	Timetable planning (work-in-progress)

(a) Master File

This is the main file which contains permanent data against which transactions are processed. Master files typically contain:

- Reference data which tends to be relatively permanent and which is processed by amending (i.e. making occasional changes in the form of the insertion of new records, the deletion or alteration of existing records).
- Dynamic data, which, as the name suggests, change frequently and is processed by updating (i.e. changing the values of the various fields).

For example, a hotel may keep a master file containing items describing the rooms (type, size, number of beds, booking charge, etc.) which will rarely change (i.e. reference data) and items of data describing the guest (e.g. name, length of stay, special requirements, etc.) which will frequently change, perhaps every day (i.e. dynamic data).

(b) Transaction Files

There are also transaction files which include input and output files for holding temporary incoming or outgoing data. Transaction files are used to update dynamic data on master files.

(c) Other Files

Some organisations keep other files such as reference, history, report and dump files. See Table 6.5 for their purpose and examples.

6.6 Organisation of Files

Files should be organised so that the tasks of file creation and maintenance, record sorting, and record removal are simple and quick.
We need to consider:

- The characteristics of the data.
- Equipment including storage.
- Available software.

There are several methods of file organisation. The two most important are serial and direct, which have already been mentioned, but will now be covered in more detail. (There are other methods — index sequential, list and inverted — but these are not part of your syllabus.)
The choice between serial and direct depends on a trade-off in terms of:

- Cost.
- Processing speed.
- Accessibility of information.

Files are very important in most activities, and they must be kept up to date so that they can provide correct information on demand.

Q. What are the basic file processing activities?

A. The basic file processing activities can be classified as follows (the example used is a stock file):

INSERT	— e.g. new stock item	⎫ FILE
DELETE	— e.g. old stock item	⎬ MAINTENANCE
CHANGE	— e.g. new price	⎭
ADD	— e.g. purchase stock	⎫ FILE
SUBTRACT	— e.g. sell stock	⎬ UPDATE

These activities are typical of most file processing applications (can you think of parallel?).
The term 'master file update' is often used loosely to mean both update and maintenance, which are sometimes combined for convenience.

(a) Serial Organisation

A serial access file has to be read in the order in which it is stored on the medium (e.g. tape). Usually data records are placed on file in a particular order (e.g. alphabetical) according to a *sort key*.

This is known as a sequential file. (NB 'serial' and 'sequential' are terms which are used as if they are interchangeable. This is incorrect.)

(i) *Processing Sequential Files*

The stages of processing and updating a sequential master file are shown in Fig. 6.3.

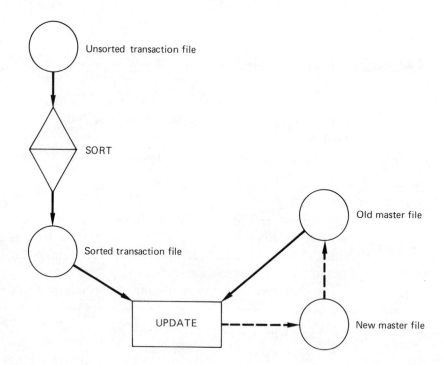

Figure 6.3 Processing a sequential master file:

1. Transactions are collected into batches.
2. They are sorted into the same sequence as the master file (MF).
3. As each transaction record is read, the master file is searched to locate the matching master file record.
4. If a match is found, the record is updated.
5. Master file records with no transactions are merely copied from the old (OMF) to the new MF (NMF).
6. The OMF is kept for backing purposes (the father to the NMF's son). The big problem of course, is that the entire master file has to be passed through even if there are only a few transactions to be processed.

(ii) *Applications*

Obviously it is impractical to use sequential file organisation in on-line systems for processing enquiries, i.e. where it is necessary to determine or update the status of a particular record. This type of application demands direct access organisation.

However, where transactions can be batched and where most records need updating sequential organisation can be used. Such an application is an organisation's payroll.

(b) Direct Organisation

On a direct access file any record can be retrieved directly without having to process other records. Records can be stored in any order, i.e. at a particular address on a direct access storage device (DASD). Sequential media such as magnetic tape cannot be used for direct organisation.

Q. How can a record be located?

A. *Addressing records* – So that a record can be stored and retrieved directly each record must have its own address. An address can be assigned by:

- Directory.
- Key transformation.

(i) *Directory*

A list of available locations on the disk can be kept so that when a new record is to be stored, it is stored at the next available location. The record key and the location are then placed in a directory (or index) for subsequent retrieval.

(ii) *Key Transformation*

Here an algorithm is applied to the key to transform it to a file address. A common method is to divide the record key by a prime number corresponding to the number of storage locations to be used. The remainder is then used as the address for the record. For example, 7 records, 11 locations numbered 0–10. Keys 3, 12, 21, 39, 44, 60, 62. The first record with key 3 is divided by 11, giving 0 remainder 3. This is placed in location 3. The second record with key 12 ÷ 11 gives remainder 1 and goes into location 1, and so on. The results appear in Fig. 6.4.

However, if we had to store a record with key 82 it would also supposedly go in location 5. But we can see that there is already a record stored at that address. Record keys that generate the same storage address are called *synonyms*. One way of handling synonyms is to store the record in the next available location and use a pointer to locate it. This is known as *chaining*. 82 would go into location 8 in Fig. 6.4.

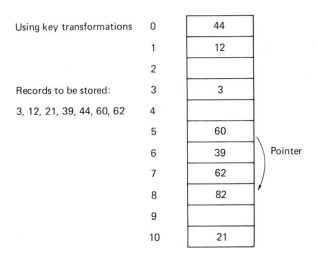

Figure 6.4 Locating records.

(iii) *Applications*

Q. Explain what you mean by 'on-line processing' and say why such applications need direct access organisation for storage.

A. Direct organisation permits the *on-line processing* of transactions (known as transaction processing) where each transaction is processed as it occurs. Hence:

- It is not necessary to batch and sort transactions.
- Each transaction is input from a terminal as it happens, and the database is updated immediately.
- Terminals can be used for information retrieval (file enquiries) with immediate response, e.g. airline reservations, banking (customer account queries).

Q. Compare sequential and direct organisation.

A. *Advantages of sequential access over direct:*

- Low-cost media (magnetic tape) can be used.
- More efficient where transactions can be batched and the activity rate is high (i.e. where most records need updating, e.g. a weekly payroll run).
- Automatic back-up files (old master file).
- It is usually easier to write programs which handle sequential files.

Advantages of direct access over sequential:

- Selected records can be accessed far more quickly in any order.
- Records do not have to be stored in any particular order, i.e. transactions don't have to be sorted.
- Several files can be processed or updated at the same time.

6.7   Storage Size Estimation

An important aspect of design is the estimation of disk storage space required to hold the files needed on-line at any one time. Disk storage has to hold:

- Segments of application programs and systems software not in main store.
- All the records used in a run, plus space for new records and expansion of existing records including overflow areas.

The file record specifications are a useful starting point for the sizing of storage. These give the average record length, but an allowance should be made for wasted space as well as future growth, and conventionally 10% is added for good measure. Clearly record type (fixed or variable) will influence storage size.

Example

Q. A products file which holds details of a toy company has 50 different product lines, each of which comes in three sizes (S, M, L) and three colours (1, 2, 3). All of these are soft toys, divided into the following categories: Animals, Dolls, Hand-Puppets and Miscellaneous, coded A, D, P or X, respectively.

The records are held on file at random and have the following fixed format (Table 6.6).

Table 6.6 Products file for toy company

	Number of characters	*Example*
Item code	3	101
Category	1	P
Description	18	Pooh Bear
Size	1	S
Colour	1	2
Selling price	6	5.00

A. Number of characters per record = 30 (approx)
Number of records
(50 products × 3 sizes × 3 cols) = 450
Required storage capacity = 30 × 450 = 13.5 K
+ 10% = 14.85 K

6.8   Worked Example — Payroll

A firm has 200 weekly paid workers on its payroll. The following stages make up the data-processing operations to convert the raw data into useful information (see Fig. 6.5 also).

(a) Data Collection

Clock cards are collected each week. These contain data on hours worked, overtime, etc. Imagine that a card consists of the following: employee's number, department code, name, hours worked for each day.

(i) *Data Entry Preparation*

The details for each employee will be keyed in and put onto a transaction file in random fashion (i.e. unsorted). An extract of the unsorted transaction file is shown in Table 6.7.

Table 6.7 Extract from unsorted transaction file

Employee number	*Department code*	*Name*	*Daily hours worked*				
054	7	Thomas	7	7	7	7	7
089	3	Hannah	8	8	8	7.5	8
007	8	Gillian	6	8	8	8	0
034	8	Stephen	7.5	7.5	7.5	7.5	7.5

(ii) *Data Validation*

The file will be checked for input errors (see Chapter 5) before being passed for further processing. Any errors will be printed out on to an error report. Errors can then be checked, corrected and re-entered.

Q. For each field on the weekly payroll transaction file state one appropriate test which might be used to validate it.

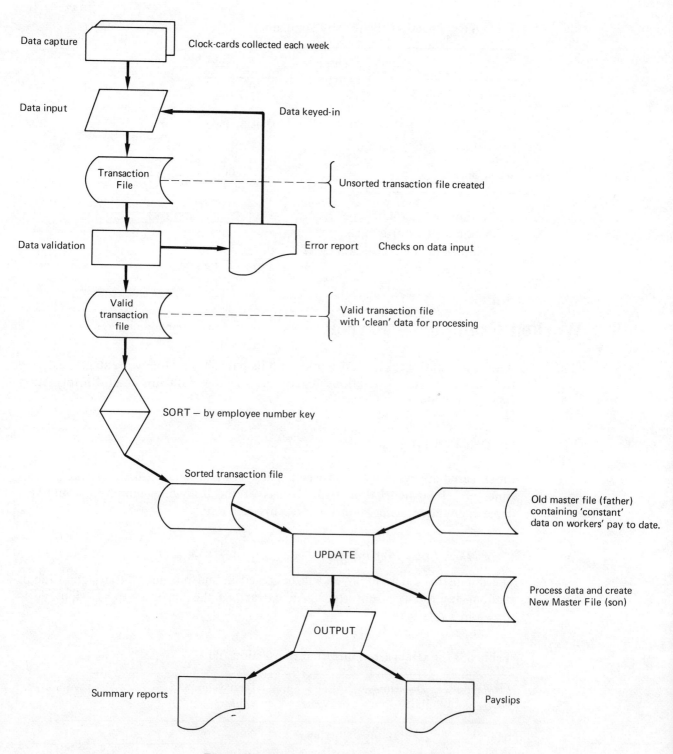

Figure 6.5 Payroll – the stages of data processing.

A. (1) Employee number   – check digit.
    (2) Department code   – range check, e.g. 1–10.
    (3) Name   – presence check.
    (4) Hours worked for each day   – range test, e.g. >5<12.

(b) Sorting

Q. Why is sorting necessary?

A. Sorting means arranging (or rearranging) data into order, e.g. names alphabetically or numbers in ascending order. Files are sorted because:

- Files are easier to update and merge if they are sorted in the same order.
- Searching a sorted file may be easier (cf. tape counters on your music cassette unit).
- People find sorted files easier to read and use.

Sorting is usually done by standard utility software (SORT programs) which are often provided by the computer manufacturer.

The payroll transaction file could be sorted in any number of ways, e.g. alphabetically by name within the department. In this case the file is sorted into employee number order — the same way as the payroll master file. An extract of the sorted transaction file is shown in Table 6.8.

Table 6.8 Transaction file sorted by employee key number (sort key)

Employee number	Department code	Name	Daily hours worked				
007	8	Gillian	6	8	8	8	0
034	8	Stephen	7.5	7.5	7.5	7.5	7.5
054	7	Thomas	7	7	7	7	7
089	3	Hannah	8	8	8	7.5	8

(i) *Example of Sorting — Bubble Sort*

A simple sort procedure in common use is called the 'bubble sort'. It can be used with numbers or names.

Q. With the aid of diagrams, explain how the following (employees) numbers would be sorted into ascending order using a systematic method such as a bubble sort: 54   89   7   34.

A. *Step (1)* — Compare each number with the next one.
   Step (2) — If the first number is bigger, swop the numbers around.
   Step (3) — Continue through each pair of numbers until the largest number is at the end.

```
54   89   7    34    No change
54   89   7    34    Swop
54    7  89    34    Swop
54    7  34    89
```

The largest number is now placed at the end.

   Step (4) — Repeat the process for the other numbers.

```
54    7   34   (89)  swop
 7   54   34   (89)  swop
 7   34   54    89
```

The process is now complete. An indicator is usually set when a swop is made. The process will stop when there is no change in the indicator.

(c) Processing Data

The file is now in the same order as the payroll master file and processing can begin. Constant data – e.g. wage rates, tax codes, national insurance payments – will be held on the master fil so that gross and net pay can be calculated. Fig. 6.6 shows how updating takes place.

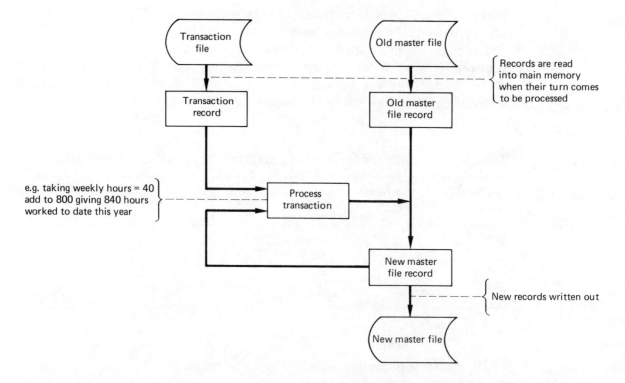

Figure 6.6 Data flow during a sequential file update.

An updating program is run which reads the master file and transaction file one record at a time. At the same time a *new* master file is created with the updated information. The old master file remains unchanged because:

- It is impractical to try to make changes on an existing sequential file (think of trying to insert one track on your music cassette).
- It can still be useful for security and back-up purposes.

(d) Merging

Q. Explain, by example, how two files are merged.

A. Merging is when two or more files are combined by interleaving their records to form one ordered file. Before merging, each data file is in order. After merging the data is again in order. For example, two files have the following record keys:

```
No. 1 file: 10    15    20    25    30
No. 2 file:  3     7    24    31    57    62    65
```

After merging, the new file will contain the following numbers in sequence.

```
No. 3 file:  3     7    10    15    20    24    25    30
            31    57    62    65
```

At each step of the merging process, the next numbers on the input files are compared. The lower number is copied on to the output file.

(e) Output

The computer can be programmed to produce:

- Payslips for weekly staff showing pay details.
- *Summary reports for management* – e.g. total wage bill, pay by department etc.; used for planning and control purposes; required for accounting and legal reasons.
- *Report of computer run* – Showing number of records processed, number of errors etc., control totals; for data processing planning and control.

6.9   File Security

Q. Define the following. (a) File security. (b) Recovery.

A. (a)   File *security* is necessary to prevent the accidental or deliberate loss of data.
(b)   *Recovery* enables data to be recovered if this does happen.

Q. How is data lost on computer?

A. Files can be:

- Destroyed by fire or other environmental causes.
- Corrupted by hardware failures (e.g. a disk-head crash which creates scratches on the disk).
- Accidently overwritten.
- Fraudulently changed.
- Updated with incorrect data.
- Accessed by unauthorised people.

Q. What are the overall guidelines for systems security?

A. The overall guidelines for systems security are:

- Restrict the number of users.
- Check the security features of the software.
- Use standard procedures so that there are fewer mistakes and it is harder to conceal alterations.
- Educate and train people to accept the importance of security.

(a) Methods of Protecting Data

(i)   *Keeping Copies*

File dumps – It is prudent to take copies of data on disk regularly by dumping files on to backing store or printer.
Generations of files – If tape is used, the updating procedure will automatically produce a new file called 'the son'. The previous master file, from which it was produced, is called 'the father', and the one before that 'the grandfather'. Usually

three generations are kept so that if data is lost or wrongly updated it can be recovered.

(ii) *Physical Safeguards*

It is important to keep files and software in a safe place to safeguard them against damage or theft.

- Magnetic media can be fitted with write permit slots or rings before data can be written on them. This prevents accidental overwriting.
- Only authorised personnel are allowed into the computer area. There are often locks to rooms and machines to restrict access.
- The distribution of printed output of confidential nature can be restricted. Shredders can be used to scrap it after use.

(iii) *Software Safeguards*

The computer's operating system can be used to restrict access to the system:

- *Passwords* — Users may have to enter a secret password as they log in to the computer. There are generally different levels of security. Some passwords give wider access than others. For example, only a few people may be permitted to update (write to) files. It makes sense to change passwords frequently.
- *Log* — The computer can keep a log of all processing activities, noting which user performed which operation. This can be used to trace the source of an error.
- *Audit trail* — In financial and accounting applications, individual transactions can be traced step-by-step through the computer system to ensure that nothing fraudulent has taken place.

6.10 Exercises

Question 6.1

(a) Explain the difference between a direct access file and a serial access file.
(b) State one advantage and one disadvantage of each type of file mentioned above.

Question 6.2

(a) Explain what is meant by the term database.
(b) Describe briefly two applications in which databases are used.

Question 6.3

In a public library, information is kept about each book. This information consists of:

- The name of the book.
- The name of the author.
- The name of the publisher.
- The ISBN number.
- The shelf classification number.

Suggest a way in which the files could be organised:
(a) When recorded on magnetic disks for processing in a computer.
(b) When recorded on small file cards kept in a drawer.   (AEB)

Question 6.4

Explain the following terms used in file maintenance. (a) Merge. (b) Transaction file.

Question 6.5

With the aid of diagrams explain how the following numbers would be sorted into ascending order using a systematic method such as a bubble sort.
87   73   5   12

Question 6.6

In a telephone directory data is organised in alphabetical order according to name. How can data be usefully organised in:

(a) A library catalogue?
(b) A list of cameras for someone who has up to £75 to spend on buying one?   (AEB)

Question 6.7

Your school decides to set up a data bank on its pupils and staff. The data bank will include data on:

(i)   each student;
(ii)   each teacher;
(iii) parents and home;
(iv)   medical records.

(a) For each of (i), (ii), (iii) give four data items to be included in the bank.
(b) How could this data be collected? Give four problems that might arise in the collection.
(c) How does a data bank such as this differ from a collection of separate files in this application?
(d) What special precuations should be taken in setting up this file and why?   (AEB)

Question 6.8

A health authority in a large city decides to keep a file concerning all children vaccinated in its area. Each child may be vaccinated against five separate illnesses. Three of the illnesses require only one injection, one requires two injections and the other, three injections. Only one injection may be given at a time, and in all cases injections must be six weeks apart. Each child's record must contain the following: name; address; type and date of all vaccinations; doctor's name.

(a) Design an index card capable of showing all this information.
(b) Give one disadvantage of storing the information this way.
(c) The file is to be computerised. Show, by means of a diagram, exactly how you would structure the data for subsequent interrogation.
(d) State which type of file (random or serial) is most suitable. Would the structure of the data in your diagram in (c) be satisfactory for random or serial access? Explain your answer.   (AEB)

Question 6.9

A paint manufacturer has a computer for stock-control purposes. Customers may place orders by telephone, post or personal visit. The orders are input through VDU terminals and despatch notes and payment invoices printed on a line printer.
(a) Give a list of the computer files required for this system, explaining their content, and the type of storage media most suitable.
(b) Draw a system flowchart to show the processing of an order from placement to payment invoice despatched to customer. (AEB)

Question 6.10

A clothing warehouse keeps a list of its contents on index cards. The information consists of:

Item number	(6 digit integer)
Item name	(up to 20 characters)
Manufacturer code	(5 characters)
Location code	(6 digits)

The information is to be stored on magnetic backing storage media, so that it becomes part of an on-line stock control computerised system.
(a) Devise a suitable data capture form for this information.
(b) Describe the data in terms of fields and records.
(c) Which backing storage media would be most suitable and why?
(d) What other field is normally added when such a system is computerised?
(e) What other information relevant to this application could be stored on the backing storage? (AEB)

Question 6.11

A second-hand car dealer wishes to keep a record of the cars he has for sale on a computer file. Each record is to contain the following details about each car: year; make; model; colour; condition; price.
(a) Show, by means of a detailed diagram, exactly how this particular data would be structured into a file for subsequent interrogation.
(b) State which type of file (random or serial access) would be most suitable for this particular application, and why.
(c) Briefly state how the file would be created; how it would be interrogated for a particular enquiry; and how data in the file could be changed.

Question 6.12

Read the following passage:

'In a shop, a microprocessor is incorporated into a cash till which is used as a point-of-sale terminal and is connected on-line to a central mainframe computer. Details of each sale are validated by the terminal before transmission to the mainframe where the data is used immediately to update the master stock file and calculate statistical information. The central computer is connected in this way to approximately 100 shops. After the shops close for the day, the central computer processes the updated stock file to produce new stock reports and other management information.'

Answer the following questions.
(i) State, giving a reason, the type of file access which would be suitable for the master stock file.
(ii) Name and describe two possible reports produced by the central computer which would be of use to management.

(iii) Describe two file security methods that could be used in case of corruption of the master stock file.

(iv) In the context of this application, why is it necessary to validate the sales data?

Question 6.13

A file contains fixed-length records relating to pupils in a school. Each record contains the following information about a pupil: name, date of birth, sex.

(a) Draw a diagram to represent consecutive records using data relating to yourself and two of your friends.

(b) When files are being updated they can become corrupted. What is meant by 'corruption' in this context? Describe one method of overcoming the effect of any corruption that might occur.

Question 6.14

(a) Explain the terms (1) masterfile and (2) generations of files.

(b) Describe a method of protecting against the loss of data due to the corruption of a master file. (L)

Question 6.15

A large company wishes to keep a personal file on each employee, which may be accessed by using visual display units. The file will contain the following details:

- Employee's name, address, age.
- Whether married or single.
- Number of children, if any.
- Employee's education qualifications.
- Salary scale and current salary.
- Name of employee's bank and account number.
- Results of medical examinations which have been carried out by the company medical staff.

(a) Suggest who in the company should have access to some or all of the data held on file.

(b) As matters of privacy are involved how would the files be protected from unauthorised access, and what assurances could be given to the employees?

(c) (i) Some names and addresses may be very short, others very long. What would be the maximum number of characters you would allow for each for entry into a computer system using a fixed-length record (justify your choice)?

(ii) In the case of 'educational qualifications' it is required to know the number of CSE, O-level and A-level examinations taken and the grades attained, together with any degrees received.

How would you encode this information for entry into the computer system, using a fixed-length record, to make use of the *least* amount of storage space? (Oxford)

6.11 Answers and Hints on Solutions

6.1 (a) *Serial access* — The process of storing or retrieving data items by first reading through all previous items to locate the one required.

Direct access — The process of storing or retrieving data items directly without having to search through other stored data first (also known as random access).

137

(b) *Direct access file*:

- advantage – speed of retrieval for data not in processing order.
- disadvantage – more complex programming required.

Serial access file:
- advantage – efficient when high proportion of records are processed in order.
- disadvantage – insertion of additional records is inefficient.

6.2 (a) Database is a collection of structured data independent of any particular application. (1) Police National Computer. (2) Local Government records.

6.3 (a) To put book data on *magnetic disk*, a *record* made up of six fields would need to be set up.
   Three fields (book name, author(s), publisher) would be variable length and would end with field markers:

Book name	*Author*	*Publisher*
THE GREAT WESTERN RAILWAY ■	TAYLOR D. ■	MACMILLAN
LOVES I HAVE KNOWN ■	SHEARGOLD D. ■	SNIPCOCK & TWEED

Where ■ denotes end of field marker.

The author field would contain a sub-field giving the number of authors would be separated by suitable symbols.
The other fields (ISBN number and shelf classification) would be fixed length fields as each will be made up of a specific number of digits. The ISBN could be used as the key field.
The last field will contain cross-reference shelf classification if a particular book covers more than one subject. It will therefore be of variable length.

(b) Two or more *file cards* would need to be written for each book. The first file could consist of all the information held in alphabetical order by author's names, with repeated cards for multiple authors. The second file could consist of the cards sorted alphabetically, according to subject.
The magnetic disk file would be more flexible because it could be searched using any of the five pieces of information as a key. (This is known as an inverted file structure.)
The file cards would be an advantage when the computer breaks down.
The use of a book could be recorded automatically on disk. Fields could be added which show the number of times it had been taken out, and the average length of time for each withdrawal. It would be too time consuming for librarians to do this manually on file cards.

6.4 (a) Two files are merged by interleaving their records to form one ordered file.

(b) A transaction file is a file of temporary data which can be used to update a master file, e.g. daily sales on a transaction file can be used to adjust stock levels on the stock master file.

6.5

87	73	5	12	swop
73	87	5	12	swop
73	5	87	12	swop
73	5	12	87	

The largest number is now at the end.
    Repeat the process:

73	5	12	87	swop
5	73	12	87	swop
5	12	73	87	

The process is now complete.

6.6 (a) Alphabetically by title/subject, or alphabetically by author, or alphabetically by book number.
     (b) Descending order of price (from £75 down).

6.7 (a)   (i)   Number, name, class, year (date of birth, etc.).
          (ii) Number, name, address, telephone number.
          (iii) Names, address, telephone number (home), work.
          (iv) Doctor, telephone number, recent illnesses, special needs.

     (b) (i) and (iii) Form completed by child and checked by parent/guardian.
                 (ii) Teacher application form.
                 (iv) Doctor (or school nurse's) records.
          NB use of codes to minimise input.
          Problems:

          1.   Ensuring accuracy of the raw data.
          2.   Getting everyone's co-operation so that data is complete.
          3.   Transcribing the data properly.
          4.   Finding the time to set up the databank.

     (c) A databank (or database) is different from a collection of separate files in the following ways:

     ● Duplicate records are eliminated.
     ● It is only necessary to store (or update) a data item once.
     ● Shared data means that different people can use them in different ways for different uses.

     (d) *Precautions* – Particular attention should be paid to:

     ● *Data validation* – It is important to ensure that data is accurate and complete because a databank is only as good as its raw data (garbage input–garbage output). Wrong decisions may be taken if the information is incorrect – e.g. an incomplete medical record which omits to mention a pupil's special disability.
     ● *File security* – To guard against accidental or deliberate loss of data.

6.8 (a) Index card:

Name:
Address:

Vaccination type   1 ☐

                    2 ☐

                    3 ☐

                                1   2
Insert dates]   4 [_____]   [_____]

                                1   2   3
in box   ]   5 [_____] [_____] [_____]

Note: Vaccination must be 6 weeks apart.

Doctor's name:

(b) It is time consuming to classify data in other ways, e.g. percentage of children vaccinated for type 3, etc.

(c) Record key:

Child number	Name	Address 1	Address 2
001	ROBINSON	999 LETSBE AVENUE	LONDON W13 0JY
6 digits	20 characters (ch)	20 ch	20 ch

vaccination type:

1	2	3	4		5				
Y/N	Y/N	Y/N	Date	Date	Date	Date	Date	Doctor's name
1 ch.	1 ch.	1 ch.	6 digits	6 digits	6 digits	6 digits	6 digits	20 ch.

(d) Random access would be most suitable. The structure of the data in(c) would be satisfactory for random access (by key algorithm or index) or serial access (by child number or name).

6.9 (a) *Computer files*:

● Stock master file.
● Customer master file.
● Possibly: Print files (various) for despatch notes, payment invoices.

Content:

● *Stock file* – Stock number, description, quantity in stock, price.

Customer file:

● Account number, name, address, telephone number, credit limit, invoice details – stock ordered, stock number, quantity.

Storage media – Most suitable is magnetic disk. For customers to place orders by telephone there must be an on-line interactive system with direct access backing store – hence disk is essential for this application.

(b) See Fig. 6.7.

6.10 (a) See Fig. 6.8.

(b) The record is a collection of related items, treated as a unit, in this case concerning an article of clothing. The records here are fixed length and are made up of four fields (number, name, manufacturer

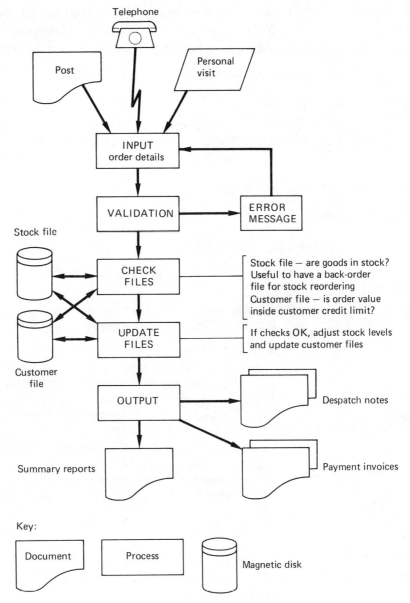

Figure 6.7 Solution 6.9(b). System flowchart — sales order processing.

and location) and 37 characters.

A field is a predetermined section of a record.

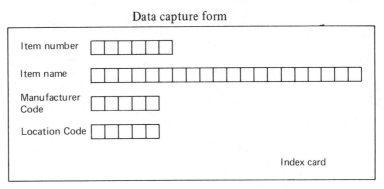

Figure 6.8 Solution 6.10(a). Data capture form

(c) Backing storage media will be magnetic disk because the system is on-line. The choice between hard disk or floppy depends on the nature of the application — the storage capacity needed, security requirements, etc.

(d) A key field to identify the record so that retrieval is made easy. The item number could be used for this purpose.

(e) Item size, colour, price, quantity in stock, reorder level, etc.

6.11 (a) Sample extract from car dealer file:

Key no.	Year	Make*	Model	Colour	Price
0123,	84,	LEYLAND ---,	MAESTRO ---,	YELLOW ---, 1,	3500
0124,	86,	FORD ------,	SIERRA-----,	BLUE -----, 3,	3000
0125,	84	AUDI ------,	QUATRO----,	GREY -----, 1,	10000
4 digits (up to 9999)	2 digits		10 characters per field (larger if necessary)		5 digits

* – Denotes space.

Condition code: 1 = very good; 2 = good; 3 = average; 4 = poor; 5 = very poor.

- The car record is made up of seven fields and 42 characters.
- It will be accessed by key number.

(b) Random (direct) access would be the most suitable for this particular application because the dealer will have to answer queries about individual cars for sale. This demands quick access to the particular record.

(c) The file can be created through a computer's editor or via a data entry program which prompts the user to enter the data step by step.

Interrogation would be by key number (see 6.11(a)). Data on file can be changed (amended, deleted) by calling up the appropriate record, making the change via the editor and filing away the update. Also a new record can be inserted into file via the editor.

6.12 (i) Direct access – permits immediate stock update.
(ii) *Reports*:

- Stockout reports – items to be reordered.
- Best-selling lines, etc. – for merchandise planning.
- Sales analysis.

(iii) File security methods:

1. Back-up copies of stock-file on disk or tape.
   Physical safeguards.
   Passwords.
2. Local file back-up until the link is restored. (Use parity checks in transmission.)

(iv) To check that data keyed-in is accurate. This is important because it will be used immediately to update the stock file and calculate statistical information.

6.13 (a)

Key	Surname	Forename	DOB	Sex
0001,	HAYWOOD ---,	GLADYS ----,	111070,	F
0002,	HAYWOOD ---,	STANLEY ---,	041271,	M
0003,	PORTER -----,	KIM --------,	181070,	F
4 digit	10 characters, etc.		6 digits	

– = Space. M=Male; F=Female.

(b) Files can be accidentally (or deliberately) erased or overwritten. One way of overcoming the effect of any corruption is to keep duplicate (back-up) copies of files. The update can then be carried out correctly a second time, using the back-up file, which, in turn, should be copied for security reasons.

6.14 (a) (1) Master file is a file of data which is the main source of information. It can be updated or amended as necessary.

(2) Generations of files — grandfather, father, son files — are the three most recent versions of a file that is periodically updated. They are retained for security purposes.

(b) See (2) above.

6.15 (a)

Access

Personnel department	All
Manager	All
Medical staff	All medical records
Employee	All records
Accounts department	All except medical

(b) *Passwords* — personal identification, levels of security.
Physical safeguards — To bar computer access.

(c) (i) Name — surname e.g.   Williamson } 25 ch.
          forename e.g.   Graham

        Address 1 —   9 Acacia Villas   20 ch.
              2 —   LONDON SE18 0JY   20 ch.

- *Fixed field length* — Name, 25 characters. Enough to cope with most names (double-barrelled plus forenames).
- *Fixed field length* — Address, 40 characters. Enough to cope with most street, town names and the post code.

NB If storage space is limited, smaller fields may be set. Long data entries would have to be truncated — e.g. use of initials instead of forenames.

(ii) Educational qualifications:

        Code C = CSE;
            O = 'O' level;
            A = 'A' level.

Sample fields:

No. of exams taken	*Grades*
C, 3,	1, 2, 1
O, 7,	A, B, A, A, C, D, E
A, 2,	B, E

7 Data Communications (or Datacomm)

7.1 Introduction

There are many situations where the user is some distance from the computer, perhaps in a different room or even a different city or country. In such cases a data communication system may be used for transmitting data to and from a computer.

A datacomm system links up computer hardware and software and telecommunications facilities. It may just consist of a terminal in an office connected to a computer in a different part of the building or it may be a very complex nationwide system of interconnected computers and terminals.

A well-designed datacomm system can improve the use of computer facilities and provide a fast and accurate service to everyone using it.

7.2 Applications of Data Communications

Q. Why do organisations need data communications?

A. Data communications are used in a variety of ways, the most important (Fig. 7.1) being:

- Enquiry/response.
- On-line data entry (transaction processing).
- Remote job entry.
- Conversational time-sharing.
- Distributed processing.

(a) Enquiry/response

This type of application typically involves people at various locations requiring access to a remote computer database. A request for information is usually made via a video display terminal, and the response should be within seconds. Examples include credit checking, law enforcement and library referencing.

(b) On-line Data Entry (or Transaction Processing)

In on-line data entry with central processing, remote terminals (usually VDUs) are placed in the user-departments and data entered directly into the computer.

144

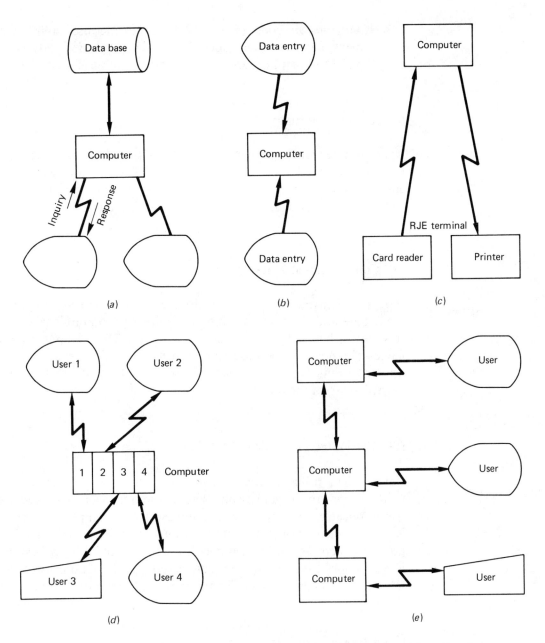

Figure 7.1 Ways of data communications usage. (*a*) Enquiry/response. (*b*) on-line data entry. (*c*) Remote job entry. (*d*) Conversational time-sharing (*e*) Distributed processing.

Transactions (e.g. customer orders) can be entered as they arrive or are created by the departments. This is often called transaction processing. On-line data entry is necessary where the computer database has to be kept right up to date and where rapid response is required. Typical applications include:

- *Reservations systems* — A clerk requests information on the availability of certain theatre seats. A central (booking) computer checks the status of the seats and responds with the information required (price, availability, non-smoking, etc.). The clerk then keys in the information necessary to make the reservation and the computer updates the file. Other reservation systems include: airline booking, car rentals, hotels.
- *Banking systems and building societies* — Use systems to give up-to-date information on the balance in an account. Deposits and withdrawals are posted instantly to the customer's account, maintained by a remote computer.

- *Manufacturing companies* — Some companies use on-line systems to link the various parts of their operation — the factories, offices and warehouses. Several thousand orders can be received and processed daily.

(c) Remote Job Entry

A remote terminal (perhaps equipped with a high-speed card reader) and line printer are linked to a central computer. Batched jobs (data and programs) are entered and transmitted to the main computer for processing. Results can then be transmitted back to the remote site for printing.

(d) Conversational Time-sharing

Here several users at remote locations can use a central computer. Responses are immediate and the user can 'interact' with the computer in question and answer sessions — hence the term 'conversational'. The computer's operating system makes this possible by allocating each user a time-slice. Each user takes turns to use processing time. This happens so quickly that everyone thinks they have exclusive use of the machine.

(e) Distributed Processing

Rather than using a large central computer, several smaller computers can be used around the organisation. The computers can be linked together by data communications and may share databases. An example of distributed computing is a network of computers in a national company, with a mini- or microcomputer in each regional office performing functions for its own area. These minis may support time-sharing, enquiry/response, transaction processing and remote job entry. Data can be sent to and from head office or other branches as required.

(f) Advantages of Datacomm

Q. What are the advantages of data communications?

A.

- Data is captured at source in computer-readable form, e.g. in a shop with point-of-sale terminals.
- Data can be collected, and information disseminated, very quickly. Data is transmitted at electronic speeds, rather than by mail or other relatively slow methods.
- Operating costs should be reduced. Data communications can replace courier services and can often eliminate the need for meetings and conferences. A company with data communications has the choice of processing the data centrally, thereby taking advantage of economies of scale.
- There is back-up data processing capacity. In larger systems, two or more computers are often connected by a data communications system. This permits priority jobs to be routed to another computer if the main computer is busy, or if one of the computers fails.

7.3 Components of a Datacomm System

Any data communications system is made up of three basic elements:

- A sender of information, e.g. a person seated at a terminal.
- A communication link, e.g. a telephone.
- A receiver of information, e.g. a computer or a person seated at a terminal.

A datacomm system is made up of five basic hardware components:

- Computers.
- Communications processors (or front-ends).
- Modems.
- Communication links.
- Terminals.

(a) Computers

There may be one or more computers in a datacomm system. The main computer, often referred to as the *host machine*, will be concerned with the basic data-processing tasks whilst other, smaller, computers handle tasks such as message switching (the transfer and routing of messages around the network), communication processing (interfacing computers and terminals with the network) or local processing.

(b) Communications Processors (or Front-ends)

Managing a data communications network is complex and often requires short bursts of activity with long periods of inactivity. Rather than tie up the host computer with such tasks, separate computers, called communications processors or front-end processors, are used. Typically, a front-end processor's tasks include:

- Connecting the host computer to communication links.
- Polling remote terminals to see if they are ready to send or receive messages.
- Accepting incoming data in different formats and converting them into a format acceptable to the computer — and back again on output from the computer.
- Performing 'store and forward' functions by storing messages from one terminal to another when the second is busy and forwarding them when the terminal is free.
- Providing error detection and correction of incoming messages.
- Performing logging of all incoming and outgoing messages, both for auditing purposes and for restart purposes after a system 'crash'.
- Assigning priorities to incoming and outgoing messages.
- Rerouting messages if a given line is busy.
- Automatically placing and answering calls to and from terminals in the system.
- Maintaining statistics concerning usage of the network, such as number of messages per hour and number of errors.

(c) Modems

Digital data cannot be directly transmitted over standard telephone lines which are designed to carry analog signals. So until the telephone system becomes fully digital modems (*mod*ulators/*dem*odulators) are used so that digital data can be sent by telephone, modulated before transmission and demodulated at the receiving end.

Modems of different types handle various different transmission speeds. One special type of cheap, low-speed modem is the *acoustic coupler* where the user places the telephone handset into the cradle of the coupler.

Modems are now quite sophisticated and can perform some or all of the following functions:

- Automatic dialling and answering of remote terminals.
- Simultaneous voice and data transmission.
- Automatic line testing and selection of other routes when a line fails.
- Minimising error rates.

(d) Datacomm Terminals

Various types of terminal can be linked to a datacomm system. They are:

- *Teletypewriters* — which are low-speed printing terminals consisting of a typewriter keyboard for input and a printer for output. These are now tending to be replaced by VDUs.
- *Visual display units* (VDUs) — VDUs consist of a keyboard and screen and can be alphanumeric or graphical. These terminals are widely used for enquiry/response, transaction processing, time-sharing and other datacomm applications. Usually they are 'intelligent terminals' — computers in their own right — carrying out local processing tasks.
- Transaction terminals are used for particular applications such as in retail stores and factories. They are used for enquiry/response and for capturing transaction data at source. These special terminals are often equipped with bar code readers as well as a keyboard for manual data entry.
- There are also portable transaction terminals, which look like large calculators. Used in such applications as stock ordering, the unit can be linked via an acoustic coupler and the data transmitted to the main computer.

Terminals were described in detail in Section 5.3.

(e) Communication Links

Data is transmitted between remote terminals and computers by means of a communications *channel* or *network*. Most organisations use the telephone network (BT) but there are other companies which offer data communication services (e.g. Mercury).

Communications traffic travels five ways, depending on the distance it has to cover:

- Along pairs of copper wires for local services.
- By microwaves (tower-to-tower) for distances about 30 miles (50 km) apart.
- Through copper coaxial cables, particularly for long-distance trunk routes over land and sea.

148

- Through optical fibres both for trunk and for local services. (Glass is cheaper than copper and, unlike copper-wire networks, is not affected by electrical interference (important in factories).)
- By satellite for very long hauls, particularly over water. (Intelstat V carries 12 000 phone conversations and TV as well.)

All transmission media are still expanding in capacity and speed.

(i) *Types of Service*

The services offered can be classified according to band width. Band width refers to the frequency range that can be accommodated by the transmission line, which in turn determines the rate at which data can be transmitted. The three classes of service can be defined as follows:

- *Narrowband* — Data may be transmitted at rates up to 300 bits per second (b.p.s.) which is sufficient for teletypewriters and other slow-speed terminals.
- *Voiceband* — Voiceband circuits are used in telephone conversations and are capable of medium transmission speeds (about 64 k b.p.s.).
- *Broadband* — Very high data rates (several million b.p.s.) can be achieved with broadband facilities which generally use coaxial cable or microwave transmission.

(ii) *Leased or Dialled Communications*

Communication facilities may be leased or dialled (switched). At a price, leasing a line from (say) BT can give the user exclusive use which is why such lines are often called private or dedicated lines.

The dial (or switch) service is very similar to the telephone service. To send a message the user dials the destination number (either a computer or remote terminal) just as for a telephone call. Because the lines are public they may be busy with other users at any given time and so the message would have to be sent a bit later. The user is charged only for the time used, with rates depending on the time of day, day of the week and distance.

The choice between leased or dialled lines is based on the analysis of costs, message volume and service requirements. In general, leased facilities make sense if there is a need to send large numbers of messages; low message volume favours dialled facilities. Leased lines provide guaranteed access, faster response (since dialling is not necessary), better quality transmission (fewer errors) and greater privacy than the dialled service. On the other hand, the dialled service does provide a wider access because of the extensive links which are available through the telephone system.

(iii) *The Telephone Service*

Q. How have computers helped to improve the telephone service?

A. Telephone networks are becoming digital which means that voices, data, telex and facsimile can all travel much faster (at 64 kilobits a second), more cheaply and accurately than with the old analog telephone systems.

This fundamental change in the telephone service with the introduction of computers into telephone exchanges and telephones provides a faster, more reliable service.

1 *PABX (Private Automatic Branch Exchanges)*

A computer-controlled switchboard (about the size of a briefcase) can provide an organisation with a superb internal telephone network, connecting branches with head office, and offering, in addition, the following types of facilities:

- *Abbreviated dialling* — For frequently dialled numbers (the computer remembers the numbers you dial often).
- *Repeat last call.*
- *Repeat last stored call* — For automatic retry if line is engaged.
- *Divert calls* — Call forwarding to other extensions/numbers, e.g. if you are in a meeting.
- *Call waiting* — Acknowledged and asked to wait.
- *Call barring* — Suppressing calls at certain times.
- *Reminder calls* — Automatic alarm.
- *Three-way (multi-way) connection* — Telephone 'meetings'
- *Cost calculations and other data processing* — Itemised billing of calls, e.g. long-distance or by extension numbers.
- *Remote control* — All facilities can be set up from any phone.

PABX can control machinery remotely; they can 'manage' energy by turning electricity on and off in specified locations, carry burglar and fire alarm signals and they can connect word-processors. Just simply automating message-taking might be a worthwhile investment, not least because only one in four telephone calls reaches the intended person at first try and eliminating the time wasted in waiting and transferring calls would mean a big rise in office productivity.

(ii) **Packet Switching**

Q. What is packet switching?

A. Packet switching is a way of evening out the flow of data between alternative pathways in computer networks. Messages sent between computers are split up into small (usually fixed length) pieces, called packets. These packets are routed around the network until they reach their destination, where they are reassembled to make up the original message.

One advantage of inter-computer communication lies in the ability of computers to store information. This means that if a required line is busy, an exchange computer can store a packet until that line becomes free again. If there are several possible routes between sender and receiver, then the exchange (or switch) can select which particular route a packet should take, re-routing packets via quieter parts of the network if necessary.

In general, the individual packets making up a message will take different routes through the network, before being finally reunited at their destination. In Fig. 7.2 a network has three minis, X, Y and Z. A user, at terminal 1, wishes to transmit a 300-character message to terminal 2. The message is divided into packets A, B and C. A and C are routed directly to minicomputer Z while packet B is routed to Z via Y.

Packet switching networks allow the user all the facilities of leased networks. They are the most common kind of network in use today because of their flexibility in routing packets along the best route currently available, thereby ensuring that lines are used to the maximum.

The British Telecomm PSS network is a packet switched service, using computers for switching only, and linking major cities in the UK. It uses the standard X25 interface and is rapidly growing in popularity.

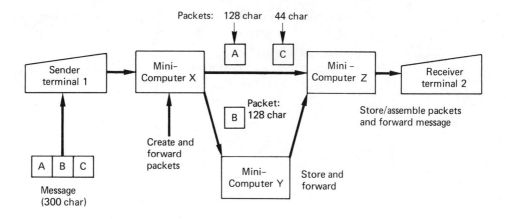

Figure 7.2 Packet switching:

- Digital exchanges.
- Lines used to maximum, re-routing of packets to quieter parts of network.

A company (e.g. ICL) can lease lines from a common carrier (e.g. British Telecom) and add value to these lines by adding minicomputers and other devices that permit packet-switching. Such networks are known as Value Added Networks or VANs for short. So VANs are communications links which process as well as carry data.

7.4 Computer Networks

(a) Point-to-point

The simplest configuration (Fig. 7.3) is where a single terminal is connected to a single computer.

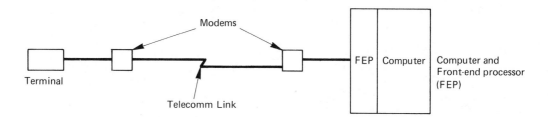

Figure 7.3 Point-to-point network.

(b) Multidrop Lines

Several terminals can be connected to a single communications line with each terminal being considered as a 'drop point'. Only one terminal can transmit at a time unless multiplexing is used (see below) and each terminal recognises its own address. The system can also feature group and broadcast addresses, e.g. messages sent to some (group) or all (broadcast) terminals. Since only one terminal can transmit at a time there must be a network line control discipline to control line usage. There are two types:

151

- *Contention* – First-come, first-served, e.g. dialled telephone system.
- *Polling* – A central computer polls each terminal in turn to see if it has a message to send.

Multiplexing enables a communications channel to be subdivided into two or more channels. Hence two or more terminals can transmit simultaneously over a multidrop line (Fig. 7.4).

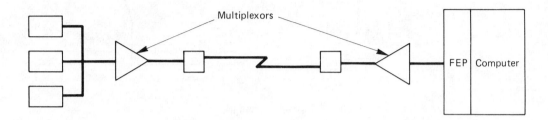

Figure 7.4 Multidrop line with multiplexor, allowing several terminals to communicate simultaneously with the computer.

(c) Loop Lines (or Rings)

Loop lines are another form of multidrop line in which several terminals are connected in a ring (see Fig. 7.8) This set-up is very effective when terminals are close together (so-called Local Area Networks) and is often used for transaction terminals such as point-of-sale terminals and factory production control terminals. If any one line breaks down, communication between all the remaining computers is still possible (assuming all the computers are switching computers).

(d) Star Network

A star network has one central message-switching computer through which all the other computers communicate (Fig. 7.5). It is a low-cost communications

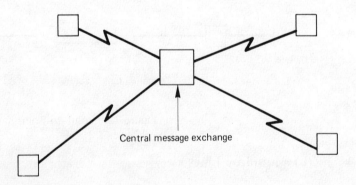

Figure 7.5 Star network.

system because it uses the minimum number of lines as well as needing only one clever computer to act as a message centre – the other computers can be smaller and cheaper. A major disadvantage, of course, is dependency on the central computer as all communication will cease if it breaks down.

(c) Selection of Facilities

The choice of network configuration will depend on a number of factors but whatever the choice it will be prudent to build in extra communications links in the network (a) to ensure reliability and (b) to share the workload.

Fig. 7.6 shows a network in which each site is linked to at least two others. It is unlikely that a fully connected network (where each computer is connected to every other computer) would be cost-effective but some extra lines are useful to guard against failure and to act as 'overload pathways' to cope with any extra workload at busy periods.

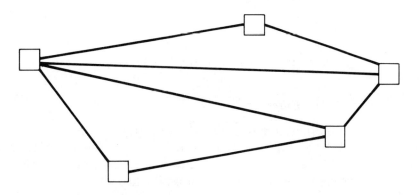

Figure 7.6 Networks with extra links (i.e. some built-in redundancy).

Local Area Networks (LANs)

Q. What are Local Area Networks?

A. Cheap micros and the development of packet-switched networks has led to the development of LANs.

A LAN, as its name implies, is used over short distances, typically within the same building, and can be of great help to the organisation particularly when it is reckoned that 80% of office mail is internal.

A LAN consists of a piece of cable (coaxial, twisted pair, ribbon or fibre-optic link) which runs around a building with connection points at regular intervals and is similar in concept to an electrical ring main. It may form a continuous loop—a ring— or start at one end of a building and finish at the other. LANs are not necessarily limited to one building.

LANs are technically capable of carrying data, text, voice and video. Although installation costs for wiring up are high, adding devices to the link is relatively cheap and easy.

A range of devices can be linked within the office. Files, printers, etc. can be attached and workstations can access greater computing power if necessary.

Users can communicate with each other using the LAN. Managers and secretaries can send messages, reports, memos, etc.; they can have quick and easy access to data files, and access via *gateways* to external databases.

Inter-company communications are also possible, enabling one company's LAN to link to another via the public network, although there may be problems due to the use of different equipment and protocols (there are several 'standards' currently in existence).

An alternative approach is to use the telephone network for data as well as voice transmission. The cable is already installed and, as well as providing links inside the organisation, contacts can be made outside, e.g. for connecting micro-computers at remote locations to a central database. However, LANs can handle data transfer rates far higher than the telephone system and are less prone to error.

Unlike a time-sharing system where users share the facilities of a large computer, LANs are not dependent on a powerful central computer. Users have their own computers for processing which will meet most of their needs. Occasionally, there will be a need to call on bigger facilities and there may be hook-ups to a company database and central computer.

LANs represent a low-cost solution for low-volume data transfer over relatively short distances.

(a) Types of LAN

Two of the best known LAN systems are *Ethernet* and the *Cambridge Ring*.

(i) *Ethernet*

Ethernet is a product of three large computer companies — Digital Equipment, Intel and Xerox — and as such may become the industry standard.

An ethernet is a straight-line network, in fact a single line of cable (known as a 'bus') to which equipment is attached.

Data sent out by a user is broadcast with the intended receiver's label — an 'identity tag' which is recognised by the appropriate device. Devices are listening out all the time (known as continuous sampling) to see if any signal is present. Ethernet LANs can be up to $2\frac{1}{2}$ km long and allow up to 1000 devices to be attached. (See Fig. 7.7 for an ethernet example.)

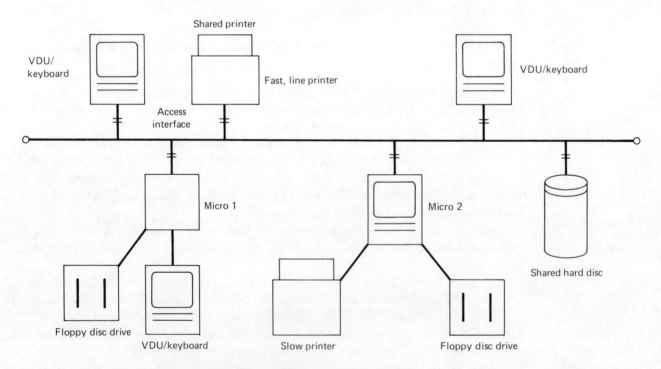

Figure 7.7 Ethernet LAN.

(ii) *Cambridge Ring*

The Cambridge Ring, developed at Cambridge University, is organised in a circle.

Messages are sent in packets around the ring and 'returned to sender' if not accepted or transmitted unsuccessfully (known as the 'anti-hogging' rule because when a packet has been round the ring it must be emptied to give another message its chance on the ring). To send a message, a user 'fills' an empty packet and puts it on the ring. Packets circulate round the ring and are sensed by each device in turn. If the destination address on the packet is matched with the device address it is output on to that device and the packet is sent back to the sender with acknowledgement.

Repeaters are needed where devices are attached and where the signal strength needs boosting.

Rings are relatively simple and cheap to set up and have proven to be very accurate (very low error rates have been recorded).

LANs can be linked with other computers via telecommunications using LAN gateways.

A typical ring configuration, including a resource manager, a central communications controller (for error detection) and a file server (to provide central filing and store and forward functions), a printing station and other devices is shown in Fig. 7.8. In addition to being a switching node of a ring, each station acts as an entry point to the network.

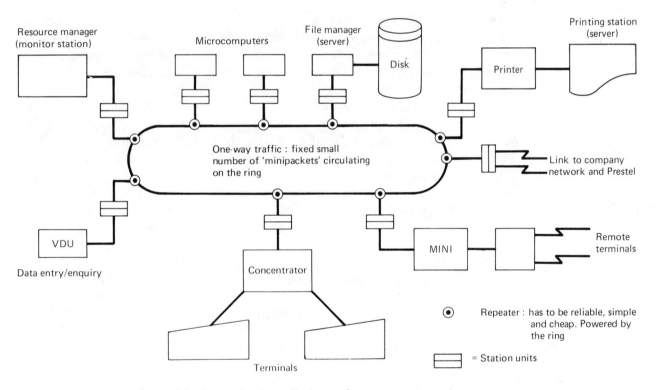

Figure 7.8 Cambridge Ring. Each interface is a repeater and ring system.

(iii) *Importance of LANs*

The reduction in the price of microcomputers means that processing power is cheap and so no longer has to be shared. LANs are therefore independent of the central processor and offer the following advantages:

- Sharing expensive resources such as printers and other peripherals. Typically one disk-drive and one printer can serve six micros.
- A coherent and expandable system, i.e. it is possible to plug in any number of workstations or nodes (subject to certain limits), all of which can be used for any application, unlike stand-alone systems.

155

- The ability to bring in information from outside, giving access to information on Prestel or any other external database.
- Greater security.

A key element is integration. Material can be extracted from an external database, tailored for a specific report, and circulated to other users for comments and amendments before final printing.

7.6 Videotex — Viewdata and Teletext

(a) Videotex

Videotex is the general term for sending and receiving information and displaying it on screen using either broadcasting (teletext) or telephone lines (viewdata).

Viewdata systems are two-way systems for transmitting text or graphics stored in computer databases, via a telephone network, for display on a TV screen. They are designed for a large number of users and are meant to be cheap, easy to use and flexible.

The cost is kept down partly by the use of low-cost terminals and networking and partly because the ease of use reduces training and support costs. Videotex systems are easy to use because they have a simple, frame-oriented approach which means that beginners or casual users can make effective use of them immediately.

Flexibility is mainly a result of the wide acceptance of standard protocols (Prestel in the UK) and the use of the voice telephone network (PSTN) as the main networking medium. Use of the PSTN for telecommunications means that systems can be implemented rapidly, often in a few weeks and can be accessed from almost anywhere.

As well as public viewdata systems like Prestel, there are also private ones. An example of a private viewdata system is at Rumbelows, who have over 500 viewdata terminals in their stores to support stock location and reordering and sales reporting. The network uses micro-based terminals which hold information on the availability of stock items and sales data to be collected by the warehouse system at night. Similarly, the travel industry incorporates viewdata into on-line reservation systems. Tour operators provide their customers, the travel agent and holidaymaker alike, with instant access to information on availability and the ability to get a quotation and make a reservation directly.

(i) *Prestel*

Perhaps the best known public viewdata system is PRESTEL. This is the two-way system run by BT. Prestel users pay the full telephone charge plus another similar charge for the computer. The system supports over 320 000 pages of information and facilities include *Mailbox*, which enables users to send messages to each other, and *Gateway* which enables them to do, for example, home banking and shopping. Schemes to attract home-users include:

- *Club 403* — For teleshopping.
- *Micronet* — Offering users computer programs (some are free, others have to be bought) as well as the usual Prestel facilities.

A stylised model is now given of the system to give an idea of its structure and purpose.

Example 7.1

Read carefully this computer system description and answer the questions which follow.

The PRESTEL computer system operated by British Telecom provides subscribers access to a vast amount of information, currently about 320 000 'pages'. A subscriber, householder or business, must possess a special VDU, or a colour TV and adaptor, which is connected to their telephone. When the PRESTEL computer is dialled up the subscriber selects required 'pages', for display on the video, by entering numbers through the keyboard. For business users a low-cost printer can be attached to the video, giving a copy of the screen display, useful for reference or showing to customers. The computer keeps a record of which pages a subscriber has accessed, and the time connected, in order that an invoice may be submitted.

Information Providers, such as WHICH magazine, the Stock Exchange, British Rail, supply new 'pages', or alter existing ones, in several ways. They may have a VDU connected on-line to the PRESTEL computer. They may have their own microcomputer with diskette storage and VDU containing working copies of their 'pages', which are transmitted to PRESTEL on-line at the end of the day. They may write their 'pages' on to special documents, rather like squared graph paper, which are sent to the PRESTEL data preparation section for batch data entry. Each 'page' occupies 1 k of storage in the computer. Memory capacity of the PRESTEL computer is 360 kbytes. Every month detailed invoices are sent to subscribers, now estimated to be about 15 000 in all. As a precaution against breakdown of backing store a safety copy of all 'pages' is taken on to magnetic tape once daily.

(a) Draw a configuration diagram suitable for the above system. Name each hardware component and explain clearly its use *in this application*, technical descriptions of equipment are *not* required. Indicate clearly the role of people using the system.
(b) (i) Estimate the capacity of backing storage.
   (ii) Each invoice averages two sheets of 60 lines. How long will it take to print these on a 800 l.p.m. printer?
   (iii) The Control Program occupies 120 k of storage and each connected subscriber occupies 3 k of store. What is the maximum number of subscribers who may be connected at one time?

Show your working for the above calculations and state any assumptions you have made.

Solution 7.1

(a) see Fig. 7.9.

(b) (i) Estimate the capacity of backing storage.

$$\text{Storage capacity} = \frac{320\,000 \times 1000}{1\,000\,000}\,\text{Mb} = 320\,\text{Mb minimum}$$

(each page occupies 1 k; 1000 k = 1 Mb)

(ii) Each invoice averages two sheets of 60 lines. How long will it take to print these on a 800 l.p.m. printer?

$$\text{Time} = \frac{2 \times 60 \times 15\,000}{800} \quad \begin{aligned} &= 2250\,\text{min} \\ &= 37\tfrac{1}{2}\,\text{hours} \end{aligned}$$

(about 15 000 invoices/subscribers; frequency, monthly)

(iii) Control program occupies 120 k of storage and each connected subscriber occupies 3 k of store. What is the maximum number of subscribers who may be connected at one time?

Memory capacity = 360 kbytes
$-$ 120 k for control
= 240 k of 'subscriber space' and 240/3 = 80 simultaneous users.

157

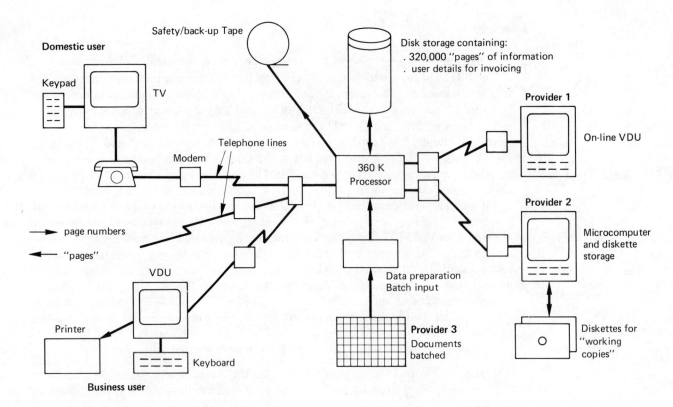

Note: This is a simple model of the real Prestel system.

Figure 7.9 Prestel.

(b) Applications of Viewdata (Videotex) Systems

Most businesses can make use of videotex for information services either within their organisation, to communicate with customers or to reach suppliers. The most popular applications for videotex are:

- *Location systems* – Directory searching, 'Yellow pages' search for items ranging from antiques to second-hand cars.
- *Teleshopping* – Stock enquiry and ordering, 'mail order' purchase of goods and services, airline, theatre-seat availability and reservations.
- *Electronic mail* – Message switching in-company or e.g. with customers and agents.
- *Telebanking* – Electronic Funds Transfer (EFT); the switching of monies to and from a bank account.
- *Telesoftware* – Downloading of computer programs/software.
- *Telepublishing* – Electronically published books, educational materials, newspapers, etc.

(c) Gateways

GATEWAYS provide communication links between the various networks and other databases. The ability to connect any terminal to any computer or service is important. This will give rise to links or GATEWAYS between the various networks similar to the one which currently allows access to private viewdata systems via Prestel.

All leading tour operators hold holiday details on private viewdata systems, whereas smaller operators use Prestel. This mixture of private and public (Prestel) databases is simplified by the use of Prestel gateways. So travel agents use Prestel for access to *all* databases, in particular to Telex and to airlines-booking systems.

Q. What is teletext?

A. This is a non-interactive (i.e. *one-way*) form of videotex transmitted as part of a TV broadcast. Frames are sent on a 'carousel' basis and therefore the number of frames is restricted to keep down the waiting time. It is used by the BBC (Ceefax) and ITV (Oracle) for newsflashes, subtitles, etc.

To receive this information, consumers can rent or purchase special teletext receivers or adaptors for existing 625-line television sets. Teletext receivers cannot, in themselves, access viewdata.

Information such as the latest news headlines, racing results, financial information, weather forecast, etc. can be superimposed over a normal programme picture or can be viewed separately. The information is stored on pages/frames which are being continually updated by computerised editing equipment. The pages are accessed by punching a code on a hand-held key pad.

7.7 Electronic Mail

Electronic mail is where a message is converted to electronic signals and sent from any data terminal via a telecom network. Electronic mail can be classified as follows.

(a) Telex (Teleprinter Exchange)

Telex carries teleprinter signals instead of speech and is a well-established service with over one million subscribers in the UK. It is under continuous development and there is now available a super telex called Teletex (not to be confused with Teletex*t*) which is effectively a network of linked text processors. This can be linked to other computer systems to provide a range of facilities.

(b) Facsimile (FAX)

FAX uses the telephone or telex network to transmit copies of an original document, e.g. GPO Intelpost.

FAX is short for facsimile transmission. Some businesses have documents which are too complicated to be easily computerised or need to be passed from one office to another remote office in a matter of minutes, rather than wait for the post to deliver them the next day — or later.

FAX enables the transmission of graphics as well as text electronically. A Fax machine is really a modified photocopier which can send images through the telephone system to another FAX machine, which reproduces it on paper. For example, it is used for transmitting photographs in the newspaper industry.

The essential requirements are a device to scan a document, encode its contents and transmit this encoded data to the required location, where they are decoded to produce a reasonable facsimile of the original.

The transmitter scans the document looking at a large number of 'dots' on each horizontal line on the document. Most devices determine the relative darkness or lightness of each dot and vary the signal passed to the telephone network.

The quality of the eventual copy will depend to a large extent on how many times the document is read or 'sampled'.

These dots are then sent in a pre-defined sequence to the receiver which 'de-codes' the dots, to produce a copy (facsimile) of the original document.

FAX currently takes around 1 minute to transmit one A4 document but machines are constantly being updated and by using digital transmission the speed and quality of transmission will continue to improve.

Although very good for graphics, FAX is inflexible compared with electronic mail for text use. This is because FAX machines can only link directly to each other; there is no central computer and therefore no mailbox facility. Annoyingly, there is no single FAX standard at present so there are also problems of com-patibility.

(c) Computer-Based Services

Increasingly businesses are using electronic mail systems (also known as com-puter-based message systems) for versatile, reliable and speedy communications rather than the telephone, telex or postal systems.

A typical electronic mail system comprises a central 'postbox' computer connected, via modems and ordinary telephone lines, to personal computers or terminals. Portable terminals are now available which can link into the network and these have increased the flexibility of access.

An electronic mail system uses special software for store-and-forward message handling, using familiar English words as commands, and a typical 'office memo' format on screen. Such a system holds messages and 'mail' in a sender's electronic mailbox (or specific area in the computer) and sends mail on command to the receiver's mailbox or to several people if needed. Therefore, it allows person-to-person communication or transmission to a defined group (using identity codes, for example). There is also a 'registered mail' facility which notifies the sender when a message has been received.

Each user has a personal mailbox number — the address to which his messages are sent on the central computer. The subscriber can dial the computer's number, connect his computer or terminal to the telephone line using the modem and type in his own mailbox number and secret password. To send an electronic letter, the recipient's number is entered, followed by the message, which is then stored and can be read when he next links up to the system (when the recipient will be told that a message is waiting in his mailbox).

Use of personal micros rather than dumb terminals means that messages can be prepared, corrected etc., before transmission which, therefore, takes much less time and costs less in connect-time charges than it would to type and send the message directly. Similarly, incoming mail can be stored on floppy disk and read at leisure.

A large company with an existing computer network could install an internal electronic mail system (remember 80% of messages are 'in-company') on its existing computer network, as most major computer manufacturers now offer the necessary software to do this. But the major growth area seems more likely to be in public electronic mail systems, e.g. British Telecom's Gold System. In addition to the message-handling service outlined this system can be used to send and receive telex messages, activate radio pagers and transmit tele-messages. There are provisions for filing messages on the central mailbox computer if you don't have a personal computer of your own on which to store them.

(i) *Applications*

- An alternative mail service.

- A complement to the telephone.
- An optional medium for conferences and meetings (alternative to travel).

(ii) *Advantages*

- Speed.
- Reliability.
- Convenience.
- Weightless, media-independent commodity.
- Doesn't depend on the simultaneous availability of both parties (sender and receiver) because messages can be stored or forwarded and retrieved from any node (terminal).

(iii) *Disadvantages*

- Currently quite costly (but not for long).
- Still not generally available.
- Psychological acceptance?
- International technical standards needed.
- Worries over data protection.

7.8 Exercises

Question 7.1

Briefly explain the function of a modem.   (AEB)

Question 7.2

What is the main difference between direct data entry and remote job entry as methods of inputing data to a computer? Mention their relative advantages and drawbacks.

Question 7.3

Acoustic coupler, Information retrieval, viewdata.
(a) Outline what each term means.
(b) Give a brief description of a way in which each can be used.

Question 7.4

Car hire

A car hire firm operates a fleet of vehicles which may be collected from and returned to any of several hundred agencies throughout Britain. At present all bookings from customers are taken by order clerks at regional offices linked to booking files in the London Computer. Each day the computer produces, for each agency, a list of vehicles due to be collected. Each day agencies phone regional offices with details of returned vehicles. As well as handling bookings the computer deals with payroll, vehicle maintenance, accounts, stock control, etc. and produces a variety of business documents and management reports.

(i) Draw a labelled configuration diagram for the above system, indicating reasons for your choice of hardware.
(ii) For reference purposes it is proposed to send copy of vehicle descriptions weekly to each agent. How could this be achieved?

(iii) Suggest ways, other than telephoning, by which agents could notify vehicle returns to the system.

(iv) Outline the stages of processing weekly payroll through the system.

Question 7.5

K Floss

K Floss plc are manufacturers of a range of cheap sweets and confections. These products are distributed to about 250 000 retail outlets by a sales force of 1000 reps who reckon to visit each retailers every 2 or 3 weeks. The reps travel with stock which they replenish from distribution centres in most large towns. A new computer system has been implemented by the company. Each morning the rep contacts a central computer by telephone and loads the sales and account details of up to 25 retailers, a day's visits, directly into a portable Teller Terminal via an acoustic coupler (a sort of modem). He can look up this detail at any time in the day to help him when making sales, and is also able to enter the day's sales into the machine for sending to the central computer at day's end. Retailers are later billed by the central computer. A sales record is about 500 characters in size, an account record up to 250 characters.

(i) What are the storage requirements of central computer and Teller Terminal?

(ii) Billing is carried out daily with the aid of a laser printer working at a rate of 250 bills/minute. What is the daily printing time?

(iii) Draw a configuration diagram for the system. Indicate clearly the names of equipment and their function in this application. Specify the component parts of a Teller Terminal.

(iv) As well as billing customers, what other use could be made of the information described above?

Question 7.6

Why is the public telephone network not always suitable for data communication between computers?

Question 7.7

Show, by means of diagrams, how computer processing has become distributed.

7.9 Answers and Hints on Solutions

7.1 A modem (modulator/demodulator) converts digital to analog data (and back again) so that computer (digital) data can be transmitted over analog telephone lines. The telephone system is becoming digital itself, so there will be less need for such converters.

7.2 Direct data entry (DDE) usually consists of a VDU and keyboard. Data is entered, checked, displayed on screen and then entered for processing. By definition the system is on-line. DDE is useful for small amounts of data.

Remote job entry (RJE) is where a job (program and data) is entered in batch mode and transmitted to the computer for processing. RJE is suitable for routine jobs and where results are not required straightaway.

7.3 (a) An acoustic coupler is a simple and cheap modem used to convert and transmit data over the telephone lines. The telephone handset can be placed into the coupler for transmission purposes. It is suitable for low speeds only and is prone to error.

Information retrieval is the process of searching, selecting, sorting or summarising information. The term implies that files are being processed merely to provide information, i.e. without the maintained data being altered in any way.

Viewdata are two-way systems for transmitting text or graphics stored in computer databases, via a telephone network, for display on a TV screen.

(b) An acoustic coupler can be used in the home to link a personal computer to a central database or another computer via the telephone system. Information, such as sports results or travel times, can be retrieved from such systems as Prestel or Travicom by having on-line terminals linked to such central databases. Viewdata systems can be used to call down information (e.g. airline costs and flight times) and to make bookings.

7.4   Car hire

(i) See Fig. 7.10.

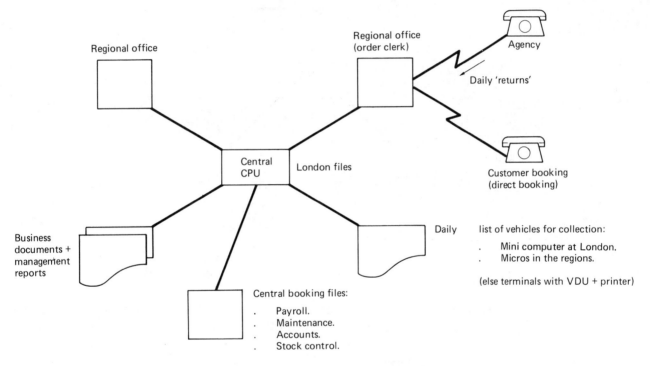

Figure 7.10 Solution 7.4(i) — Car Hire firm.

(ii) Post.
Computerlink to regional offices for distribution.
SORT vehicle file by price, car type.

(iii) Telex, computer link, post (too slow), drivers.

(iv) See Fig. 7.11.

7.5   K Floss

(i) Storage requirements:

- *Teller terminal*:
  25 retailers (maximum) × 750 characters = 1875 chs

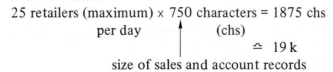

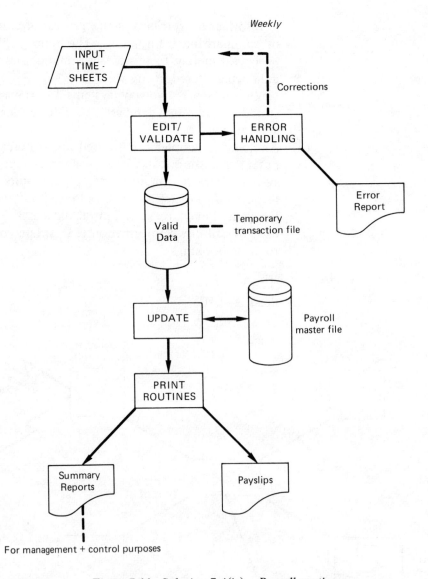

Weekly

Figure 7.11 Solution 7.4(iv) – Payroll routine.

- Central computer must cope with $\frac{1}{4}$ million retail outlets. Hence capacity
  = 250 000 x 750 chs = 187 500 000 chs or 187.5 Mb
- *Alternative calculation*:
  Each teller terminal = 18.75 k (for 25 shops)
  x 10 000 (250 000 retailers/25) = 187.5 Mb

(ii) Number of bills per day (max)
  = 25 calls x 1000 reps
  = 25 000 bills per day
  ∴ Daily printing time = $\frac{25\,000 \text{ bills}}{250 \text{ bills per minute}}$ = 100 mins,
  i.e. 1 hr 40 min

(iii) See Fig. 7.12.

(iv) Other uses:

- *Sales/marketing analyses* — e.g. sales by outlet, outlet type, representative and other performance measures), region, etc.
- Stock reordering/purchasing.
- Warehouse/van loading.
- Accounting.

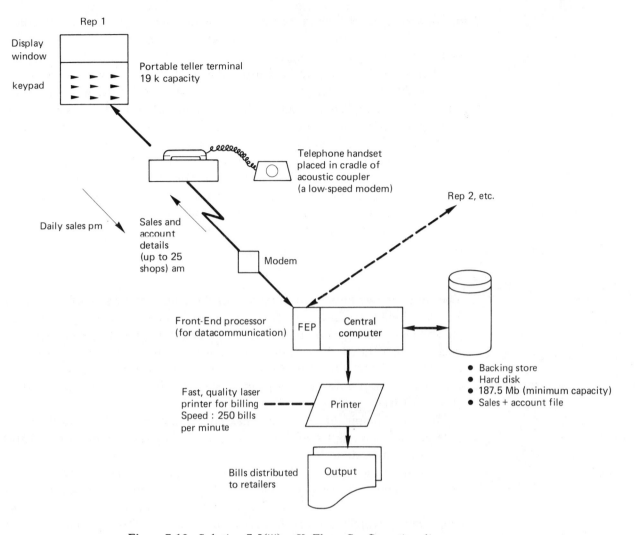

Figure 7.12 Solution 7.5(iii) — K. Floss. Configuration diagram.

7.6   Although it is possible to use the public telephone network to exchange data directly between computers, in practice this is not done because of:

1. The high costs.
2. The slow speed of data transmission.
3. The high error rate.

Each of these difficulties can be overcome.

1.   Firstly, the high cost can be offset by sharing. A set of terminals can be connected to a *multiplexor* which allows the sharing of a communications line between several terminals (See Fig. 7.4). There are two basic approaches to multiplexing:

- *Frequency division* — Where the channel is divided into narrow frequency bands.
- *Time division* — Where the channel is assigned successively to the active users.

This is achieved by giving each terminal a fixed (short) length of time to use the line. This means that, at any one time, the line can be carrying pieces of data from any or all of the terminals. Messages from each terminal can be broken up and sent bit by bit with each terminal 'taking turns' to send a piece of a message. The speed of transfer of data between two computers is much greater than that between a terminal and a computer. For this reason, multiplexing doesn't tend to be used for inter-computer communication. Nevertheless, the principle remains important — messages can be split up and transmitted piece by piece.

2. The second disadvantage of using the public telephone network — the slow speed of data transmission — can be overcome by using private lines, where computing equipment is directly connected together so that no dialling up is needed. Such circuits are often called *hard-wired* (because they cannot be easily switched between other pieces of equipment). Hard-wired lines improve speed, but only at the expense of flexibility.

3. The third drawback — the high error rates in a public telephone network — can again be overcome by the use of private lines. These are, of course, much more expensive than using the normal telephone service but this is not necessarily a problem if the equipment can be shared between several users.

7.7 *The development of computer systems*

The following examples are intended to show how the design of computers has developed from the original single-user, single-process system. This growth reflects how computer tasks have been separated out. Processing has become distributed. A centralised system is where the hardware, software and data are kept at one site. A single-user, central-site system might be as in Fig. 7.13(a) but one step beyond this would be a multiple-user system (Fig. 7.13(b)).

Of course, some of the terminals can be distributed but this does not detract from the point that they are slaves to a central computer. Fig. 7.13(c) takes such a system further still by including a *front-end processor* to control the time-sharing between terminals and the message flow between computer and users (which is why an alternative name is communications processor). Additionally, Fig. 7.13(d) shows a *concentrator* (a type of *multiplexer*) which receives messages from many different channels, stores them temporarily and transmits them when the outbound line becomes available.

Rapid advances in technology and the lower costs of processing have led to the development of distributed data processing where computer power can be placed where the user wants it.

The advent of low-cost microprocessors has led to the development of the *intelligent terminal* which is similar to the ordinary (dumb) terminal in that it has a keyboard and screen, but which can also do some processing of its own, e.g. to validate and format data. A typical distributed data processing system is shown in Fig. 7.13(e).

Another development is the idea of a *back-end processor* which is a separate computer to deal with access to backing store so that the main computer can concentrate on program execution.

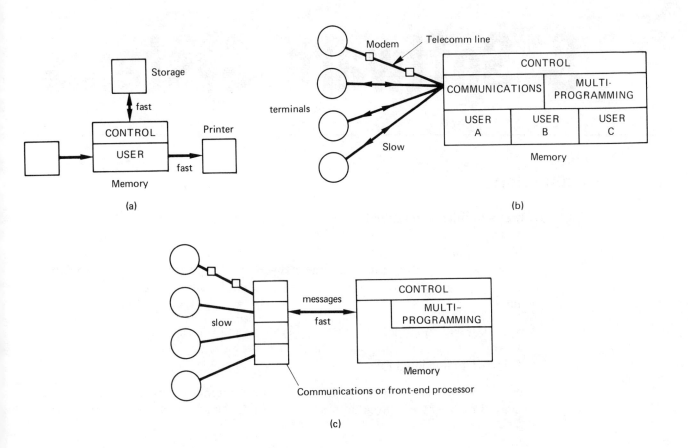

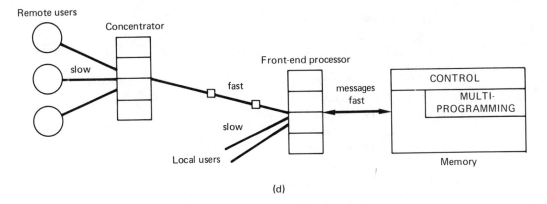

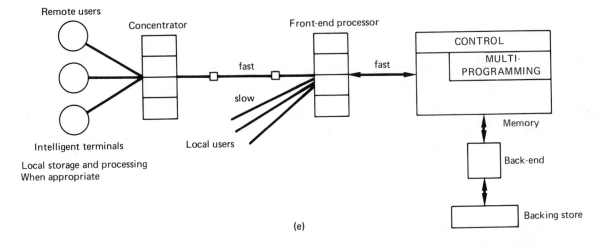

Figure 7.13 Solution 7.7. The development of computer systems. (*a*) Single user, central site. (*b*) Multiple users, some distant access. (*c*) Front-end processor. (*d*) Remote users, concentrators: (*e*) Distributed processing and 'backends'.

8 Software Systems

8.1 Introduction

A user's problems can only be solved by a computer if they are stated in the form of a program, i.e. a concise set of instructions which tell the computer what to do.

When computers were first invented it was necessary to use machine language but this was very difficult and time consuming. To overcome these problems computer programs and techniques called software were developed. Software includes:

- Systems software such as operating systems and translators.
- Applications software to solve particular problems.
- Programming languages.

These software systems improve the efficiency of computer use, reduce the cost of and time spent on programming and ease the man–machine 'interface', i.e. make computers easier to use.

(a) Types of Software

There are basically two types of software:

- *System software*, including:
  - Operating systems.
  - Translators.
  - Utilities and service programs.
  - Database management systems (DBMS).
- *Application software*, including:
  - User application programs.
  - Applications packages.

8.2 System Software

System software affects the control and performance of a computer system. It is usually provided by the manufacturer and has three main aims:

- To make the best use of the hardware.
- To provide for such common functions as language translation, sorting and report production.
- To provide simple 'user-interfaces' so that the user need not be too concerned with the inner workings of the computer.

(a) Operating Systems

The operating system is the most important type of system software and can be defined as a set of programs which coordinate and control computer operations.

It makes it easier for people to interact with the computer. Operating systems are often specific to the manufacturer but there are standard ones such as CP/M and MSDOS.

(i) The Main Functions of an Operating System

- Job control:
  - The location and loading of programs.
  - Providing for continuous processing.
  - Passing control from one program to the next.
  - Job queuing.
  - Maybe a priority system involving interrupts.

  The overall function of job control is especially important where there are several users (a multi-user environment).
- Memory management:
  - Calling into main storage programs and subroutines.
  - Storing, retrieving, erasing and copying data files or programs on magnetic storage.
  - Supporting various file organisation methods.
- To keep details of resource use; e.g. a log of:
  - The number of files stored.
  - Where they are kept.
  - How much storage space is free, etc.
- To produce error messages.
- Input/output control, including interrupt handling and the efficient use of input and output devices.
- Multi-programming: schedules and controls the running of several programs at once.

(ii) Supervisor

The main component of an operating system is called the supervisor or monitor (in single-user systems) or executive. Typical supervisor's functions are:

- Loading programs and data into main memory from backing storage.
- Scheduling the sequence of jobs to be run for maximum efficiency.
- Communicating with the human operator via the console.

The actual tasks performed by the supervisor depend on the type of processing being used.

Types of Processing

(i) Single-User Systems

These are typically small microcomputer systems which have *monitors*. They allow one user to operate one program at a time in an interactive, conversational mode, e.g. CP/M.

(ii) Batch Processing

Here jobs to be run are typically stacked on magnetic tape of disk. A special command language called a job control language (JCL) is often used to identify jobs and tell the supervisor what is required. At the beginning of each job, the JCL will provide such information as the program to load and what data file to copy, etc. Each job control statement is typed into the file using the system's editing facility.

Jobs (programs and data) are not processed until fully input. Jobs are entered and stored in a batch queue and then run one at a time under the operating system.

When batch jobs are entered from remote terminals this is known as remote job entry (RJE).

(iii)   *On-Line Processing*

Various users access the computer from local or remote terminals. The operating system must identify the terminal and see if the user is authorised, load any programs required and log the user off at the end.

This means that the computer and terminals are linked *interactively*; if the program allows the user to enter data or look at results before continuing with the next step it is sometimes known as *conversational mode*. Many computers use batch and on-line processing at the same time and the supervisor must be able to control both types of processing.

(iv)   *Multi-Programming (or Multi-Tasking) Operating Systems*

Processing one program at a time can be wasteful of resources because the fast CPU and the slow input/output devices work at vastly different speeds. To overcome this problem, multi-programming systems were devised.

Multiprogramming is where one or more programs are being processed apparently at the same time. Programs take turns at short bursts of processing time. When one is using the CPU, another may be using peripherals. It involves the use of *interrupts* to pass control from one program to another. So a multi-programming operating system can switch the fast CPU from one program to another during processing rather than having a program in CPU waiting for slow input and output devices.

(v)   *Time-sharing*

A time-sharing system permits many users to have apparently simultaneous use of one computer. Each user is allowed a 'time-slice' — a brief period when access to the CPU and conversational facilities are available. The computer checks each terminal in turn by *polling* or 'round-robin' to see if the user needs it. This happens so quickly, and CPU speeds are so fast, that the individual user *thinks* he has continuous use of the system. The *response-time* may be slowed, however, if the system is busy with many people's work.

The majority of operating systems are multi-access time-sharing (MATS) systems, e.g. UNIX.

(vi)   *Real-time Systems*

Real-time systems process data so quickly that the results are available to influence the activity currently taking place. Possible applications are airline reservations, where a customer's booking is completed and the files updated before another transaction can be processed, and process control, e.g. in a chemical plant it may be necessary for a system to react immediately to a change — if a chemical is too hot, for example, corrective action must be taken straight away.

Real-time systems must therefore be fast and reliable. They have complex and expensive operating systems and usually involve *multi-processing* (where two or more CPUs are present in the system sharing the 'workload') and a front-end processor which handles the communications problems (linking with remote terminals) so that the main CPU can concentrate on other tasks.

Some Examples of Operating System Functions

(i) *Spooling*

Many jobs can be *stacked* on devices and instructions as to priority (if any) given to the operating system. Processing of various jobs will continue automatically via the supervisor. If a particular program requires the printer a lot, the supervisor will write the output to disk for printing later on as a separate job. The transfer from disk to printer will happen automatically, usually as a *background job* when some other main application program is running. This technique is known as *spooling* (Simultaneous Peripheral Operations On-Line) and is a good example of how the operating system controls resource use (Fig. 8.1).

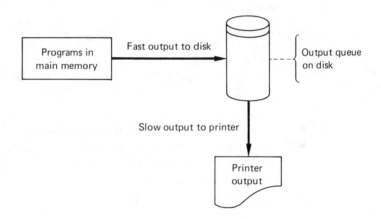

Figure 8.1 Spooling.

(ii) *Buffering*

All input and output devices are much slower than the CPU and so they contain storage spaces, called buffers, for the data being input or output at the time. These temporary storage spaces allow the CPU to carry out processing at the same time as data is being input and output. Buffering is a good example of how an operating system is able to make efficient use of hardware which inevitably operates at different speeds.

(d) Translators

Before programs can be executed they must be translated into machine language – the binary patterns of 0's and 1's. A program written in any language other than machine language is called the *source* program which is translated into machine language (known as the *object* program) by systems programs called translators. Fig. 8.2 shows these relationships.

171

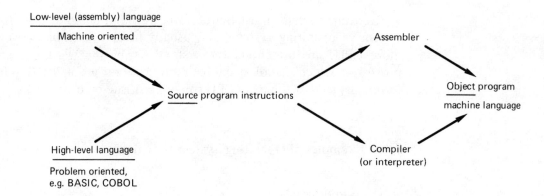

Figure 8.2 Program language/translator relationships.

Q. Distinguish between the main types of translator.

A. There are three types of translator:

- *Assemblers* – Convert *low*-level assembly programs to machine code.
- *Compilers and interpreters* – Convert high-level language programs to machine code.

COMPILERS:

- Translate the *whole* source program at once before it can be run.
- Ensure that the program need only be translated once.

INTERPRETERS:

- Translate the source program one instruction at a time.
- Ensure that the source program will be translated every time the program is executed which is, therefore, slower than compiling.
- Are often found on small computers.
- Are helpful for line-by-line fault-finding when developing programs.

Translators also provide supporting functions such as:

- Identifying syntax errors, i.e. by providing *diagnostic* messages (see Chapter 9).
- Working out where to store the object program and its data.
- Providing links to other programs or routines.
- Printing a listing of the source and object program.

(e) Utilities (or Service) Programs

Utilities are systems software programs which provide a useful service by performing common tasks and routines.

Q. Give some examples of utilities.

A. Some of the most typical are:

- SORT, e.g. arranging records in alphabetical order.
- MERGE, e.g. combining files.
- COPY, e.g. file copied from tape to disc.
- DUMP, e.g. copy contents of main store on to output device, e.g. printer.

- EDITOR, for file maintenance, i.e. the correction and alterations of existing data, e.g. the insertion/deletion of records in files.
- LIBRARY, e.g. to catalogue, control and maintain a directory of the various programs used by the computer system.

The above utilities are often referred to as *housekeeping routines*.

- System aids:
  - Tracing and debugging – For testing and finding errors.
  - Evaluation tools – To measure and improve the performance of the computer.
  - Subroutines – Sets of instructions that perform a specific task, e.g. a mathematical calculation. They can be called by the user program when needed.

(f) Database Management System (DBMS)

A database was defined in Chapter 6 as a collection of files, logically structured to meet the information needs of an organisation.

Package programs are available called database management systems (DBMS) which are a general set of programs for managing a database.

It helps the user to set up, maintain, access and protect the database by separating it from the applications programs. This would otherwise be a very complex process.

Two languages are used to communicate with the database:

- *A data description language (DDL)* – Used to give the DBMS standard descriptions of data – called a *data dictionary*.
- *A data manipulation language (DML)* – Used to provide the DBMS with requests for data insertions, deletions, amendments and removals.

A DBMS makes the database easy to use; people need not worry about how the data is stored.

8.3 Application Software

Application programs are written to solve particular problems. There are basically two types:

- *User application programs* – These are *custom* programs written by the user, or a software house under contract, to perform a specific job.
- *Application packages*:
  - These are *prewritten* programs purchased 'off the-shelf' by the user.
  - They are generalised programs for solving common business problems and can be used by a wide variety of users with little or no modification.
  - They are particularly suitable for routine applications such as word processing, financial modelling (spreadsheets), data management, payroll, stock control, etc. The range and variety of packages continues to increase. Packages now exist for specific types of organisation, such as building societies, estate agents, car dealers, solicitors, etc. They are very important to non-specialists, in the home or the small business and for beginners. A particularly important development is *integrated* software which incorporates data management, word-processing and financial modelling (spreadsheets) into one package.

Advantages and disadvantages of packages

(i) *Advantages*

- Save time, effort and expense of programming.
- Tried and tested.
- 'User-friendly' and easy to run.
- Quick results.

(ii) *Disadvantages*

- Designed to meet the needs of a number of different users. May not be *exactly* suitable but there are extra MODULES to suit particular needs.
- Poor documentation (sometimes).
- Is the package reliable? — ask current users.
- Support/guarantee—what can you do if things go wrong?

(b) How the Package is Supplied

An application package usually consists of:

- A program on tape or disk.
- Documentation which should specify:
  - How to set up the package.
  - How to use it.
  - Any technical details if you need to make amendments.

(c) Factors Influencing the Choice of Package

- *Cost.*
- *Compatibility* — Does it fit in with the existing system? An organisation should pick the program that most closely meets its requirements.
- *Contract* — In some cases it is possible to negotiate a program maintenance contract for 'after-sales' service so that, for example, changes or improvements can be incorporated easily.
- *Popularity* — What do existing users think of it?
- *Test-drive* — A trial run with your own data to ensure that the package does what it is claimed to do.

8.4 Programming Languages

A computer 'works' by executing a series of instructions — the program. A program can be written in a variety of programming languagues.
In order of development there are three generations of languages:

1. Machine. ⎫
2. Assembly. ⎬ Low-level languages
3. High-level languages. ⎭

(a) Low-Level Languages

(i) *Machine Language*

A manufacturer designs a computer to obey just one language, its machine code, which will be represented inside the computer by combinations of binary digits. The set of binary codes which can be recognised by the computer is known as the machine code *instruction set*.

Before looking at machine language in a little more detail it is helpful to know something about how the computer's control unit fetches, decodes and executes instructions.

1 The Fetch–Execute Cycle

This is the timed process by which the control unit retrieves an instruction from store, decodes it and carries it out. To do this the computer has:

- *An addressing system* for main memory. Each memory cell has an absolute address so that data can be selected from the right location.

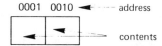

- *Registers* which are special-purpose storage locations used for the temporary storage of addresses, instructions and data during the fetch–execute cycle.
- *Buses (or highways)* – These are the links which connect the parts of the CPU together so that messages can be sent to and from the various units. There may be address, data and control buses.

Q. Fig. 8.3 shows a diagram of a computer control unit.

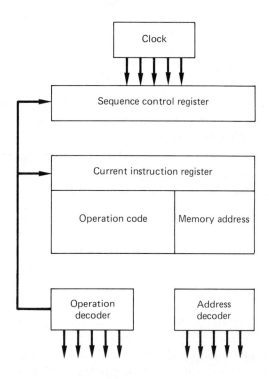

Figure 8.3 Computer control unit.

175

(a) Explain the function of each of the sections in the diagram.
(b) Explain what happens at each of the two important steps of the instruction
cycle: fetch, execute.   (AEB)

A.
(a) The *clock* synchronises (times) all the various sections by generating pulses
at a constant rate.

The *sequence control register* is the register which contains the address of
the *next* instruction to be fetched. It is also known as the *Program Counter*
or Instruction Address Register.

Once the instruction has been fetched the value of the program counter is
incremented (i.e. 1 is added to it), as the control unit normally fetches instructions in sequence. If the instruction executed causes a branch to an
instruction in another part of the program the value of the program counter
is changed to the address of the new instruction.

The *current instruction register* is used to hold the machine instruction
which is currently being interpreted by the control unit.

The *Operation Code* is the part of the machine code instruction that
specifies the operation to be performed.

Instruction format:

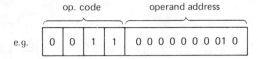

The *memory address* is the identification of a memory location. The
decoders translate the internal binary codes in the control unit to or from
external signals for peripheral input or output actions such as printing,
reading, etc.
(b) The *fetch/execute* cycle is the process of getting (fetching) an instruction
from store, decoding it and carrying it out (executing it).

The *fetch* phase is the part of the cycle in which the instruction is copied
to the ALU and decoded.

The *execute phase* is the part of the cycle in which the instruction is
obeyed.

OTHER REGISTERS

Besides the registers mentioned in the question there are other important ones
found in computers which you should know about.

Registers in the ALU – An *accumulator* is a register which stores values so that
logical, arithmetic or data transfer operations can be carried out. For example,
if two numbers in locations X and Y are to be added and the result stored in Z,
instructions with the following functions will usually be fetched and executed:

1. Load contents of location X into accumulator (acc).
2. Add contents of location Y to contents of acc.
3. Store contents of acc in location Z.

REGISTERS USED IN FETCHING AND EXECUTING

The *memory address register (MAR)* contains the address of the location being
used when data or instructions are being transferred to and from store.

The *memory data register (MDR)* contains the value of any data or instruction
being transferred *within* the computer. The MDR is also known as the memory
buffer register.

176

2. Machine Code Instructions

A machine code instruction is one which directly defines a particular machine operation and can be recognised and executed without any intermediate translation.

The instruction format of a machine code instruction has two main parts:

- A function (or operation) code.
- An address (operand).

The function code tells the control unit of the CPU what to do with the item held in the address.

e.g., for one computer
        4 A 2   1 8 7

             instruction   address
             (op. code)

might be the hexadecimal machine code instruction for: 'Add the contents of storage location 187 to the contents of register 2.'

The absolute address of each store location is a binary number which can be decoded so that when data is required from a memory cell the right location is selected.

The relative address of a store location is the address *relative* to some base address. Subscripted variables may be stored in this way.

Example 8.1

A microprocessor has 8-bit function codes and 16-bit addresses. How many different instructions and how many locations can be directly addressed?

Solution 8.1

The number of different instruction codes using 8 bits = 2^8 = 256.
The number of different addresses using 16 bits = 2^{16} = 65534.

In any machine code instruction there may be a number of ways in which the address (or operand) part can be carried out.

Example 8.2

In any machine code the range of locations which may be directly addressed is limited. With the aid of an example, explain why the address range is limited, and indicate two ways in which the address range can be extended.

Solution 8.2

Example:

Function code	Address	$101_2 = 5_{10}$
0 0 1 0	0 0 0 1 0 1	

(10 = (say) Load Accumulator)

Direct addressing is where the address specified in the instruction is the actual address of the location to be used. In the example above the instruction would load the *contents* of location 5 into the accumulator.

  NB The number of bits available for the operand address has been limited to 6 by using four bits for the function code. (Therefore the number of different instruction codes = 2^4 = 16 in this case.) Direct addressing is simple, fast and effective, but the number of addressable locations is limited — in our example to 2^6 = 64 locations. This problem may be overcome by alternative methods of addressing.

  Indirect addressing is where the address specified in the instruction is that of a location which in turn contains the required address. In our example the *address* we want will be found in location 5.

INDEX ADDRESSING (OR ADDRESS MODIFICATION)

In this method the required address is obtained by adding the contents of the address part of the instruction to a number stored in a special address register (or index register). The sum becomes the address location to be used.

OTHER ADDRESSING MODES

Immediate addressing. Here the address is the actual operand. For example,

function code	operand
0 0 1 0	1 1 1 1 1 1

  LOAD

MEANS LOAD the accumulator with the *value*.
(i.e. the actual number) 1 1 1 1 1 1.

Implied addressing. There is no address part (e.g. BREAK and CLEAR instructions) where it is obvious what the operand is.

3 An Instruction Set

A typical machine code instruction set will usually contain instructions to:

● *Transfer data* — Between accumulator and store; between accumulator and peripherals; and between registers.
● *Perform arithmetic and logical operations* — Add, subtract; increment, decrement; compare; shift; AND, OR, etc.
● *Branch or jump to another part of the program* — Conditionally (*IF*); unconditionally (always).

178

Example 8.3

A computer has a 4-bit operation (function) code for its instructions. Part of its instruction set is as follows:

Op. code	Meaning
0 0 0 1	Load accumulator with the number given (immediate)
0 0 1 0	Add contents of location to accumulator (direct)
0 0 1 1	Add number given to accumulator (immediate)
0 1 0 0	Store contents of accumulator in location (direct)
0 0 0 0	Halt program execution

The following program is executed:

Instruction address	Op. code	Address (operand)
0 0 1 0 0 0	0 0 0 1	0 0 0 0 0 0
0 0 1 0 0 1	0 0 1 1	0 1 0 0 0 0
0 0 1 0 1 0	0 0 1 0	0 1 0 0 0 0
0 0 1 0 1 1	0 1 0 0	0 1 0 0 1 0
0 0 1 1 0 0	0 0 0 0	—

Before execution, location 0 1 0 0 0 0 contains the value 0 0 1 1 1 1. Draw a table to show the effect the program has on the accumulator and the locations 0 1 0 0 0 0 and 0 1 0 0 1 0.

Solution 8.3

Instr. address	Op. Code	Operand	Acc.	Location 010000	Location 010010	Notes
001000	0001	000000	000000	001111	?	Load acc (immediate)
001001	0011	010000	010000	001111	?	Add to acc (immediate)
001010	0010	010000	011111	001111	?	Add to acc (direct)
001011	0100	010010	011111	001111	011111	Store acc (direct)
001100	0000	—				Break

NB The contents of location 010000 remain the same throughout (non-destructive read).

- The first instruction clears the accumulator.
- The difference between the 2 add instructions; add *immediate* adds 010000 to the accumulator, add *direct* adds the contents of location 010000 (i.e. 00111) to the accumulator.
- The Break instruction stops the control unit from fetching more bit strings.
- The program is difficult to read and understand in binary. Where bits are in groups of 6, octal could be used (or hex when the number of bits divides by 4, e.g. on 16-bit micros).

4 Advantages and Disadvantages of Machine Language

Advantage: It makes fast and efficient use of the CPU.
Disadvantages – Machine language programming is:

- Usually limited to one machine.
- Very long.

- Time consuming.
- Difficult to read and understand binary codes, because:
  - All operation codes have to be remembered.
  - All memory addresses have to be assigned.
  - It is difficult to amend or find errors.
  - There is a one-to-one relationship between written and machine instructions.

(ii) *Assembly Language*

Because of the disadvantages of machine languages, assembly (or symbolic) languages were developed.

Assembly is a *'low-level'* language because it is still close to the machine, there is one instruction for each computer operation. Instead of using binary digits (or some other number representation such as hexadecimal), assembly typically uses:

- *More meaningful symbols* — Mnemonic codes, e.g. SUB for subtract.
- *Symbolic addresses* — The name for the data to be used in the operation, e.g. GROSPAY.

e.g. Assume 10 is the function code for jump in a machine code instruction set.

10 0 0 0 1 1 1 would therefore mean JUMP to location 7.

If the program is changed, the instruction at address 7 may have to be moved, so that the jump instruction will have to be altered.

In assembly it is possible to use a label; e.g. JMP LOOP might mean jump to the location whose symbolic address is LOOP. Even if the program is changed the jump instruction will still be the same, even though the absolute (i.e binary) address of LOOP may be different.

1 Advantages of Assembly

- It is useful for writing, e.g. operating systems, games programs, where a fast and efficient use of the CPU is needed.
- It may be used for security reasons. Fewer people understand it, therefore fewer people can copy and amend it.
- Mnemonics and symbols make it easier to use than machine code.
- Symbolic addresses can easily be changed or moved around without upsetting the rest of the program.

(b) High-Level Languages

The limitations of the low-level languages — machine code and assembly — led to the development of *high-level* languages which are:

- 'User-friendly' ('people-based').
- Similar to English with vocabularies of words and symbols.
- 'Problem' rather than 'machine' based.
- Shorter than their low-level equivalents. One statement translates into MANY machine code instructions.

There are many high-level (people-based) languages in use today.

The *choice of language* depends on:

- Purpose, e.g. business, educational.
- Facilities provided, e.g. meaningful variable names, control and data structures, error checking facilities.
- Ease of learning and use.
- Popularity — availability of compilers/interpreters.
- Documentation provided.
- User acceptance.

The most popular high-level languages are now briefly reviewed.

(i) COBOL — Common Business Oriented Language

COBOL consists of four divisions:

1. *Identification division* — Where the program name, author, date and other details are given.
2. *Environment division* — Which specifies the equipment used when the object program is compiled and executed.
3. *Data division* — Describes the data to be processed (format and characteristics of files and data items).
4. *Procedure division* — Specifies the actions required to process the data, including input/output, arithmetic, data movement and sequence control. Reserved words are used to link the actions to the data division.

1 Advantages

- It is widely used.
- It is designed for business.
- It has an American National Standards Institute (ANSI) standard and is therefore portable (i.e. it can be used on different types of computer).
- It is easy to read.
- It has a pool of skilled programmers.
- It supports structured programming.

2 Disadvantage

Even simple programs are long.

(ii) BASIC — Beginners All-purpose Symbolic Instruction Code

1 Advantage

- Developed as an instructional language and is therefore simple and easy to use.
- An interactive language used with time-sharing systems.
- *The* language of micros.

2 Disadvantages

- Needs a standard; there are too many 'dialects'.
- Some versions offer limited facilities in term of:
  - Structured programming.
  - Meaningful variable names.

(iii) FORTRAN – FORmula TRANslator

1 Advantages

- Intended for scientific, engineering and mathematical applications.
- Statements are in the form of mathematical equations.
- It has a standard.
- It is fairly widely used.

2 Disadvantage

It is not really suitable for business.

(iv) C

1 Advantages

- Well structured and compact.
- Portable.
- Closely linked to the popular UNIX operating system.
- Ideal tool for systems programming.

2 Disadvantages

- Not easy to read.
- Difficult to learn.

(v) LISP – LISt Processing

1 Advantages

- Flexible.
- Many artificial intelligence (AI) languages are developed from LISP, including LOGO and PROLOG, POP-2.

2 Disadvantages

It is *not* suitable for:

- Commercial data processing.
- Some real-time applications.
- Interactive programs, e.g. games.

(vi) RPG – Report Program Generator

RPG is based on file, input, calculation, output specifications.

1 Advantages

- Produces reports from files quickly.
- Easy to use.
- Developed by IBM.

2 Disadvantages

It is not good for handling complex files or arithmetic.

(vii) *PASCAL*

1 Advantages

- A recent language (1973), developed after the concepts of structured programming became popular.
- Uses a 'top-down' approach, including procedures and functions.

2 Disadvantages

- It is not too easy to learn.
- It has poor file-handling.

(viii) *Other Languages*

- ALGOL – ALGOrithmic Language, cf. FORTRAN.
- PL/1 – Programming Language 1, from IBM.
- APL – A Programming Language; maths/finance.
- FORTH – Can be developed as it is used.
- ADA – 1979; based on PASCAL.

(ix) *User-Oriented (Author) Languages*

Recently user-oriented or *query* languages have been developed to permit non-specialists with only a little training to write programs and access data, e.g. a credit control manager to know which of his customers owe more than £1000 and have owed the money for more than 3 months.
He/she might write the following:

SELECT CUSTNAME, CUSTNUM FROM CUSTDATA
WHERE DEBT > 1000
AND MONTHS > 3

It is not too difficult to understand this 'pseudocode' which can permit users to 'write' programs using 'natural' language. PILOT is an example of an author language available on micros.

Table 8.1 Summarises the main points of high- and low-level computer languagues

183

Table 8.1 Computer languages—Memory sheet

	Low level		High level
	Machine code	*Assembly*	
Symbols	Hexadecimal, decimal, octal or binary	Mnemonics	Similar to English and mathematical symbols
Example	1011 10100011	LDA TOT ADD TOT2	LET COST=PRICE*QUANTITY LET C=P*Q
Format	*Function address*	*Function address*	Various
Translator to object code	None required	Assembler	Compiler or interpreter
Features	+ : Faster to execute, compact to store − : Requires knowledge of the computer used • Difficult to learn, write and amend • Boring and time consuming		+ : Easier to learn and use shorter programs − : Longer to translate and execute
Uses	Where fast and efficient use of the CPU is needed, e.g.: • Writing operating systems • Controlling peripherals • Writing games programs		COBOL – Business BASIC – Education FORTRAN – Science, engineering

8.5 Exercises

Question 8.1

Explain the difference between machine code and assembly. (AEB)

Question 8.2

(a) Explain what you understand by a machine code instruction.
(b) A certain computer uses 16-bit words. One word in main store contains the following string of bits:

```
0000001100010101
```

Stating any assumptions that you make, describe how the contents of the above word might be interpreted as either: (i) an integer; or (ii) a machine code instruction; or (iii) two characters.

(c) Describe the cycle of operations which is necessary for the execution of a sequence of machine code instructions.

Question 8.3

(a) Explain what is meant by symbolic addressing in relation to assembly languages.
(b) State the advantages of programming in an assembly language rather than in machine code.

Question 8.4

(a) Give examples of two distinct machine code instructions, which perform different types of operation. For each, describe the stages in the execution of the instruction.

(b) (i) Explain what is meant by the term register in relation to the central processing unit of a computer.

(ii) Describe the functions of the various registers which are used during the instruction, execution cycle.

Question 8.5

Integers and instructions are held in 8-bit words in a computer's store. For integers, the most significant bit is the sign bit and negative numbers are held in twos complement form. For instructions, the three most significant bits are used to hold the function (or operation) code and the remaining bits represent the address. The following instruction set is used:

Instruction	Function
001 Address	Load content of specified location into the accumulator.
010 Address	Subtract content of specified location from content of the accumulator and leave the result in the accumulator.
011 Address	Add content of specified location to content of the accumulator and leave the result in the accumulator.
111 Halt	

A section of the computer's store contains the following bit patterns:

Location	Content
00001	001 00101
00010	010 00110
00011	011 00111
00100	111 00000
00101	000 00101
00110	000 00010
00111	111 11101

Given that the first four locations contain instructions and the rest contain data, complete the table below by decoding each instruction and converting to decimal the binary content of the remaining three locations.

Location	Content (decoded)
00001	
00010	
00011	
00100	
00101	
00110	
00111	

Execute the program giving the binary content of the accumulator immediately after each instruction has been carried out.

Store location of instruction	Content of accumulator after each instruction has been executed
00001	
00010	
00011	
00100	

Question 8.6

Define: (a) multi-programming; (b) multi-access. (AEB)

Question 8.7

(a) How does a source program become an object program?
(b) Clearly explain the difference between a compiler and an interpreter. (AEB)

Question 8.8

What are the main functions of an operating system?

Question 8.9

Using a programming language of your choice list what you consider to be its main advantages and disadvantages.

Question 8.10

Explain: (a) spooling; (b) buffering; (c) monitor; (d) real-time.

Question 8.11

There are various levels of programming used to communicate with a computer: Machine code; Low level; High level.

Explain the difference between the above three levels referring to storage space required, ease of programming and debugging, ease of use and any other relevant information.

Question 8.12

What are the benefits of application packages? Can you see any drawbacks in their use?

8.6 Answers and Hints on Solutions

8.1 *Machine code* directly defines a particular machine operation without having to be translated.

Assembly is the process of converting a program written in assembly language into machine code.

8.2 (a) A computer is designed to obey just one language — its machine code — represented inside the CPU as patterns of binary digits. A machine code instruction is one which directly defines a particular machine operation and can be recognised and executed without any intermediate translation.

(b) (i)   00000011 00010101 = 789_2 in straight binary. Equally it might represent another integer in some other code – e.g. 4-bit BCD.

      (ii)   The 16-bit word could be an instruction made up of, for example, a 6-bit function code and a 10 bit address. The number of different instruction codes using 6 bits = 2^6 = 64. The number of different addresses possible using 10 bits = 2^{10} = 1024.

      (iii)   the 16-bit word could be made up of two 8-bit bytes each representing a character. The left-hand 8 bits (00000011) might, for example, represent 'C', the right-hand, 'U' (the 21st letter of the alphabet).

(c)   See text for description of the fetch–execute cycle.

8.3   (a)   Addresses and operands can be replaced by names (or labels) by the programmer, which can be used instead of an absolute address. Such a label is called a symbolic address. Programs are more easily changed if symbolic addressing is used (see 8.3 (b) also).

      (b)   Mnemonics and symbolic labels are easier to remember and understand, therefore programming is quicker and more accurate. Programs written in assembly can easily be changed or moved to another part of store without changing the addresses of all the operands. This is because assembly uses symbolic addressing.

8.4   (a)   Data transfer instruction: LOAD ACCUMULATOR – transfer data from a location in store to the accumulator. Data must be copied into the MDR and then the accumulator. A load instruction will consist of a function code and an operand address specifying the address of the data item to be loaded. For example:

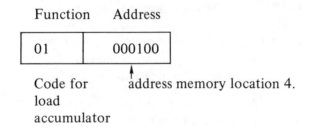

Function   Address

| 01 | 000100 |

Code for   address memory location 4.
load
accumulator

Arithmetic instruction:

ADD A – add contents of a location to the contents of the accumulator A.

Data for processing is taken from storage, as directed by the control unit, and passed via the MDR into the accumulator in the ALU. The ALU then performs the required operation on the data (in our case adding) and leaves the result in the accumulator.

NB: The instructions are in words rather than in machine code to ease understanding. They will, of course, be stored by the computer in binary form.

(b)   (i)   A register is a special-purpose storage location. Registers are used to store addresses, instructions and data in the fetch–execute cycle.

      (ii)   There can be many registers in a computer. The most important ones are:

- Program counter.
- Current instruction register.
- Accumulator.

See text for details.

8.5

Location	Content (decoded)
00001	Load content of 00101 (i.e. 5) into acc.
00010	Subtract content of 00110 (i.e. 2) from content of acc and leave result in acc.
00011	Add content of 00111 (i.e. −3) to content of acc (3) and leave in acc.
00100	Halt
00101	101 = 5
00110	10 = 2
00111	<u>1</u>11 11101 = −128 + 125 = −3

Store location of instruction	Content of accumulator after each instruction has been executed	Explanation
00001	00101	5
00010	00011	5 − 2 = 3
00011	00000	−3 + 3 = 0
00100	00000	Halt

8.6 (a) *Multiprogramming* is a method whereby two or more programs are apparently processed simultaneously, but are, in fact, taking turns to use the CPU. This is controlled by the operating system. For example, whilst one program is waiting for an I/O operation to be carried out, another may be using the CPU.

(b) *Multi-access* is a system which allows several users to have apparently simultaneous access to the computer. This system is used mainly for interactive work on a time-sharing basis.

8.7 *The source program* is the program written by the programmer using a programming language; it must be assembled, compiled or interpreted (i.e. translated into 'computer language') before it can be executed. The translated version is known as the *object program*.

8.8 The operating system is a control program which allows a number of programs to be run on the computer without the need for operator intervention. The main functions are: job control, memory management, maintaining resource use, showing error messages, input/output control, multiprogramming.

8.9 BASIC

Advantages	Disadvantages
Easy to learn and use	No standard (too many dialects)
Good for the beginner	Some versions offer limited facilities in
Very popular − the	terms of:
language of micros	• Structured programming.
Most systems support	• Meaningful variable names.
BASIC, i.e. they have	
an interpreter/compiler.	

8.10 (a) *Spooling* is the temporary storage of input or output data on tape or disk to adjust for the different operating speeds of peripheral devices or when queuing output for printers, etc.

(b) *Buffering* is the use of a store area (the buffer) to hold temporarily data being sent between two devices, e.g. a terminal and the CPU, to compensate for differences in working speeds.

(c) *Monitor* is a control program (usually in single-user systems, e.g. micros) which schedules the use of hardware required by the program being run.

NB: Monitor is also the TV-like display unit often found in micro systems; either answer is acceptable.)

(d) *Real-time* is a system which can receive continuously changing data from outside and process it quickly enough to influence the outcome (e.g. the process control, aircraft control).

8.11

	Storage space	*Ease of programming/use etc.*
Machine code	Compact to store 'machine language'	Very difficult to learn, write, and amend. Machine specific. Fast and efficient execution.
Low level	Requires assembler	Still difficult.
High level	Compilers/interpreters needed	Easy to learn and use, shorter programs.

8.12 Applications packages

Benefits:

- Pre-written.   } Save time, effort and
- Tried and tested. } expense of programming
- Wide variety.
- 'User-friendly' and easy to run.
- Quick results.

Drawbacks:

- May not meet exact needs.
- Poor documentation.
- Reliability/support.

9 The Programming Task

9.1   Introduction

There is a lot more to programming than writing code, and examiners are prone to ask questions about other aspects of programming. This chapter will also help you to plan and undertake any practical programming work that might form part of your syllabus. The principles and practices that make up the programming task may be divided into a number of steps:

9.2   Steps in Programming

Example 9.1

Describe each step in the programming task.

Solution 9.1

See Fig. 9.1. A description of each step now follows.

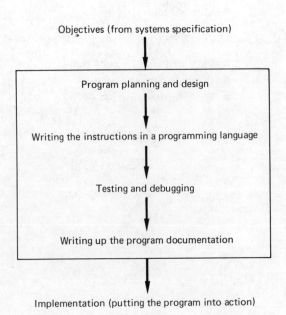

Objectives (from systems specification)

Program planning and design

Writing the instructions in a programming language

Testing and debugging

Writing up the program documentation

Implementation (putting the program into action)

Figure 9.1   Steps in program preparation.

(a) Objectives in Writing Programs (Defining What the Program Must do)

The programmer will usually receive *system documentation* which provides a general set of specifications for a computer program. It is vital to understand the problem and to be sure of the aims and objectives of the program. In particular the program should be:

- *Workable* — It should do what it's supposed to!
- *Efficient* — It should be written economically.
- *Easy to read and understandable* — Use lots of comments.
- *Easy to change* — Ideas for improvements/changes should be easy to fit in if necessary.
- *Portable* — Easily transferable on to another type of machine (often language-dependent).

There should be documentation to help:

- The programmer.
- The user.

(b) Program Planning and Design (Table 9.1)

Before coding a program, the programmer should plan the solution to the problem in detail and write down the processing logic. (Do you sit at a terminal and make a program up as you go along? Why is this a *bad* habit?!)

Programming is a tiring, expensive and time-consuming task and special techniques have been developed to ease the programmer's task, as follows.

(i) *Systems Documentation*

A carefully written systems specification can aid programming by including processing procedures and sample input and output layouts.

(ii) *Structured Program Design*

The task of program design is aided by the use of standard programming aids. These include:

- *Structure charts* — Which divide the program up into modules.
- *Flow (logic) charts* — Which show the processing logic often at several levels, e.g. outline charts showing the overall logic and detail charts showing the detailed logic of each program section.
- *Other* — Decision tables, pseudocode, etc.

(iii) *Writing the Instructions in a Programming Language (Coding)*

Time and money can be saved by using existing library routines, subroutines, subprograms and other programming aids (e.g. report generators) and incorporating the code into the new program.

(iv) *Testing and Debugging the Program*

This includes deciding on the test data and procedure to be used. There should be a test plan for each program module as well as a system test for the entire program.

Coding and testing are made easier by the use of high-level languages and compilers which identify syntax errors. Trace routines can be used to isolate coding errors.

Table 9.1   A checklist for program design

- It pays to put effort into program design, rather than trying to get a badly designed program to work.
- Use logical steps; write the program in modules.
- Use sensible identifiers.
- Use variables for one purpose only.
- Avoid clever tricks.
- Structure program clearly to make it understandable.
- Include adequate comments in code.
- Test to check for errors. Correct them as quickly as possible.
- If necessary examine the critical parts of the program for efficiency (look at loops, etc.).

(v)   *Writing up the Program Documentation*

All stages of the program should be carefully documented. This is because:

- Revision of the program may be necessary because of an enforced change (e.g. new tax rates from the Budget may affect a payroll program).
- The organisation's circumstances might change.
- Other people may think of ways of improving the program.

Therefore, program documentation is essential so that:

- Revisions can be made.
- Efficient processing can take place.

Not least, it acts as a reference manual for program maintenance — program authors can leave or go on holiday!

Program documentation typically includes:

- A *description of the problem* to be solved by the program.
- A *program abstract* which describes briefly the various tasks which the program performs, the files used, etc.
- A *program description* which gives details of the program including structure charts, systems flow charts and program flow charts as well as the program listing. The listing should also indicate the meaning of each variable used in the program (sometimes known as a data dictionary).
- *Operating instructions* on how to run the program.
- A *summary of the program controls* which are built into the program.
- A *test plan and data used* to test the program for accuracy. A note should be made of any approved changed made during testing.

9.3   Structured Program Design

Program design using the *top-down* approach involves developing a structure chart showing the overall framework of the program, with each level showing progressively more detail. The program is separated into modules, one for each main function. Modules are developed, starting with the top and moving down the hierarchy (Fig. 9.2). This method ensures that all modules link in together as the program develops.

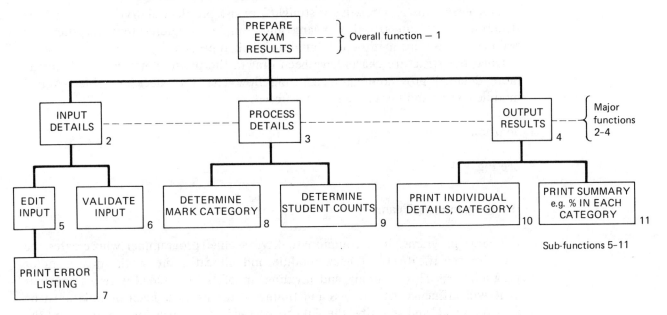

Figure 9.2 Structure chart — a first step in program design. NB: There are lower levels of detail, not shown.

(a) Developing Structure Charts

Example 9.2

This example will be used to illustrate how a program might develop using structured program design. It is less complex than many problems so that the basic methods can be clearly shown.

A teacher wants to process examination results. For each candidate the input consists of a candidate name, code (a three-digit number) and a mark out of 100. For each student the required output is name and code number followed by a FAIL, PASS or CREDIT message. The pass mark is 40 and the minimum mark for a credit is 70 in each paper.

At the end of the results the percentage of candidates failing in each category should be shown. All marks are recorded as whole numbers and a dummy value of −1 terminates the input.

Suggest suitable test data.

(a) Draw a structure chart for this problem.
(b) Draw a flow chart for this problem.

Solution 9.2(a)

See Fig. 9.2.

Module 1 defines the overall function of the program. *Modules 2–4*, on the second level, divide up the main function of the exam system.

Module 5–7 — All the candidate details have to be entered and checked for accuracy before processing. For example, we might wish to trap wrong code numbers (which must be three-digits) or marks which are over 100, entered accidentally.

Modules 8–9 — The category of fail, pass or credit has to be determined and a count kept of how many students fall into each category.

193

Modules 10–11 – Output will consist of individual candidate details, including whether they have passed or not, together with summary results – in this case the percentage number of students in each category.

Of course, this is a relatively straightforward problem and you may find the structure chart quite trivial. For large and complex programs, however, there is a real need to use this methodical, building-block approach.

Once the structure charts have been drawn, the programmer can move to the more detailed programming logic using flow charts or decision tables. Actual module coding and testing can then proceed.

Solution 9.2(b)

See Fig. 9.4.

(b) Programming Teams

For large programs, it is common to have a chief programmer who creates the program specifications of each module and allocates the work to a team of programmers. This planning and dividing up of the workload is very important as it will influence the success and timing of the project. Each module must be self-contained, and describe the data to be used, the processing required, and the output. Each module is tested individually and tested again with the previously finished sections. Testing goes on right up until the program is finally complete, when a full *systems test* will be carried out to check that everything is working correctly together.

(c) Structured Programming Procedures

The main features of structured programming are that any program can be written using just three logical structures, which are: Sequence, Selection, and Repetition (Fig. 9.3). These features make modules short and simple, and programs easier to write and test:

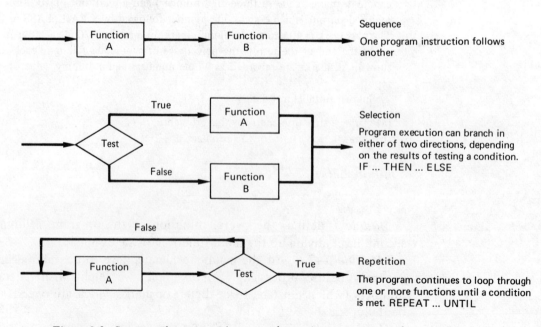

Figure 9.3 Structured programming procedures. Any program can be written using only three logical structures.

- Each module should be designed to fulfil a single, well-defined task, e.g. to edit the candidate's input data or to format and print an error message.
- Each module has only one entry and one exit point.

(d) Flow Charting

The flow chart for the examination results example is shown in Fig. 9.4. This is the next stage on from the structure chart and shows the programming logic in more detail. There are alternative aids and techniques which programmers use such as decision tables. Note how the flow chart illustrates the three logical structures.

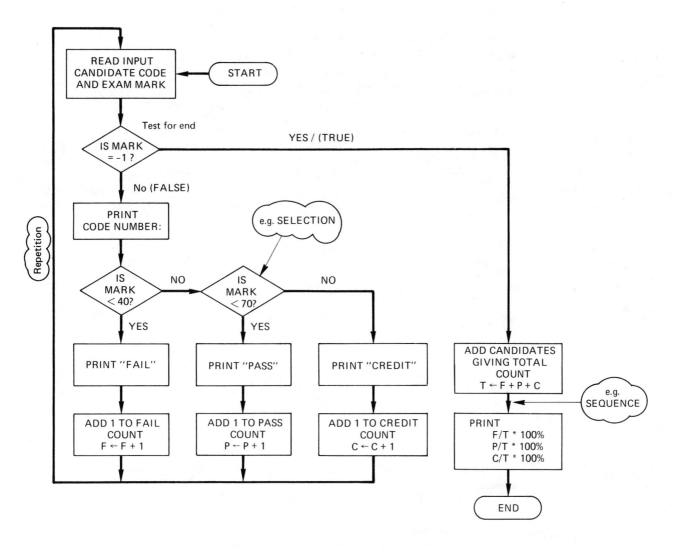

Figure 9.4 Flow chart to process examination results. Suitable test data: marks to cover each path in the flow chart e.g. 35, 50, 75 and −1. NB: Validation checks could be devised to check for marks < 0 or > 100 and candidate codes that are not three-digit numbers.

Flow charts show a sequence of steps involved in a process. They are made up of boxes of standard shapes linked to show the order of processing. Each box contains a brief note stating what the operation is. When applicable, further explanation can be given alongside.

Example 9.3

Distinguish between system and program flow charts.

Solution 9.3

There are two types of flow chart:

- Systems flow charts
- Program flow charts – which, in turn, can be used to show a program in outline or in detail.

(i) *Systems Flow Charts*

These show the computer system overall. This includes descriptions of the:

- *Inputs* – Including collection and preparation of data.
- *Processes* – Calculations, sorts, merges, etc.
- *Files* – The backing store and files used.
- *Outputs* – Reports, listings, etc. produced.

For a sample systems flow chart see Fig. 6.5 (page 130).
The standard symbols used in systems flow chart are shown in Fig. 9.5.

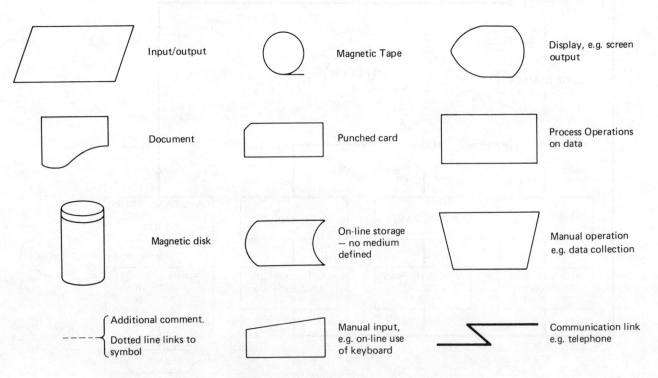

Figure 9.5 Standard symbols for system flow charts.
NB There are also procedural flow charts that show the steps in a manual process.

(ii) *Program Flow Charts*

These show the sequence of operations carried out by a computer program.

An *outline* program flow chart or block diagram shows:

- The start and end of the program.
- The input/output operations.

- How the data is processed.
- The main sections of the program.

A *detailed* program flow chart shows all the operations carried out by a computer program, step by step. In theory, it should be sufficiently detailed for the program code to be written directly from it. Hence, a detailed program flow chart will represent an *algorithm*, i.e. a series of instructions which solve a specific problem.

For a sample program flow chart see Fig. 9.4. The standard symbols used in program flow charts are shown in Fig. 9.6.

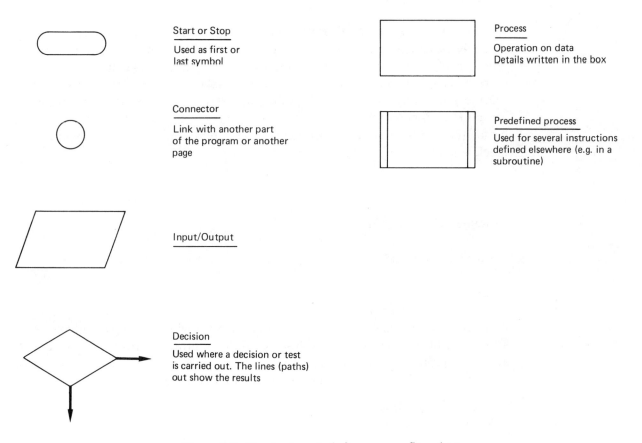

Figure 9.6   Standard symbols for program flow charts.

Tips when drawing flow charts:

- Use standard flow charting symbols.
- Use a template – this also saves you having to remember what each box shape represents.
- Try to keep logic flow from top to bottom and from left to right.
- Use arrows to indicate flow (direction).
- Use connectors to reduce the number of flowlines.
- Use English (avoid BASIC–like statements).
- Add notes if necessary, but don't clutter your diagram.
- Lines should, ideally, be vertical or horizontal.

9.4   Writing the Instructions in a Programming Language — Coding

After program planning and flow charting the program must be coded. This is usually done on preprinted forms. It is important to remember that the program *listing* is one of the best sources of program documentation. Some languages, e.g. COBOL, are very like English and are particularly easy to read. Others such as FORTRAN and the simpler versions of BASIC can be much improved by the inclusion of comments in the listings. For example, the REMark statement can be used for explanatory notes etc. in the BASIC language. A program listing which includes carefully written up notes is sometimes called a self-documentating program.

(a) Using Existing Code

We have seen how the complexity of business problems usually results in a group of analysts and programmers tackling one program. Complicated problems are most readily solved by breaking application programs down into simpler and more manageable tasks. Sometimes these smaller units (subprograms or subroutines) already exist and can be called upon as required by the main program. Structured programming techniques make extensive use of subroutines and have been found to be of value in reducing programming time as well as enabling the quick amendment of programs.

Example 9.4

What is a subroutine?

Solution 9.4

Programming time and effort can be eased by borrowing existing chunks of code. These so-called subprograms or library routines provide programs which solve everyday problems, such as sorting a list of names alphabetically, and can be easily adopted when needed. Basically there are two types:

- Open subroutines.
- Closed subroutines.

(i) *Open Subroutines*

An open subroutine is *copied* into the main program (your program) whenever it is *called* (or referenced) by the programmer. Fig. 9.7(a) shows an example of where a subroutine has been called two times at different points in a program. Note that the same section of coding is inserted at the two locations in the program. This approach is generally used for fairly short bits of coding.

(ii) *Closed Subroutines*

In lengthy programs it is often necessary to use a group of instructions frequently, and at different points in the program. To avoid repeating the instructions and to save time and computer memory it is possible to separate out the repeated instructions and branch to them. This process is referred to as a *closed subroutine* (Fig. 9.7(b)).

A closed subroutine is a *separate-program* in computer memory. Each time the programmer calls a closed subroutine, data is 'passed' to the subroutine for calculation, worked upon and 'returned' (passed back) to the main program. This is

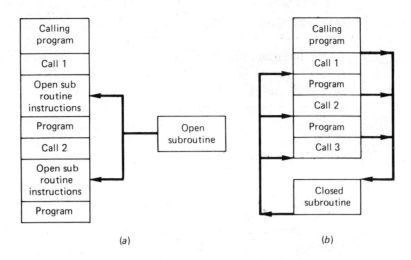

Figure 9.7 Comparison of open (*a*) and closed (*b*) subroutines.

done by means of links between the two programs. Closed subroutines are very important in programming and are used in large and complex work.

(b) Program Generators

For many kinds of application, a program generator can reduce the program development time. Applications intended to produce reports are particularly suitable for software generators.

From a preset specification, generators will produce a program which will create a defined output from a given output. The high-level language RPG works on this principle but it is not suited for all applications.

Computer manufacturers and software houses have devoted considerable efforts to the development of improved generators. However, there have been some notable failures to remove the software constraint.

9.5 Testing and Debugging the Program

The program must be tested and errors (bugs) removed – this process is called *debugging*. Finding bugs can be a frustrating and time-consuming task; even the smallest error in program code will usually cause the program either to produce incorrect results or not to run at all.

Careful planning and coding will reduce errors and spending time on program design is worth while in the end. However, a program rarely runs perfectly the first time it is tried.

Example 9.5

What are the main types of error in computer programs?

Solution 9.5

There are two main types of error in computer programs:

- *Syntax errors* – Errors in the use of program *language*.
- *Logical errors* – Errors in the program *logic*.

(a) Syntax Errors

Every programming language (like any natural language) has a set of rules concerning formal spelling, punctuation, naming of variables and other conventions that must be obeyed by the programmer. An error in language usage (similar to a spelling or punctuation mistake) is called a syntax error, e.g. in BASIC when using the INPUT statement, all variables must be followed by a comma, *except* the *last one*.

- *Correct form* – 10 INPUT A, B, C
- *Incorrect form* – 10 INPUT A, B, C,

Although this is a tiny error, it is enough to halt the execution of the program.

Translators convert the program into machine-code and will produce error messages if there is a mistake in the code. There are three types of translator:

- *Interpreters* translate one instruction at a time and so the program will be halted when a syntax error is met and an error message produced.
  This line-by-line fault-finding is helpful when developing programs.
- *Assemblers* (for low level)
OR
- *Compilers* (for high-level languages).
  Check the whole program and if there are any errors, even in the last line, it will not be possible to run the program until all the errors are corrected. Error messages, called the *diagnostic*, will be output indicating the nature of the error and the location (line number) where it was detected.

(b) Logical Errors

Although the interpreter will detect syntax errors, it will not find errors in programming logic. Thus a program with an error-free listing may still contain logical errors which produce incorrect results or cause the program to be aborted during execution, e.g. when using the logical IF statement in BASIC we wish to go to line 100 when the variable HOURS is greater than 40 we would use the statement:

30 IF HOURS > 40 THEN GO TO 100

an accidental reversal of the 'greater than' sign, i.e.

30 IF HOURS < 40 THEN GO TO 100

would still allow the program to be executed but would produce incorrect results because of the logic error. Only by careful testing can this type of error be identified.

A logical error can lead to one of two results:

- The program will produce wrong results but will finish normally.
- An unusual condition will be encountered (e.g. attempting to divide by zero) that leads to a premature end of the program. This type of error is known as a *run-time* error (in contrast to the diagnostic printed out by the compiler at *compile-time*!).

(c) Program Testing

Example 9.7

What are the main stages in program testing?

Solution 9.7

There are several stages in testing a program:

- Desk checking.
- Compiler (or assembler) system checking.
- Program run with test data.
- Diagnostic procedures, if needed.
- Full-scale (system) test with actual data.

(i) *Desk Checking (The Dry Run)*

Having just written the program, the programmer should be familiar with the required logic, therefore time spent working through the program on paper can often pick up logic errors which otherwise would cause extra work at a later stage. This is sometimes called a *dry run*.

(ii) *Translator System Checking*

After the program has been desk-checked it is keyed into the computer for interpretation (e.g. compilation). As mentioned, syntax errors are detected at this stage and indicated by diagnostics. The programmer corrects these errors and re-submits the program until an error-free listing is obtained.

(iii) *Program Run with Test Data*

Trial runs with test data should include all important variations and extremes of data, including data with errors, so that all paths and error conditions are tested. The program should not 'grind to a halt' if incorrect data is read in; rather a helpful error and retry message should be output (see Fig. 9.6 for suitable test data in our examination results question).

(iv) *Diagnostic Procedures*

For complex programs, diagnostic procedures, such as *trace routines*, may be used to help find logical errors. A trace prints out the results at each processing step in the program being tested, such as the value of selected variables and an indication of various paths taken in the program. If a trace routine is not available, the programmer can insert instructions in the program to print out intermediate results at key points. As most errors occur on data input it is a good idea to print out data after reading to ensure that they have been read correctly.

(v) *Full Test with Actual Data*

As part of the 'acceptance trials' new programs are typically run in parallel with the existing system for a short time so that results can be compared and adjustments made. The systems test is made using actual input data. The program can now be formally accepted and put into action in the organisation's system.

9.6 Exercises

Question 9.1

A small company act as agents for a larger firm, and earn commission on sales at a rate of 5%. The company employs three staff each earning a basic of £140 per week, has fixed overheads of £250 p.w. and other costs of 2% on sales. The flow chart in Fig. 9.8 represents the algorithm for a subroutine producing the profit (P) and the % profit on sales (R). S represents weekly sales, I income, V variable costs, E expenditure.

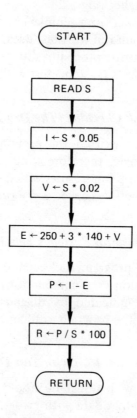

Figure 9.8 Flow chart for sales agency. ← = 'becomes'; e.g. C ← C + 1, replace (contents of C) by (contents of C) +1.

Complete the trace table and determine the profit and % profit on sales for each of the values of S.

Trace Table

S	I	V	E	P	R
50000					
200000					
125000					

Question 9.2

(a) Give two items of essential documentation you would provide with a program you have written.
(b) Who might find these useful, and why?

Question 9.3

With suitable examples explain fully each of the following programming terms: loops; conditional jump; subroutine.

Question 9.4

During the construction and running of a computer program, syntax and logical errors may occur; for each type of error:

(a) Explain the nature of the error.
(b) Give a suitable example.
(c) Describe how each can be dealt with so that the final program is correct.

Question 9.5

(a) Explain what is meant by the term dry run.
(b) Why is it good practice to do a dry run?

9.7 Answers and Hints on Solutions

9.1 *Trace table*

S	I	V	E	P	R
50000	2500	1000	1670	830	1.66
200000	10000	4000	4670	5330	2.67
125000	6250	2500	3170	3080	2.46

9.2 (a) *Program documentation* might include:

1. *A program description* – Including a listing of the program and the meaning of the variables together with any supporting flow charts, structure charts, etc.
2. *Operating instructions* on how to run the program.

(b) (1) would be useful to a programmer or systems analyst for program maintenance and improvement. It should be easier to make changes to a program if there is a clear and well-annotated program description.

(2) would be useful to anyone wishing to run the program. The operating manual should show the user what to do, including in those circumstances where things go wrong and error messages result or the computer halts.

9.3 LOOPS

A part of a program which can run repeatedly is called a loop. Short programs using loops can therefore process lots of data.
In programming there are WHILE-DO loops (Fig. 9.9(a)), REPEAT-UNTIL loops (Fig. 9.9(b)) and FOR-NEXT loops.

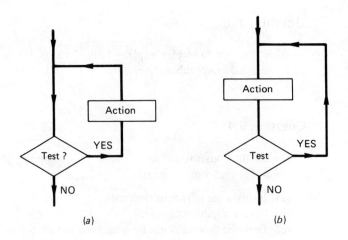

Figure 9.9 (*a*) WHILE loop. (*b*) REPEAT loop.

Example: WHILE loop:

```
WHILE SALES <> 0
DO TOTAL=TOTAL+SALES
ENDWHILE
PRINT TOTAL
DATA 50, 75, 33, 0
```

The program extract above adds individual sales figures together and prints the total. This loop will be repeated WHILE the data is non-zero.

Example: REPEAT loop. An alternative loop is the repeat loop:

```
REPEAT
FAHREN=(CENT*9/5)+32
PRINT FAHREN
UNTIL DATA = −1
DATA 25, 20, 10, −1
```

The program extract converts temperatures from centigrade to fahrenheit.

Example: FOR–NEXT loop:

```
FOR P = 1 TO 10
PRINT P,P*0.15,P*1.15
NEXT P
```

This is known as a finite loop in that it will go round a certain number of times—in our example 10—before moving down to the next instruction. The program extract above will show a price list, VAT cost, and total cost for items valued £1 to £10 in steps of £1.

CONDITIONAL JUMP

A conditional jump will occur *IF* a specified condition is met:

```
10 IF AGE <17 THEN GOTO 40
20 PRINT 'O.K. TO DRIVE A CAR'
30 GOTO 50
40 PRINT 'TOO YOUNG TO DRIVE A CAR'
50 . . . .
```

The program will jump from line 10 to line 40 *if* age is less than 17. Note, in contrast, the *unconditional jump* on line 30; the program is sent to line 50 always.

A subroutine is a group of instructions which can be used several times and at several different points in a program. Subroutines are written for common procedures within lengthy programs.:

50 GOSUB 1000 (calls subroutine)

. . .

100 GOSUB 1000 (calls subroutine)

. . .

1000 REM SUBROUTINE

1100 RETURN (to program line after call)

. . . = Body of subroutine.

9.4   (a) and (b)
(1)   A syntax error is an error in language usage like a spelling or punctuation mistake, e.g. missing quote marks or commas.
(2)   A logical error is syntactically correct and so the program will run but incorrect results will be produced, e.g., FC=VC+TC (where FC= fixed cost, VC=variable cost and TC=total cost). This is logically incorrect. It should be: TC=FC+VC, but the computer wouldn't notice this.
(c) The translator (compiler or interpreter) will reject syntax errors producing (hopefully) useful error messages. Mistakes in the code can then be corrected. Logical errors can only be found by careful testing, e.g. comparing computer results against your own predictions (*see* also 9.5).

9.5   (a)   A dry run or desk check involves working through a program on paper to see what the program is doing at each step. It is useful to write a trace table showing the sequence of instructions and the data values as you work through.
(b)   A dry run can help you to check that the program is logically correct. It can also save a lot of extra work at a later stage.

10 Program Writing in Basic

10.1 Introduction

The BASIC (Beginners All-Purpose Symbolic Instruction Code) language was developed as a teaching language and is therefore simple and easy to use. It is *the* language of micros and is particularly suitable for interactive work.

However, there are many versions (or 'dialects') of the BASIC language, some of which offer only limited facilities allowing only short variable names and making structured program writing difficult.

What follows is a revision of minimal BASIC. We take a standard subset of the language and apply it to a series of problems. This will be easy to learn and will give you quick results.

10.2 The BASIC Language

Learn the BASIC reserved words – Look at Table 10.1. This show a dozen or so reserved words in BASIC. Make sure you know at least these; there are, of course, others but this should be enough to get you by. BASIC is much easier to learn than a foreign language because there are only a few new words and symbols to learn.

Learn the main rules – If you misspell a BASIC word or make a grammatical mistake (such as forgetting a comma) this can stop the program. So learn and check the main rules of syntax (the grammar) carefully.

Statements – Each instruction is known as a statement. In some languages several statements can be put on one line.

Reserved words – A reserved word is an identifier which the programmer cannot use because it is part of the vocabulary of the programming language and, therefore, has special meaning to the translator: e.g. PRINT, LET.

An identifier is a name or label chosen by the programmer.

A variable is an identifier associated with a particular storage location. The value of the data item can change.

A constant is a data item which does not change.

Variables and constants are either numbers or names (character strings).

An expression is a statement which has to be worked out by the computer.

Statement format:

```
(i)        (ii)         (iii)
10         LET   A = B + C
```

(i) Statement (Line) number

Table 10.1 Essential BASIC

Reserved word	Example	Purpose
REM	REM wages calculation REM check routine	To describe what the program is doing; not acted on by the computer.
INPUT	INPUT N$, A	Enables data to be entered whilst a program is running.
READ } DATA }	READ X, Z$ DATA 15, 'PETER'	Used jointly to enter data.
LET	LET I = F * 12 LET A$ = 'JOAN' LET P = Q	Puts given value into named memory location; known as an assignment statement.
PRINT	PRINT F$, B PRINT 'HELLO'; A$; 'NICE DAY' PRINT C, C * 2, C * C	To output information , ; to separate items.
END	END	To finish a program.
GO TO	GO TO 999	Unconditional transfer of control.
IF. .THEN	IF P=20 THEN GO TO 100 IF N$='THOMAS' THEN GO TO 650 IF A > $\emptyset$ THEN T = T+A IF N < $\emptyset$ THEN PRINT 'OVERDRAWN'	Conditional action depending on result of test.
FOR } NEXT }	FOR P = 1 TO 10 NEXT P	Finite loop.

(ii) Operation code e.g. INPUT, LET, etc.

(iii) Operand — the rest of the statement made up of variables or constants.

(a) Reserved Words in BASIC

(i) *The LET Statement*

This is known as the *assignment* statement.

The LET places the given value into a named memory location:

	Memory name	Locations contents
10 LET G = 2	G	2
20 LET P = G * 3	P	6
30 LET Q = P	Q	6
40 LET A$ = 'DOUGIE'	A$	DOUGIE

NB: The equals sign does not mean equals in the mathematical sense, rather it is an assignment symbol.

Thus 10 LET X = 99 implies 'move the value 99 into the place called X'.

10 LET C = C + 1 means 'add 1 to the number already in C and store the result in C'.

(ii) *The REM Statement*

REMarks are included in a BASIC program by using REM statements. Remarks describe to people what the program is doing and help to explain how the program works and what each section is supposed to do. They are not acted on by the computer so syntax is unimportant.

(iii) *INPUT and OUTPUT*

The INPUT statement allows the user to enter data as the program is running. When BASIC executes an INPUT command it displays a ? on the screen and waits for a response from the keyboard. Commas are used to separate items. For example:

10 INPUT A$, N
RUN
User enters (e.g.)————►WEBSTER, 36

For output *the PRINT statement* is used to output information, messages or instructions, on to screen or printer.

A comma (,) or semi-colon (;) are used to separate items. Quote marks 'surround' strings. For example, if X and Y have the values 5 and 7, 10 PRINT X, Y would result in the following screen output:

     5   7

A computer divides each line of output on the screen (or printer) into print zones. The number of zones will depend on the make of computer. A comma forces the next data (in our case Y) to be printed on the same line as X but in the next free print zone.

10 PRINT X ; Y would result in:

     57   the semicolon causes the two numbers to be printed without a gap.

40 PRINT 'TREVOR FRANCIS' would give:

       TREVOR FRANCIS

50 PRINT 'TREVOR FRANCIS' ; X would give:

       TREVOR FRANCIS 5

(iv) *READ . . . DATA Statements*

READ AND DATA are jointly used to enter data.
The READ statement fetches values from the DATA Lines. Values are assigned to variables in the sequence in which they are read. For example:

10 READ N$, A, B

999 DATA 'NAOMI', 17, 34

Variable	Contents
N$	NAOMI
A	17
B	34

It doesn't matter where the DATA lines appear in a program although, conventionally, they are usually written at the end.

(b) Branches and Loops – The IF. . . THEN and GO TO Statements

(i) *Branches*

A *branch* or *jump* breaks the normal sequence of the program. The jump may be *conditional*, i.e. dependent on the result of same test, or *unconditional* – GO TO line number.

In BASIC a conditional branch uses: IF condition THEN action, where the action is taken IF the condition is true; otherwise the program carries on in sequence to the next statement. For example:

```
100 GO TO 200 – unconditional
150 IF A >10 THEN GO TO 1000
  170 IF A$ = 'END' THEN PRINT 'BYEBYE'
```

Some versions of BASIC allow IF . . . THEN . . . ELSE:

```
IF AGE> = 17 THEN PRINT 'OK TO DRIVE' ELSE PRINT
'TOO YOUNG TO DRIVE A CAR'
```

(ii) *Loops*

A program *loop* is a sequence of instructions that is executed repeatedly until a specific condition is satisfied.

A *nested loop* is a loop contained within another loop. (In extended BASIC there are REPEAT and WHILE loops: *REPEAT* loop *UNTIL* condition is true; or *WHILE* condition is true *DO* loop).

Most high-level languages have easy ways of writing loops. Here is a BASIC program extract which uses the *FOR. . . NEXT* loop:

```
10 PRINT 'COST', 'VAT', 'TOTAL'
20 FOR P = 1 TO 10
30 PRINT P, P*0.15, P*1.15
40 NEXT P
```

This program prints out costs from £1 to £10 together with VAT charges and total prices in steps of £1.

Here is an example of a nested loop. If P = Price and V = VAT rate what does this program do?

```
10 FOR P = 1 TO 10
20   FOR V = .10 TO.20 STEP .05
30     PRINT  P, P*V, P* (1+V)
40   NEXT V
50 NEXT P
```

Inner loop | Outer loop

(c) Rogue (or Dummy Values)

A rogue value is a specified value at the end of a list of data items which is used to terminate further input:

- It should have a value which will not be confused with the real data.
- It should have the same format as the rest of the data so that it can be read without halting the program.

For example:

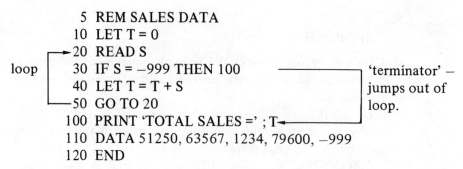

```
   5 REM SALES DATA
  10 LET T = 0
  20 READ S
  30 IF S = −999 THEN 100
  40 LET T = T + S
  50 GO TO 20
 100 PRINT 'TOTAL SALES =' ; T
 110 DATA 51250, 63567, 1234, 79600, −999
 120 END
```

loop

'terminator' – jumps out of loop.

(d) Operators and Precedence

The *relational operators* in BASIC are:

Sign	Example	Meaning
=	IF N = ∅ THEN	Equal to
<	IF P < Q THEN	Less than
>	IF A > 16 THEN	Greater than
< =	IF Z <= 5 THEN	Less than or equal to
> =	IF K >= 100 THEN	Greater than or equal to
<>	IF A$ <> B$ THEN	Not equal to

Basic arithmetic operators:

Order of precedence		Example
( )	Brackets	$(X − Y) *7$
↑	Exponentiate	$X\uparrow2$
* and /	Multiply and divide	$(P*Q)/C$
+ and −	Add and subtract	$A + B − 4$

For example, LET C = (F − 32) * 5/9 converts Fahrenheit to celsius.

(e) Running a BASIC Program

There are several *system* commands which you need to execute a BASIC program. Typically these are:

Command	Purpose
RUN	Executes current BASIC program
LIST	Lists the program code
NEW	Clears memory
SAVE	Stores a copy of the current program on backing store
LOAD	Recalls a SAVED program

NB: These are system not BASIC commands and therefore do not need a line number.

10.3 Worked Example — Gas Bill

The following program computes a gas bill from two meter readings supplied as DATA. The bill comprises a standing charge of £12.50 and the cost of gas used at rates of 7p per unit on the first 150 units and 3p per unit on further units.

```
  1   REM **JOHN MUIR
  2   REM **GAS BILL
 10 READ M,N
 20 DATA 1900,2550
 30 LET U=N-M
 40 LET L=U-150
 50 IF L>0 THEN GOTO 80
 60 LET L=0
 70 GOTO 90
 80 LET U=150
 90 LET X=U*7/100
100 LET Y=L*3/100
110 LET Z=X+Y+12.5
120 PRINT "UNITS","CHARGE"
130 PRINT U,X
140 PRINT L,Y
150 PRINT "ST.CHG",12.5
160 PRINT "TOTAL",Z
200 END
```

Answer the following:
- (i) Draw a trace table showing how the computer works through the program.
- (ii) Write down carefully all print-out produced at a terminal by the program.
- (iii) How would you amend the program to use meter readings 2780 and 2850?
- (iv) The standing charge is raised to £15.00; the number of units charged at the higher rate is reduced to 120; charges per unit become 8.1 and 3.4p. Write down the lines you would use to amend the program accordingly.
- (v) Write down the lines to amend the program so that it accepts meter readings entered via the keyboard when the program is run.
- (vi) Write lines to amend the program to loop and calculate the bills for several sets of meter readings.

(a) Answers

(i) A trace table aims to show how the computer will work through the program and shows what will be in each of the variable 'boxes':

Line number	Variable	Contents
10	M	1900
	N	2550
30	U	650
40	L	500
80	U	150
90	X	$10.5 - (150*7/100)$
100	Y	$15 \ - (500*3/100)$
110	Z	$38 \ - (10.5+15+12.5)$

These variables are explained in the following legend:

M,N	=	1st and latest meter readings
U	=	number of units used/then 150 units
L	=	Units used above 150
X	=	Charge for 150 units
Y	=	Charge for extra units at cheap rate
Z	=	Total charge

(ii) Hence it should be possible to predict exactly what the output will be. The format will be determined by the use of space commands, in this case commas.

Now type in the program and see if your 'guestimate' matches with the computer run:

```
>RUN
UNITS          CHARGE
150            10.5
500            15
ST. CHG.       12.5
TOTAL          38
```

(iii) This simply involves changing line 20 to:

DATA 2780, 2850

You might like to do another 'trace' and try to predict the answer before you run the program again. For interest the result will be as follows:

```
>RUN
UNITS          CHARGE
70             4.9
0              0
ST. CHG.       12.5
TOTAL          17.4
```

Note that there are no units charged at the cheap rate because only $2850 - 2780 = 70$ units were used.

(iv) This involves six changes as follows:

40 LET L = U−120	These lines change the high/cheap rate threshold.
80 LET U = 120	
90 LET X = U*8.1/100	These lines change the unit prices.
100 LET Y = L*3.4/100	
110 LET Z = X+Y+15	These lines change the standing charge.
150 PRINT "ST. CHG.", 15	

(v) 10 PRINT "ENTER FIRST, SECOND METER READINGS"
20 INPUT M,N

These lines will overwrite the existing lines 10 and 20 on read/data. The user now has the facility to enter any meter readings. A useful supplementary would be to think how to ensure that the latest meter reading is greater than the first and to trap such errors. For example:

25 IF M <= N THEN GO TO 30
27 PRINT "IMPOSSIBLE TO HAVE NEGATIVE UNITS − TRY AGAIN"
28 GO TO 10

Of course you could introduce range tests or tests of reasonableness to improve the accuracy (or at least the validity) of data input. In business, controls and checks like this are very important.

(vi) 170 LET T=T+Z   ——►Accumulates individual bills
180 PRINT "ANYMORE BILLS(Y/N)" ——► Determines if there are any
190 INPUT A$ more bills to enter.
200 IF A$ = "Y" THEN GO TO 10
210 PRINT "GRAND TOTAL= " ; ——► Prints out the total when
220 END   there are no bills left.

In order to calculate a grand total an accumulator has been introduced (line 170). This has to be inside the loop so that it can add any number of Zs — gas bill totals. The response to line 180 will determine whether the program loops back to line 10 for another bill or ends by printing out the grand total.

10.4 Subprograms

A subprogram is a set of program instructions which carries out a specific task, but which is not a complete program in itself. To work it must be used with the main program. Subprograms are also referred to as routines, subroutines, procedures or functions.

Modular programming is an approach to writing programs which divides up a task into separate sections or modules (subprograms) to perform a specific job. In theory, amendments are easier to make because individual sections can be corrected without having to work through the whole program (see Chapter 9) for more details).

(a) Procedures

In some versions of extended BASIC, e.g. BBC, it is possible to use procedures. A procedure is a group of BASIC statements which can be called by name from any part of the program.

Using procedures allows you to break down a problem into manageable sections and to call them up when necessary.

```
10  PROCSTART————► call START
20  REPEAT
30  PROCMAIN————► call MAIN
40  UNTIL STOP
50  END
60  DEF PROCSTART
      .
      .
      .
100 ENDPROC
110
120 PROCMAIN
      .
      .
      .
200 ENDPROC
```

(b) Functions

Functions always calculate a result (a number or a string).
Functions are of two types:

- Built-in (or standard) functions.
- User (or programmer) -defined functions.

(i) *Built-in Function*

This is a subprogram which carries out a task such as the calculation of a mathematical function. It is always available and is part of the program language translator. For example:

SQR (X) returns the positive square root of X.
INT (X) returns the largest integer not greater than X.
e.g.   INT (1.3) = 1
       INT (−1.4) = −2

(ii) *User-Defined Function*

This can be created by the programmer within a program. The general form of statement for defining a function is:

- DEF FN X = Expression.
OR
- DEF FN X (parameter) = Expression.

Where X is a single letter and a parameter is a simple numeric variable. For example, the following function D corrects a value to 2 decimal places (useful where pence/money is concerned):

```
10     DEF FND(N) = INT (N * 100 + .5) / 100
  :
  :
  :
1000  PRINT "TOTAL BILL  = " ; FND (I)
1010  PRINT "TOTAL VAT = "; FND (V)
```
Lines 1000–1010 use the function defined in line 10 to print monetary values defined to the nearest penny.

(c) Subroutines

A subroutine in BASIC is a section of program that is entered by a GOSUB statement and exited by a RETURN statement which sends the computer back to the statement immediately after GOSUB. A GOSUB statement can call for certain complex calculations not suitable for defined functions:

```
50   GOSUB   1000
  60

1000  REM SUBROUTINE TO TEST RANGE OF INPUT
1005  REM CHECKS HEIGHTS OF STUDENTS IN INCHES AND
      CHALLENGES INPUT DATA BELOW 4'8" OR ABOVE 6'8"
1010  IF H<56 OR H>80 THEN PRINT "CHECK THIS"
1020  RETURN
```

The values passed between a program and a subroutine are called *arguments* or *parameters*.

A *library subroutine* is already available to any user of a computer system as part of the software. It can be *called* when necessary.

(i) *Advantages of Subroutines*

- Routine operations can be carried out several times in different parts of the program without having to repeat all of the instructions.
- Different programs can use the same program segment (not true in some versions of BASIC).

10.5   Arrays (see also Chapter 6)

An array is a set of storage locations referenced by a single identifier.

(a) Dimension

The limits of an array or 'array bounds' are declared in a DIMension Statement, e.g. in BASIC: 5 DIM Z (20) declares a one-dimensional array with 20 elements. 10 DIM X (15,25) declares a two-dimensional array with 15 rows and 25 columns. One-dimensional arrays are sometimes called lists or vectors. Two-dimensional arrays are sometimes called tables or matrices.

(b) Elements and Subscripts

Individual elements of an array are referenced by combining one or more *subscripts* with the identifier, e.g.:

STUDENT (20) is an *element* in the array STUDENT.
SUBJECT (2,4) is an element in the two-dimensional array SUBJECT.

(a) Worked Example

Q. Below is a program segment in the language BASIC, designed to accept numbers which should be between 0 and 15 and convert them to percentages of 15.

```
 5  DIM N(100)
10  INPUT N
20  FOR I = 1 to N
30  INPUT M (I)
40  IF M(I) > 0 AND M(I) < 16 THEN 70
50  . . . . . .
60  GO TO 80
70  P(I) = (M(I)/15)* 100
80  NEXT I
```

Q. What is happening in lines 5–30?

A. In the program, line:

5 sets up space for an array with up to 100 elements.
10 allows the user to define how many items there should be in the array (up to 100).
20 sets up a FOR . . . NEXT loop to go round N times.
30 allows the user to enter values into M (1), M (2), M (3), etc. respectively up to M (N).

Q. What happens at line 40?

A. *IF* the number input is more than $\emptyset$ (i.e. positive) and less than 16 *THEN* the program accepts the number and jumps to line 70 where the percentage calculation is carried out.

Q. What statement should be included at line 50?

A. An *error* message, e.g.:

50 PRINT "OUT OF RANGE, NUMBER MUST BE BETWEEN 0 AND 15".

Q. In your test data the first number input is 6. Complete the test data to check this program segment giving the reasons for your choice.

A. Test data should include numbers which are:

< 0
> 15
as well as 'legitimate' data.
Note: The ordering (or sorting) of an array is demonstrated in the next section.

10.6 Common Methods of Sorting

Q. Sorting routines are used frequently in computing. Describe the steps of an algorithm to sort an alphanumerical file into alphabetical key order.

A. Sorting a list of numbers or names into some order is a very common task. In BASIC a DIM statement (for DIMension) has to be used to specify the maximum length of the list if this is greater than 11 (so technically line 5 is not essential in the example).

After reading into N (line 10) the actual length of the list, lines 20–40 read N strings (names) into the list S$. Data begins at line 170.

The sorting technique used here sorts adjacent pairs of names. In lines 70–80 X$ and Y$ become the first and second of a pair of entries at positions J and J + 1. If the first entry (X$) does not exceed the second entry (Y$) no swop is made (line 90 causes a jump to line 120). However, if X$ *is* greater than Y$ then the interchange is carried out in lines 100–110.

By working all the way down the list once (the first pass) swopping out-of-order pairs, it is certain that the last entry will be the nearest to Z and the end of the alphabet. The next time through, the next-to-last becomes the next nearest to Z and so on; there is no need to re-examine the last pair, since it is guaranteed to be in order. Thus the J-loop (lines 60–120) becomes shorter each time, since its upper limit is N–I.

Finally, the alphabetical list of names will be printed out in lines 140–160. The trailing colon in line 150 causes the names to be printed close together on the same line to save space.

```
5    DIM S$(100)
10   READ N
20   FOR I=1 TO N
30       READ S$(I)
40   NEXT I
50   FOR I=1 TO N-1
60       FOR J=1 TO N-I
70           LET X$=S$(J)
80           LET Y$=S$(J+1)
90           IF X$<Y$ THEN 120
100          LET S$(J)=Y$
110          LET S$(J+1)=X$
120      NEXT J
130  NEXT I
140  FOR I=1 TO N
150      PRINT S$(I):
160  NEXT I
170  DATA 10
180  DATA "Jibson", "Robinson", "Rushbrooke"
190  DATA "Gilchrist", "Jones", "Lopez"
200  DATA "Smith", "Buckner", "Haywood"
210  DATA "Whitehead"
220  END
```

10.7 Simple File Handling

Quite often file handling commands vary according to the machine-type, so check your manual. The following commands apply to BBC BASIC.

(a) Some BBC BASIC File Handling Commands

OPENIN	:	opens a file so that it can be read.
OPENOUT	:	opens a new file so that it can be written to.
INPUT	:	reads data from file.
PRINT	:	writes data to file.
EOF	:	indicates the end of file.
CLOSE	:	closes the file.

Data files are very important, particularly in business, and are often kept *separate* from programs rather than as data lines.

(b) Why Have External Files?

- They are easier to create/amend and update than having to change DATA lines.
- Several programs can use the data file in different ways.

10.8 Exercises

Question 10.1

(a) Give and explain two examples of reserved words e.g. IF.
(b) Outline three considerations which should be given when choosing the names of variables to be used in a program.   (OLE)

(c)   A = RND (X)

This is a statement in a programming language which produces a random number and assigns it to the variable A.

Give and explain one example of a situation in which the random number function would be used.   (AEB)

Question 10.2

Read the BASIC program below, then answer the questions which follow.

```
1    REM EXAM PROGRAM
2    REM JOHN MUIR
10   LET T1=0
20   LET T2=0
30   LET T3=0
40   LET  N=0
50   READ N$
60   IF N$="END" THEN GOTO 150
70   READ A,E,S
80   LET T1=T1+A
90   LET T2=T2+E
100  LET T3=T3+S
110  LET M=(A+E+S)/3
120  LET N=N+1
130  PRINT N$,M
140  GOTO 50
150  PRINT
160  PRINT "ACCOUNTS", "ECONS", "STATS"
170  PRINT T1/N,T2/N,T3/N
200  DATA "CHAS", 60,40,50,"ALTHEA",35,60,40
210  DATA "DAVE",50,40,15,"DONNA",80,70,60
220  DATA "END"
999  END
```

(a) Draw a trace table for the above program and write down carefully all that is printed out when the program is RUN.

(b) What is the purpose of this program?

(c) A fourth subject, COMPUTING, is to be included in the processing. What changes are necessary? Write out your amendment lines.

(d) If all the data for a whole class is stored in a separate computer file rather than DATA statements what amendments to the program are needed?

Question 10.3

Below is part of a table

46220	Jane Coton	4	f	24
46221	Peter Hole	3	m	25
46222	Bob Lomas	4	m	36
46223	Dave Sheargold	1	m	37

Using a flow chart or program segment show how the data may be read into a two-dimensional array.   (AEB)

Question 10.4

(a) For a named high-level language explain:

(i) How variable names are constructed.

(ii) The input and output statements.

(b) (i) For the named high-level language, provide the programming instructions to read exactly 20 data items into a one-dimensional array and print the average.

(ii) Rewrite the instructions to read in an unknown number of items (not exceeding 100) into a one-dimensional array. Make clear how the end of data would be recognised.   (OLE)

Question 10.5

Sorting routines are used frequently in computing. Describe the steps of an algorithm requested to sort a file into ascending number order.   (AEB)

Question 10.6

Using statements in a high-level language (e.g. BASIC) show how to:

(a) Declare an array name Z with 15 elements.
(b) Assign to the first 10 consecutive elements of array Z the odd number values 1, 3, 5, etc.

Question 10.7

The gross remuneration of a company's salesmen comprises a basic salary and certain additional payments and bonuses as follows:

Salesmen with over 5 year's service receive a 10% addition to their basic salary each month.
London salesmen receive an additional allowance of £100 per month.
Monthly bonus payments are made and calculated as follows:

Monthly sales (£)	Bonus as a percentage of monthly sales
0–2500	0.5
2501–5000	1.0
>5000	1.5

You are required to prepare a flow chart to calculate the gross monthly remuneration of a salesman.

Question 10.8

Draw a flow chart and write a program to read in a series of positive and negative numbers, ending in the rogue value –999, and to count and print out the number of positive and the number of negative numbers read in. (0(zeros) are counted as positive numbers).   (AEB)

Question 10.9

Draw a flow chart and write a program to illustrate the process to read any amount of dollars and convert it into sterling. The output must be in pounds and pence as integer values.

Question 10.10

ABC Ltd, with warehouses in London and Birmingham keeps its inventory file on a computer. Each record on file contains, inter alia, the following items of data:

(i) Stock number.
(ii) Warehouse location (London or Birmingham).
(iii) Balance of stock.
(iv) Cost price per unit of stock.
(v) Three months' history of sales.

The last record is a dummy record numbered 99999.

Draft a flow chart and write a program which would read the file sequentially and, for the Birmingham warehouse only, print out:

1. A schedule listing balance of stock and value of stock for all those items for which no sales have been made in the past three months.
2. The grand total in value of all such items.

Question 10.11

```
1    REM JOHN MUIR
2    REM TRAVEL DISCOUNTS
5    LET T1=0
7    LET T2=0
10   READ N$,R$,A
20   IF R$="Z" THEN 110
30   IF R$="Y" THEN 60
40   LET D=A*10/100
50   GOTO 70
60   LET D=A*15/100
70   PRINT N$,A,D
80   LET T1=T1+A
90   LET T2=T2+D
100  GOTO 10
110  PRINT "TOTALS",T1,T2
200  DATA "THOMAS COOK", "X", 1470
210  DATA "SKYBLUE", "Y",300
220  DATA "THOMSONS", "Y",5000
230  DATA "ALLTRAVEL","X",550
240  DATA "Z", "Z", 0
250  END
```

This program calculates discounts on customer accounts.

(i) Work through the program, writing out a trace table and also writing down carefully all output produced at a terminal when it is run on the computer.
(ii) Which lines in the program set up and allow exit from a loop?
(iii) What extra lines would you insert in the program to put an appropriate heading above the program output?
(iv) The discount for X accounts is to become 12.5% and for Y accounts 20%. What changes should be made to the program?
(v) What changes are necessary in order that the program takes account details from a file called SALACC?

Question 10.12

A small company acts as agents for a larger firm, and earn commission on sales at a rate of 5%. The company employs three staff each earning a basic of £120 per week, has fixed overheads of £250 p.w. and other costs of 2% on sales.

The following program is a 'model' used to calculate weekly profits.

```
2    REM* MONEY MODEL
3    REM* JOHN MUIR
10   READ S
20   LET I=S*0.05
30   LET V=S*0.02
40   LET E=250+3*120+V
50   LET P=I-E
60   LET R=P/S*100
100  PRINT "PROFIT",P
110  PRINT "PROFIT ON SALES",R;"%"
200  DATA 50000
999  END
```

(i) Write down clearly all that the program would output to the user.

(ii) Write down amendments which cause the program to repeat the calculation for 5 weekly cycles.

(iii) Average Profit over the 5 weekly cycles are required. Write suitable amendments.

(iv) The company takes on a second agency for which commission will be 7% of sales, another employee being appointed to cope with the new work.

What changes are needed to the original program above?

(v) What changes are required so that values of income and expenditure are produced for the user?

Question 10.13

The following is a description of the procedure for dealing with delivery charges for goods bought from AB Ltd.

For the purpose of determining delivery charges, customers are divided into two categories, those whose Sales Region Code (SRC) is 50 or above, and those with an SRC of less than 50.

If the SRC is less than 50 and the invoice amount is less than £1000, the delivery charge to be added to the invoice total is £30. But if the invoice value is for £1000 or more, the delivery charge is £15.

If the SRC is equal to or greater than 50 and the invoice total is less than £1000, the delivery charge is £40. For invoices totalling £1000 or more, however, the delivery charge is £20.

Prepare a flow chart and decision table of the above procedure.

10.9 Answers and Hints on Solutions

10.1 (a) The IF ... THEN statement gives conditional transfer of control, where the action is taken IF the condition is true. Otherwise the program will continue in sequence, e.g. 10 IF A > 10 THEN 30.

The REM (REMARK) statement is used to describe what the program or program extract is doing; it is not acted upon by the computer. For example:

10 REM Line 20 converts degrees fahrenheit to celsius
20 LET C = (F−32)*5/9

(b) • Not reserved words.
• Use meaningful names (subject to the constraints of the language, e.g. P = Price; N = Number).
• Not too long.

(c) Simulation, e.g. coin-tossing:

```
10 LET A = RND
20 IF A< 1/2 THEN 60
30 PRINT 'TAILS'

_ _ _ _ _ _ _ _ _ _

60 PRINT 'HEADS'
```

- Useful for simulation and games programs to test probability.
- Can generate *test* data.

10.2 (a)

Line number	Variable 'box'	Trace table contents			
40	T1,T2	PASS 1	2	3	4
	T3,N	Variables initialised i.e. to $\emptyset$			
50	N$	CHAS	ALTHEA	DAVE	DONNA
70	A	60	35	50	80
	E	40	60	40	70
	S	50	40	15	60
80	T1	60	95	145	225
90	T2	40	100	140	210
100	T3	50	90	105	165
110	M	50	45	35	70
120	N	1	2	3	4

Output *LINE 130*		LINE 160 LINE 170	ACCOUNTS 56.25	ECONS 52.5	STATS 41.25
Pass: 1 CHAS 50 2 ALTHEA 45 3 DAVE 35 4 DONNA 70		*LEGEND* T1 = Total for accounts (A) M = average student mark T2 = Total for econs (E) N$ = name T3 = Total for stats (S) N = count T1/N,T2/N etc. Examination average mark			

(b) The purpose of this program is twofold. It calculates:

- The average mark for each student.
- The average mark for each examination.

(c)
```
35 LET T4 = 0
70 READ A, E, S, C
105 LET T4 = T4+C
110 LET M = (A+E+S+C)/4
160 PRINT "ACCOUNTS", "ECONS", "STATS","COMPUTING"
170 PRINT T1/N, T2/N, T3/N, T4/N
```
200–210 Fictitious marks have to be added to each student's records. There must be four marks in each because of line 70.

(d) This answer depends very much on the type of machine you have, so check your manual.

In BBC BASIC, the following amendments are necessary:

10 X = OPENIN ('BECMRC')	!	opens a file called BECMRC so that it can be read
20 REPEAT	!	sets up a loop
30 INPUT #X,N\$,A,E,S,C	!	reads data from file
40 PRINT N\$,A,E,S,C	!	Prints the details
50 UNTIL EOF#X	!	Loops back to line 20 until end of file (EOF) is found
60 CLOSE#X	!	closes the file
70 END		

External file record format:
     e.g.   CHAS, #60, 40, 50, 75
            name   marks for 4 subjects

10.3   FOR I = 1 TO 4
         FOR J = 1 TO 5
            READ T\$ (I,J)
         NEXT J
       NEXT I
       i.e. four rows
       and five columns in table.

10.4   (a) (i) Variable names
            In ECMA (European Computer Manufacturers Association)
            BASIC variables are constructed as follows:
            one or two characters, the first of which must be a letter.
            Numeric variables are named by a letter followed by an optional digit.
            String variables are named by a letter followed by a dollar sign.

            e.g.s X   A5   V(3)   S(X,X+Y/4)

                   P\$ subscripted numeric variables

       The following are illegal in ECMA BASIC

            PRICE − too long
            6A   − names cannot begin with a digit
            RU   − two letters are not acceptable
       Note: BBC BASIC allows longer, and therefore meaningful, variable names.
         (ii) Input and output statements
            e.g.   INPUT X   INPUT X, N\$,Y(2)   INPUT A,B,C
                   7.2   2, LUCAS, −5   5, 10, 20
       The *INPUT* statement allows the user to assign values to variables
       whilst the program is running. Data items are separated by commas.
            The *PRINT* statement produces *output* on screen or printer in a
       consistent format.
            TAB or the punctuation marks comma and semi-colon can be
       used to separate the items printed.
            e.g. PRINT X, Y
               PRINT 'THE AVERAGE MARK = ';A; ' FOR THE COM-
               PUTER TEST'

```
4b)i
   10   DIM X(20)
   20   LET T=0
   30   FOR J=1 TO 20
   40      READ X(J)
   50      PRINT X(J)      :optional
   60      LET T=T+X(J)
   70   NEXT J
   80   LET A=T/20
   90   PRINT "THE AVERAGE =";A
  100   END

  ii) Changed lines

   10 DIM X(100)
   30 READ X(J)
   40 IF X(J)= -1 THEN GOTO 80    :-1 set as terminator
   65 LET C=C+1                   :counter
   70 GOTO 25
   80 LET A=T/C
```

10.5   See program on alphabetic sort in text and:

- Replace the string variables S$,X$,Y$ by numeric ones – S, X and Y.
- Change the data to numbers.

10.6   (a) and (b)

10 DIM Z(15)	reserves space for 15 elements
20 LET P = 1	sets P to 1
┌ 30 FOR N = 1 TO 10	sets up a FOR . . NEXT loop for 10 elements
│ 40 LET Z(N) = P	transfers contents of P to Z(1), Z(2) etc
│ 50 LET P = P + 2	Increments P by 2 giving 3, 5 etc
└ 60 NEXT N	Increments N by 1 until 10 is reached

10.7   See Fig. 10.1.

10.8   See Fig. 10.2.

Program:

```
10  READ N
20  IF N = -999 THEN GO TO 50
30  IF N>= 0 THEN P = P+1
    ELSE G = G+1
40  GO TO 10
50  PRINT "No OF POSITIVE NUMBERS =" ; P
60  PRINT "No OF NEGATIVE NUMBERS =" ; G
70  END
80  DATA lines . . . .
```

10.9   See Fig. 10.3

Program:

```
10  INPUT "ENTER DOLLAR AMOUNT TO EXCHANGE" ; D
20  INPUT "EXCHANGE RATE (e.g. type 1.6 if $1.6 = £1)?" ; R
30  LET P = INT (D*R*100 + .5)/100
40  PRINT "YOU WILL RECEIVE" ; P ; "POUNDS"
50  INPUT "ANOTHER GO ? (Y/N)" ; A$
60  IF A$ = "Y" THEN GO TO 10
70  PRINT "BYE BYE"
80  END
```

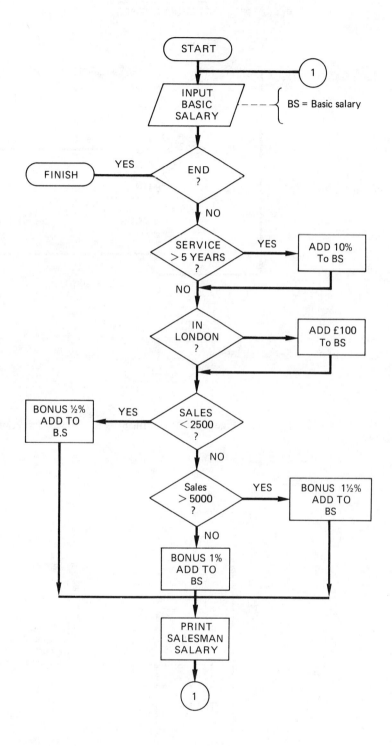

Figure 10.1 Solution 10.7 Salesmen's salary flow chart.

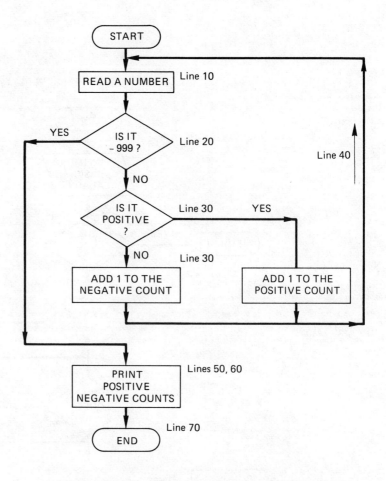

Figure 10.2 Solution 10.8 Flow chart: counting numbers.

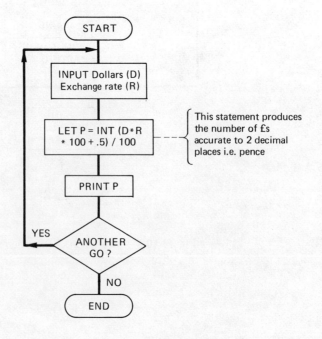

Figure 10.3 Solution 10.9 Flow chart: money conversion.

10.10 See Fig. 10.4.

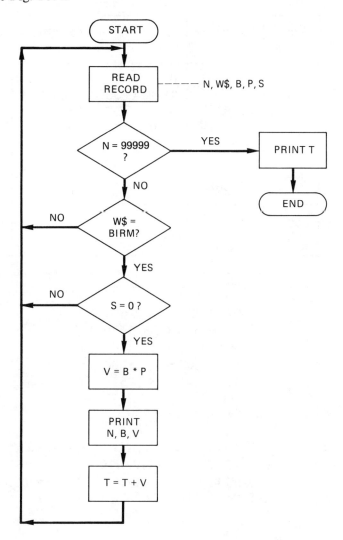

Figure 10.4 Solution 10.10 Flow chart: warehouse – inactive stock. N = Stock number; W$ = Warehouse; B = Balance of stock; P = Cost price; S = Sales (last 3 months); V = Value; T = Grand total value.

```
1   REM Answer question 10
2   REM In ECMA BASIC using DATA lines
3   REM N= stock Number,W$=Warehouse location (either L for
4   REM London or B for Birmingham),B=Balance of stock,P=Price
5   REM Sales history for last 3 months
7   PRINT "Stock no.", "Balance", "Value"
10  READ N
20  IF N= -999 THEN GOTO 100
30  READ W$,B,P,S
40  IF W$<>"B" THEN 10
50  IF S<>0 THEN 10
60  V=B*P
70  PRINT N,B,V
80  T=T+V
90  GOTO 10
100 PRINT
110 PRINT "Total value = ";T
200 DATA 1234,"L",20,2.5,100
210 DATA 1235,"B",50,3.7,0
220 DATA 1236,"L",100,1.0,50
230 DATA 1237,"B",50,0.5,75
240 DATA 1238,"B",55,1.0,0
500 DATA -999
999 END
```

10.11

Line number	*Variable*	*Contents*		*Trace table*		
5/7	T1,T2	0				
10	N$	THOMAS COOK	SKYBLUE	THOMSONS	ALLTRAVEL	Z
	R$	X	Y	Y	X	Z
	A	1470	300	5000	550	0
40	D	147				
60			45	750	55	
70	PRINT		LINE	See below		
80	T1	1470	1770	6770	7320	
90	T2	147	192	942	997	
110	PRINT		LINE	See below		

(i) *OUTPUT*

```
THOMAS COOK 1470 147
SKYBLUE      300  45
THOMSONS    5000 750
ALLTRAVELS   550  55
TOTALS      7320 997
```

(ii) Set up – Line 100
Exit – Line 20

(iii) 3 PRINT"COMPANY","AMOUNT","DISCOUNT"

(iv) 40 LET D = A*12.5/100 (X accounts)
60 LET D = A*20/100 (Y accounts)

(v) DELETE DATA lines and line 20

```
   8 X = OPENIN ("SALACC")
   9 REPEAT
  10   INPUT #X,N$,R$,A
 100 UNTIL EOF#X
1900   CLOSE#X
```

} in BBC BASIC

10.12 (i)

Lines	*Variable*	*Content*
10	S	50000
20	I	2500
30	V	1000
40	E	1610
50	P	890
60	R	1.78

Output: PROFIT 890

PROFIT ON SALES 1.78%

(ii) 7 FOR C = 1 TO 5
115 NEXT C
1000 DATA 50000, 100000, 75000, 50000, 150000 (i.e. five data items)

(iii) 70 LET T = T + P
130 PRINT 'AVERAGE PROFIT = ';T/C

(iv)　10 READ SI,S2 (where S1=sales for agency 1; S2=sales for agency 2)
　　　20 LET I1 = S*0.05
　　　35 LET I2 = S*0.07
　　　40 LET E = 250 + 4*120 + V
　　　45 LET I = I1 + I2
(v)　80 PRINT 'INCOME=';I
　　　90 PRINT 'EXPENDITURE =';E

10.13　See Fig. 10.5.

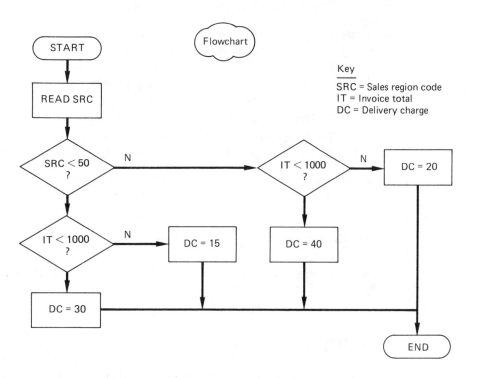

Decision table

		Rules			
		1	2	3	4
Conditions	SRC <50?	Y	Y	N	N
	Invoice<£1000?	Y	N	Y	N
Actions:	Delivery £15		√		
	"　　20				√
	"　　30	√			
	40			√	

Delivery charge procedure
DATE...　2 CONDITIONS
　　　　　4 ACTIONS
　　　　　4 RULES

Flowchart

Key
SRC = Sales region code
IT = Invoice total
DC = Delivery charge

Figure 10.5 Solution 10.13　Flow chart and decision table: delivery charges. Advantages of decision tables over flow charts:

- Easy to amend.;
- Good for finding ambiguities and incomplete routines.
- Simple, concise.

11 Computer Applications

11.1 Introduction

A computer application is any particular use made of a computer as part of a system. Nowadays this can cover a wide range of things. Generally examiners leave it up to you to pick an application (see questions 11.1 and 11.2) so obviously you will need to study one or two topics in detail.

Sometimes a question will be on a particular area, e.g. schools (questions 11.3–11.6), simulation (questions 11.7), science and engineering (questions 11.8 and 11.9), libraries (question 11.10).

Outline answers are given for each of these.

11.2 Worked Example — A Doctors' Surgery

For any typical computer application you should know:

(a) The general purpose of the application.
(b) Why computerisation was desirable.
(c) The computer system and its role.
(d) The data-capture methods used and why.
(e) The files used and the data kept on them.
(f) The backing store used and why.
(g) The programs and details of the computer operations carried out.
(h) The computer output, its format and how it is used.

We will use a doctors' surgery to answer this question.

(a) The General Purpose of the Application:

The computer is used to maintain a patients file, with details of each patient held in one record.

(b) Why Computerisation Was Desirable

- To maintain and update thousands of patients records.
- To speed up the retrieval of information about a patient.
- To improve the accuracy of records held.
- To improve the efficiency and quality of service.

A manual system would involve keeping a card index with a card for each patient.

NB: For any given application, it is helpful to know how a manual system would work and its drawbacks, so that you can make useful comparisons with the computer system.

(c) The Computer System and its Role

The size and nature of the computer system will depend on (amongst other things):

- Cost.
- Number of users.
- Storage requirements.
- Number of computer applications run.

A small-business microcomputer system should be adequate for a surgery. A typical configuration might be:

- Microcomputer 128 K RAM.
  – with an option to network extra terminals.
- Dual disk drive.
- Floppy disks (or Winchester disk).
- Quality printer.

For a small surgery, a disk-drive and floppy disks would probably suffice, although a larger practice, with several doctors, might warrant a Winchester-disk based system with on-line terminals in each doctor's office, as well as reception (Fig. 11.1).

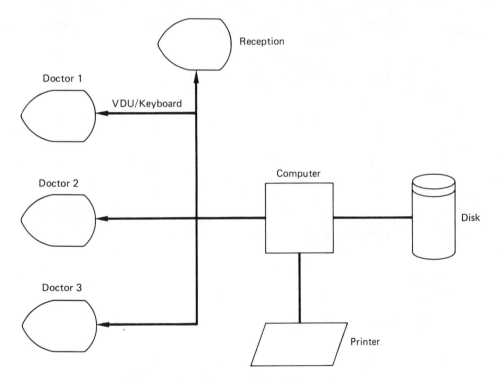

Figure 11.1 A typical computer configuration for a dotor's practice.

(d) The Data-capture Methods Used, And Why

Data capture refers to the collection and recording of data for computer use.
The patient record card will be filled out by entering name, address, telephone

number, date of last visit, date of birth, sex, occupation, doctor, NHS number, family group and brief medical history. This can be done by the doctor and/or receptionist. The patient details are read from the card and are then keyed into an on-line terminal (keyboard plus VDU) in a 'fill in the blanks' operation by the receptionist.

The patient card can then be filed for legal or archival purposes.

(i) *Data Editing/Verification/Validation*

Data editing — allows the user to inspect and alter the program or data.

Verification — This is the act of checking that the data entered is the same as the data stored, e.g. a visual check of a patient's card with the information recorded on the computer record.

Validation is used to detect any data which is inaccurate, incomplete or unreasonable. For example:

- Blood type (A or O or B etc.).
- Pulse rate (range test).
- Date of birth (Days not $>$ 31; Month not $>$ 12, etc.)

(e) The Files Used and the Data Kept on Them

In the doctor's application the patient master file will be stored on magnetic disk using direct organisation. An index could be used to record the location of each record in the file.

Periodically, duplicate files will be taken and stored in a safe place on magnetic or floppy disks. They are used for back-up purposes if the main file is lost or destroyed in any way.

Estimated storage capacity : patient file
e.g. 5000 patients × 100 characters per record = $\frac{1}{2}$ Mb.

(f) The Backing Store Used and Why

Data contained in main memory will be passed to some storage device or medium. Backing store is secondary storage which keeps the programs and files not currently in use.

A disk-based system will be needed by the surgery because the doctor will require *direct-access* to an individual patient's record. Using a serial medium (e.g. magnetic tape) would involve a time-wasting search for the appropriate record.

(g) The Programs and the Details of the Computer Operations Carried Out

Most data processing will involve the following operations:

Sorting — Sorting puts data items or records into a predetermined sequence, e.g. an alphabetical list of patients.

Classifying — Classifying places data elements into categories to help understanding, so that people can plan and make decisions. For example, the doctor may have to contact all patients suffering from a particular illness, e.g. diabetes, or people with a rare blood group, etc. The computer can classify patients accordingly and, when necessary, print out the appropriate list.

Summarising — This operation produces totals so that useful statistical information may be extracted. Monthly summary reports, e.g. number of patients examined, etc. can be printed and used for resource planning.

Arithmetic and logical operations — The computer can also be used for arithmetic or logical manipulation of the data. For example, if the surgery set up a check-up procedure for 'heart' patients, the computer can determine when a given time period has elapsed and issue reminder notices to the appropriate people.

Retrieving — This is the opposite of storing. It entails finding a record in store, accessing it and moving it to computer main memory, e.g. retrieving a particular patient's record for terminal display. A record *key* is normally used for speedy retrieval.

Any data about the patient which has changed since the last visit can be entered as well as the 'date of the last visit' field. This on-line procedure greatly speeds up the process compared with a manual system.

In sum, a program, or suite of programs, will be needed to maintain the patient file and perform various operations such as sort/classify/retrieve/summarise on it.

Additional software may also be available to help produce such things as reminder letters for despatch to patients, address labels for correspondence, and appointment diaries for each doctor.

(h) The Computer Output, its Format and How it is Used

Information can be presented in the form of:

- Printed reports.
- Screen displays
- Graphics.
- And even speech output.

In the doctors' surgery system, output might be:

- *Screen display* — Of a patient's record for information retrieval and updating.
- *Printed reports/lists* —
  - Monthly summaries of resource use for planning and control.
  - List of house calls.
  - Appointments diary.
- *Printed labels/letters* —
  - Address labels for correspondence.
  - Personalised standard letters, e.g. reminder letters for check-ups, vaccinations or for patients at risk.

Of course, other applications can be added to the system described as need and experience develop, e.g.:

- Payroll and financial control.
- Prescription and safety checks.

Drugs that are issued in repeat prescriptions to particular patients can be monitored and warnings of potential cross-reactions given. Analysis could be by age/sex group or for a specific group of drugs.

11.3 Worked Example — The Electronic Office

Offices are important. Information handling is reckoned to involve over one-third of the UK workforce and one-half of an organisation's running costs. Furthermore, it is estimated that the average manager spends 80% of the time communicating in some way and that 20-30% of time is wasted in looking for information. To make matters worse, 1-5% of information is misfiled.

So labour-intensive office life has been rightly seen as a prime target for *IT* (Information Technology). But there are no 'quick fix' solutions to the office productivity problem. Buying an expensive piece of office automation (like a word processor), sacking several secretaries and demanding more from the rest is a sure way to fail. In fact, concentrating on clerical workers, particularly secretaries, misses the point.

Typing is only a small part (about 15%) of a secretary's job; far more important is the general administration (around 30%) he or she performs (Fig. 11.2).

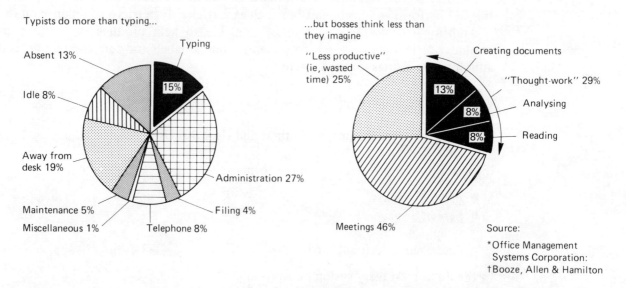

Figure 11.2 Office productivity.

Though great strides have been made to churn out more paper more quickly (and IT was supposed to save trees?!) few people have begun to think about trying to improve the quality of information printed on it, or to find out whether others bother to read it.

So to improve office productivity we need to:

● Reduce the flow of paper, aiming ultimately to abolish it (can you think of reasons to keep paper?).
● Ensure that data is captured (keyed in) only once.

Capturing data is expensive, storing/retrieving data is relatively cheap. The data will be accurate and up to date if held only once in a database:

● Concentrate on executives/managers.
● Managers waste time (Fig. 11.2).
● They are expensive (about 75% of office costs).
● Bosses are far less productive than most of them assume (nearly half their time is spent in meetings).

So better organisation, in terms of prepared agendas, agreed discipline, restricted numbers, etc. is needed to lessen such time-consuming tasks and allow more 'think time'.

- Prepare for the electronic office.

  Aim for multifunction workstations on every desk (in fact IBM reckons that one for every three workers will do).

These workstations will consist of a keyboard, VDU, disk drive and printer (maybe voice I/0 and touch-screen facilities in the future) and permit easy access to databases and therefore the storage/retrieval of information — the preparation, editing and output of reports as well as the usual clever analytical tricks which computers are renowned for. Linked workstations facilitate electronic messaging and mail as well as teleconferencing. (The latter has been seen by some as an alternative to business travel but it is hard to put a value on personal contact.)

The main function of the office is information handling, and IT offers a single solution to replace old working methods. The combination of computing and communications means that information (voice, text, picture or data) can be stored, retrieved, displayed and communicated entirely in electronic form.

(a) Word Processing (WP)

Q. (a) What is word processing (WP)?

(b) List some typical uses.

(c) Indicate the main facilities offered by WP software.

(d) What are the hardware requirements for a WP system? Distinguish between stand-alone and shared-resource configurations.

(e) How does WP affect the people in an organisation?

A. (a) Probably the most widespread use of computing, certainly in the office, is word processing (WP). In essence, WP is the use of a computer-based system to do all of the tasks (and more) that a typewriter usually does. The production of letters and other similar documents is a costly office activity. Electronic typewriters (which, incidently, can be linked up with WP systems) helped to obtain speedier and more consistent results; however, a great deal of a typist's time is still spent making corrections and redrafting documents.

WP is essentially a special application of the editing facility available on computers. This facility (text editing) allows alteration or correction of the text without the need for complete retyping because programs and data to be amended can be held in the computer's memory whilst the changes are being made.

Its use produces far greater productivity in that it restricts the need for retyping to error corrections and author changes. Furthermore, it allows typists to type at full speed secure in the knowledge that any errors can be easily put right. Standard letters or paragraphs can be called from store and merged with individual customer or client details to make up a 'personal' quality letter — quickly produced error free, stylish and 'clean' (Fig. 11.3).

(b) Typical uses of WP include the storage and/or production of:

- Standard letters.
- Standard documents, e.g. contracts with the use of pre-defined paragraphs and the inclusion of variables, e.g. names.
- Staff lists, price lists, overdue notices.
- Regularly updated reports and manuals.
- One-off documents and short memos.

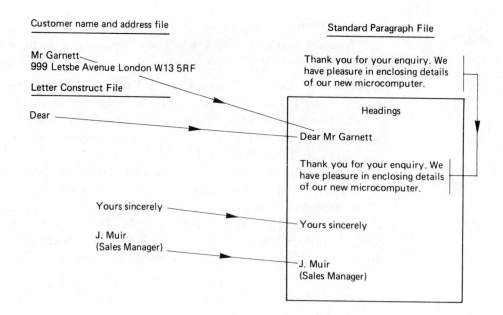

Customer name and address file

Mr Garnett
999 Letsbe Avenue London W13 5RF

Letter Construct File

Dear

Yours sincerely

J. Muir
(Sales Manager)

Standard Paragraph File

Thank you for your enquiry. We
have pleasure in enclosing details
of our new microcomputer.

Headings

Dear Mr Garnett

Thank you for your enquiry. We
have pleasure in enclosing details
of our new microcomputer.

Yours sincerely

J. Muir
(Sales Manager)

Figure 11.3 Constructing a letter.

(i) *WP Software*

Software can come either 'bundled' (as part of a WP system) or separate. It can be in the form of a program on disc or as an add-on ROM chip (e.g. WORD-WISE for the BBC micro).

WP packages (the best-known and best-selling of which is WORDSTAR) are sold at various levels of sophistication and it is important to check what they offer and which operating system they run with, to ensure that your computer can use them.

A. (c) The main facilities of a WP system can be categorised as in Table 11.1

A. (d) *WP Configurations – basic components*

The basic components of a WP system are the same as any other computer:

● A computer, with a keyboard and screen (VDU).
● A printer.
● Backing store, usually a disk drive.

Printers have to match the quality of good typewriter copy, particularly for external use (e.g. letters to customers), and the market tends to be dominated by quality daisywheel printers.

Keyboards have to be professional (i.e. typewriter) size and often feature user-programmable and special keys for ease of use and routine entries.

Screens (VDUs) are offered in a range of sizes (usually large for constant use), colours (green, brown etc.) and have tilt/swivel features. Highlight tricks such as black on white are also available.

Backing store tends to be disk (either floppy or hard) for two reasons: words take up a lot of space and businesses need to 'access' data quickly. Such demands rule out tape systems for WP. Floppies are usually seen in small-business systems and a single disk can now hold up to 1 Mb of data (about 750 pages of output). Hard disks are more expensive but have a much greater capacity. They are also more reliable than floppy disks because they are contained in sealed, dust-free units.

Table 11.1 Main facilities of a WP system

Main facilities	*Examples*
Input Fast, easy entry	HELP menus Automatic underlining Decimal tabulation (aligning numbers)
Reduces problems of text layout	Forms design Indentation Page length control (page breaks) Page numbering Centring Titles/headings Line length/word-division (at the end of line) Bottom, top, left, right margins/justification Automatic paragraphing
Spelling checker (on the more sophisticated systems)	Phrase recall Thesaurus Check against 'known' words in store
Arithmetic facilities	Add, subtract, divide, multiply, etc.
Storage Documents are usually stored on floppy or hard disk for easy retrieval, amendment and/or printing	Automatic saving Back-up Records management Command file capability
Editing Modification of text	Add/delete/correct/'cut and paste' Search and replace (global or selective), e.g. find every occurrence of *recieve* and change to *receive* Phonetic search 'nearest fit' Full-screen cursor control
Use of stored text with keyed text to create document	Merge text from another source Select from files
Output Quality printed text Print format handling	Autocopy Multiple printing Several 'top' copies No sign of correction fluid Part document printing Proportional character spacing Variable line spacing
Automatic paper-handling functions	Spooling-background printing Automatic single sheet feed Bold type

WP configurations vary from general-purpose micro systems to dedicated systems. The differences can be measured in terms of cost, support/training and the level of sophistication. A small stand-alone system based upon a home computer can cost under £1000 (including software) whereas a dedicated business system, supporting a large number of workstations, can cost well over £10 000. Shared-resource systems (Fig. 11.4) usually consist of several intelligent terminals using the extra power and storage of the shared minicomputer. Using the mini's communications facilities

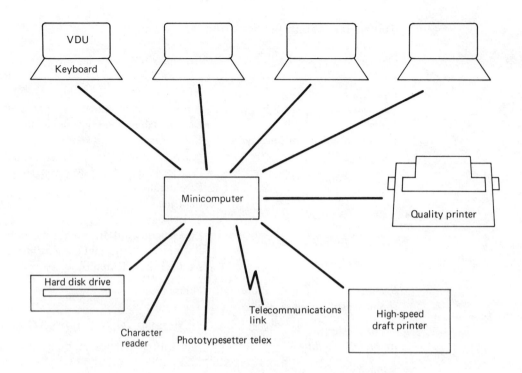

Figure 11.4 Shared-resource configuration.

access can be gained to timesharing services and data networks, so enhancing the electronic office capability.

A. (e) *Effect on People and the organisation*

WP may change working relationships. However, traditional male reluctance to learn keyboard skills or lose status may slow organisation change. Most typists agree that a move to WP leads to an increase in job satisfaction although there may be a danger that typists will be pooled and managers lose the status of having a personal secretary.

11.4 Driver and Vehicle Licensing Centre (DVLC) Swansea

Road vehicles in Great Britain must have a registration number and licence (tax disc).

Drivers must hold a driving licence to ensure that they are medically fit, over 17 years old and not disqualified by the courts.

(a) Disadvantages of the Old Manual System of Licensing

Originally, each local authority was responsible for driver and vehicle licensing.

This meant that when the owner of a vehicle moved to a different area or sold the vehicle to someone living elsewhere the vehicle records had to be transferred from one local authority office to another. Not only was this wasteful and expensive, there were often difficulties in tracing vehicle details quickly.

Additionally, because local authorities work independently of each other, it was not difficult for a disqualified driver to get a driving licence from another local authority by making false declarations.

The growth in the numbers of vehicles and owners over the years meant that the sheer volume of data was too much to handle for a manual system.

(b) The Computer System

Hence, DVLC Swansea was set up. It is a central, computer-based system, dealing with all driver and vehicle licensing in this country.

(c) Data Collection

To get a vehicle or driving licence an application form has to be sent to DVLC. (Fig. 11.5). Page two of the form includes, amongst other things, questions on health, traffic offences etc., all of which is manually coded at DVLC in the 'official use only' section.

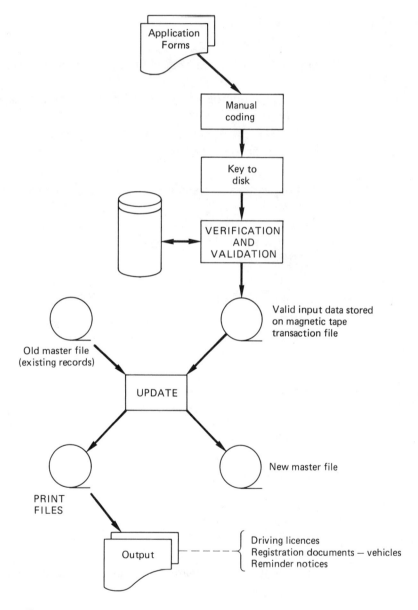

Figure 11.5 DVLC systems flow chart. Driver application procedure.

(d) Data Preparation

The information on the application form must be translated into a form that the computer can understand. Operators key in the information using VDU or teletype terminals linked to a number of small computers, where data is held on magnetic disc. This is an example of a 'key-to-disc' system. During the data-entry stage, the computer carries out a number of checks to ensure that the operator is typing in valid data. Any unchecked data is later verified (i.e. retyped) to check for errors. Further validation checks are then carried out automatically by the computer, such as a comparison between town and post-code. Any incorrect information will be overwritten and only accurate information is transferred from disk store to magnetic tape for later processing by the main computers. Information is stored in two stages so that error checks can be carried out.

Some documents, such as the reminders sent out by the centre do not have to be keyed. This is because the reminder form is printed by the computer with information coded as marks which can be read by a document reader when the form is returned.

Provided that the application form is correctly completed and the conditions are met, a driving licence will be issued.

Q. How is the driver number made up from the information entered?

A. The driver number is made up of the applicant's: (a) full name; (b) date of birth; (c) sex.
The following example shows the driver number along with the name and date of birth, which are changed to help identify the algorithm used to form the driver number.

(e) The Driver Number Algorithm (Fig. 11.6)

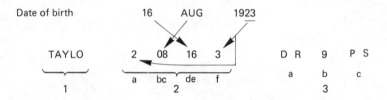

Figure 11.6 Driver number algorithm.

The sections of the driver number are as follows:

1. The surname is truncated to five characters.
2. The date of birth and sex code. This is coded from the day/month/year in the form de/bc/af. If the applicant is female then 50 is added to the month before coding.
3. (a) First two forename initials. The number 9 is used as a space-filler, if necessary.
   (b) Tie-breaker. This is usually the number 9, but if the previous sections generate a number which has been used already then the number will be set to any number working from 8 down to 1.
   (c) Check/security code.
       These last two characters are derived mathematically from the previous sections. These allow the driver number to be checked as a valid number. For security reasons the code is not the one used by DVLC.

(f) Processing and Output

The magnetic tapes containing the information from the valid application forms are then run together with the existing DVLC master files. A new, updated master file is produced and the computer also prepares magnetic tapes containing the information to be printed (the print files). The print tapes produced each day are run through high-speed printing machines which produce driving licences, vehicle registration documents and driver and vehicle licence reminders in continuous stationery form.

(g) People and DVLC

Q. List the people that might be interested in the information held by DVLC.

A.

- Police — for tracing suspect/stolen vehicles.
- Tax authorities to find last known address of tax evaders.
- Car manufacturers to call in cars needing safety checks.
- Insurance firms/garages — mailing lists, etc.

Q. Should these people be allowed to gain access to DVLC? How can they be stopped from doing so?

A. There is a trade-off between an individual's right to privacy and a society's right to protection, e.g. by allowing police to trace stolen cars.

Protection can be achieved by creating laws restricting the right of access to computerised data banks (The Data Protection Act).

11.5 Banking

Banks are suppliers and users of masses of information. Cheques are no more than information about the transfer of money.

Each major bank has a computer which stores its customers' accounts and usually each branch has a terminal connected to this computer. Most banks also send out a daily summary of the balances of its customers' accounts, often on microfiche. Periodically (usually monthly) each customer is sent a statement showing the balance of money in the account and the details of all transactions since the last statement.

Cheques are produced with some details printed on them in MICR characters (see section 4.7(c)(iv)). When a cheque is paid in, the amount written is also encoded in MICR by the bank clerk. The cheques are then forwarded to the Inter-Bank Clearing House where they are sorted by computer for distribution to the correct banks and for payment.

(a) Electronic Funds Transfer

Such information can be easily processed and transmitted electronically (known as electronic funds transfer (EFT)).

The trend is to link up bank branches with each other, with other banks and eventually with customers so that EFT can happen.

(b) Developments in EFT

(i) *Automated Teller Machines (ATMs)*

ATMs disburse cash automatically when a customer inserts a plastic card and types in a personal identification number (PIN code). They improve service by providing banking outside office hours and cut transaction costs. ATMs are on-line, i.e. continually linked to the bank's central computer. Every withdrawal is instantly logged on a large customer-account database. Withdrawals can be made up to a customer's credit limit. Other services offered include: instant readout of balance, cheque book or statement request and some permit the switching of funds from one account to another (e.g. from current to deposit). ATMs are now shared between several banks and the next step is to make them international.

(ii) *Home Banking*

Computer terminals in the home can be linked to a bank's central computer by telephone or cable. Hence balance enquiries, money transfers – e.g. bill payments to local shops etc. – could be made at home.

(iii) *Point of Sale (POS)*

POS will enable a customer in a shop to pay for goods with an electronic plastic card which, linked to the bank's computer via a terminal in the shop, will instantly check the customer's credit limit and if all right, debit the bank account. Again no paper need change hands.

(iv) *Problems with EFT*

Standards – There is a need for standards; for example, plastic cards are currently read by different ATMs in different ways. Some use magnetic strips and some use optical readers.

Reliability – What use is any EFT system if it fails to work? Fortunately, great technical advances have been made and, for example, ATMs are now robust, reliable and working properly for a much greater proportion of the time.

Database integration – With home banking, for example, customers want access to all their accounts. To date, separate accounts have been stored on separate files, so there is a need to group them together in a database.

Security and privacy – Already lots of money has been embezzled by computer fraud. Similarly, 'secret' information on accounts is potentially available to others. No system will ever be perfect but more emphasis is being put on database security.

Acceptance – Although acceptance of ATMs by customers has been good (witness the queues during banking hours) there is still a general question of whether people will take to a paperless (if not cashless) world.

11.6 Exercises

Question 11.1

Describe a major data-processing application of computing that you have studied. In your answer you should make clear:

(a) The nature of the output from the system.
(b) The use to which this output is put.
(c) The nature of the inputs to the system.
(d) The method of data capture.
(e) Details of any information held on back-up store, together with the medium or media used.
(f) Why computerisation was desirable.

Represent the flow of data through the system by means of a systems flow chart (you may use any appropriate symbols).

Question 11.2

For any application of computers which you have studied:

(a) List four main objectives that the computerised system was designed to meet.
(b) Discuss briefly the success (or failure) of the system to meet these objectives.
(c) Describe the likely causes of success (or failure). (L)

Question 11.3

(a) Outline suitable computer facilities for use in schools, explaining what hardware, software and processing methods might be used.
(b) For any *two* of the following show how in one way the computer may be used to help them:

Head teacher.
Secretary.
Librarian.
Subject teacher.
Teacher in charge of 'tuck shop'. (AEB)

Question 11.4

A school has a microcomputer which is used:

 (i) In the teaching of Computing Studies.
 (ii) In the teaching of other subjects, e.g. simulating and displaying events in Science or Geography, or information retrieval in History.
(iii) For school administration by the school secretary, e.g. keeping a record of all the pupils in the school.

Below is a list of features of the computer system. For each one, explain which of the three uses above will be affected favourably or adversely by the feature.
(a) The system has a maximum of 32 K 8-bit bytes of usable RAM.
(b) The system uses cassette storage and has no discs.
(c) The system has an assembler.
(d) The high-level language interpreter produces poor error messages.
(e) The visual display unit is a 12 inch black-and-white television.
(f) The printer produces a poor-quality dot matrix output rather than typewriter quality printing. (L)

Question 11.5

Write an essay on the use of computers in schools. Include in your answer:

(a) The various application areas.
(b) The hardware and software components.

(c) The benefits.

(d) The training that would be required by both staff and students in order to use the system. (OLE)

Question 11.6

A *school* has a disk-based microcomputer system.
Suggest applications in each of the following categories:

(a) School administration.
(b) Teaching in disciplines other than computer studies.
(c) Teaching slow learners.

Question 11.7

Real-life situations are often *simulated* using a computer. Choose a simulation from science, business or commerce. Explain that simulation in detail, showing:

The purpose of it.
How it operates.
Who uses it.
Why it is used.
The disadvantages of it. (AEB)

Question 11.8

'There are many stages in any modern engineering project. Whether it is a road, a bridge, a motor car or a computer there are at least three stages where computers can help the engineers – in the planning, in the design and in the construction itself.' (*Living With Computers* – Blakeley & Lewis)

Show how computers could help architects and engineers in the choice of the site, the design and construction of a school, explaining each of the following stages;

Planning and surveying.
School design.
Testing materials used in construction.
School construction.

In each case refer to the hardware used and explain any advantages and disadvantages in using that hardware. (AEB)

Question 11.9

Using computers, it is possible to automate the running of a railway system.

(a) Which operations do you consider should be controlled by computer and why?
(b) Which operations should be carried out by people and why?
(c) What advantages and disadvantages might an automated system have for:

(i) The passengers?
(ii) The non-managerial railway staff?
(iii) The railway management?

Question 11.10

A local County Library Service has decided to install a computer system. It decides on an On-line Real-time system with terminals in each of the 15 branch libraries linked to the main-frame at Library Headquarters. The system is designed to control lending and borrowing as well as book re-ordering and receiving.

(a) State what hardware would be suitable in each branch library and say why.
(b) Explain suitable methods of collecting data in the following situations:
  (i) When a customer borrows a book.
  (ii) When a book is returned.
  (iii) When a new book is introduced to a branch library.

(c) State three files that would be needed at headquarters, indicating their contents and the purpose they serve.
(d) Give two advantages of this system over a manual system for:
  (i) Customers using the library.
  (ii) Running the County Library Service.   (AEB)

Question 11.11

Each of the following in their jobs collects and stores data. Choose *one* and answer the questions below.

Cartoonists.
Detectives in a murder hunt.
Pharmacists in a large hospital.

(a) What aspects of the job would be assisted by the use of a computer?
(b) What data is collected and how can it be stored without a computer?
(c) If the job was computerised, suggest what hardware would be suitable for data capture and storage.
(d) Choose one aspect of the job and draw a system flow chart to show data capture, processing and information output.   (AEB)

Question 11.12

For each of the applications stated below, say whether the method or processing would be *off-line, on-line, real-time*. In each case explain one reason for your choice.

(a) A Water Authority's flood warning system.
(b) A branch of a large clothing firm using Kimball tags.
(c) One of a series of car components warehouses linked to the head office by terminal.
                    (AEB)

11.7 Answers and Hints on Solutions

11.1   See text – doctors' surgery or DVLC examples.

11.2   (a)   DVLC objectives:

- To reduce administration costs.
- To reduce the delay in issuing licences.
- To trace details of vehicles more quickly.
- To ensure that drivers are qualified.

(b) and (c)
The original system was badly planned, too big and the personnel requirements were wrongly predicted. Certain parts of the system didn't work

and had to be suspended until improvements were made. After 2 years or more of 'teething troubles' the system is now operating reasonably well in terms of the objectives laid down in (a).

11.3 (a) and (b)   Microcomputers (perhaps networked).
Interactive processing, shared printer, disk drive.
Software — applications packages for:

- Timetabling and other resourcing (head teacher).
- Stock control and accounting (tuck-shop teacher).
- Word processing (secretary, subject teacher).

11.4 (a) The small RAM size will have an adverse effect where programs take up a lot of memory, e.g. in graphics or simulation applications in science, etc.

(b) This will have an adverse effect on all applications which need direct access, e.g. the school secretary may want the record of an individual pupil. With cassette storage a search is necessary.

(c) An assembler translates language into machine code; this may be an advantage in teaching Computer Studies, where a low-level language (assembly) is used to teach programming, or to demonstrate the nature and meaning of machine code.

(d) Poor error messages are annoying to anyone, but will be particularly confusing to a non-expert, e.g. the history or geography teacher.

(e) This display will hinder everyone, but prevents colour output — a particular disadvantage in science and geography demonstrations.

(f) Poor output will affect school administration as the pupil records will be produced by printer.

11.5 (a) Some application areas:

- Timetabling and resource management.
- Student records and performance.
- Computer-assisted learning. (In-class demonstration packages.)
- Word processing.

(b) Microcomputer(s), disk drive, printer, applications packages.
(c) Benefits — speed, cost-effectiveness, accuracy.
(d) Training (students):

- Keyboard familiarity.
- Using packages.
- Importance of correct data input.

   Staff:

- As above.
- Use of disk drive and printer, perhaps some programming knowledge.

11.6 (a) Monitoring student records or exam entries.
(b) Information retrieval, e.g. history dates.
(c) Graded spelling exercises, timed arithmetic tests with percentage success rate.

11.7 Simulation is a method of studying the behaviour of a system by using a computer-based model of it.

Purpose – Design analysis, reduce cost and time taken to design vehicles.

How it operates – Engineers use a screen and light pen or keyboard to introduce design changes etc. and can work in 3–D. Design criteria – such as weight, safety and aero-dynamism – can be tested on screen using powerful computer techniques. It is simple and quick to redraft and improve designs.

Who uses it – Designer, to test loads, stresses, etc. Engineers, for tooling and jig information. Outside suppliers, to check on specifications. Quality controllers, use data to monitor manufacturing processes and quality.

Why it is used – No need to use costly prototypes. You do not have to crash real cars to test their safety.

Disadvantages – People are dubious about model-based testing. Hence destructive tests are often performed on 'the real thing' (in this case a car) to prove its capabilities to sceptics.

11.8   *Planning and surveying* – Information storage. By storing past designs and data on disk, architects can build up libraries of easily accessible information. In theory, computers should eventually be able to take over the job of making sure that building designs conform to local building codes.

School design – Computers can quickly translate schematic plans into realistic drawings of buildings. A 3–D model of a building can be stored in memory, called up, rotated or enlarged according to the designer's wishes. Drawing and modifying schematic plans is quick and easy by computer. This is important for architects. For example, designs for the new terminal at London's Heathrow Airport required 1500 plans, each of which went through an average of ten changes and several modified versions.

Testing materials used in construction – Computer modelling can help designers learn how their buildings will react to stresses such as high winds. This saves a lot of time and money that would otherwise have to be spent on building and testing model structures.

School construction – As a designer plans a building, the computer can keep track of how many doors, window panes and tons of cement he has to put into it. It can also draw up construction schedules using Network (Critical Path) Analysis. And all this helps to find overall costs and examine possible cost savings. A complete Computer Aided Design (CAD) system is still very expensive, but prices are falling.

11.9   (a)   By computer:

- Signalling, breaking – safety.
- Tickets – calculated and printed, useful for sales analysis.
- Timetable production systems.
- Typesetting – printing timetables.
- Scheduling locomotives, rolling stock and train crews.
- Payroll and accountancy, standard routine systems, management information.
- Stock control.
- Engineering systems – factory scheduling, bridge design, track maintenance, etc.
- Reservations.

(b) By people:

- Customer 'services'
- Driver for passenger confidence.

(c)   (i)   Advantage — a cheaper, more efficient service.
Disadvantage — breakdowns cause greater disruption?

    (ii)   Advantage — more interesting jobs, satisfaction of a better service.
Disadvantages — fewer jobs, less room for initiative.

  (iii)   Advantage — better for planning and control.
Disadvantage — initial costs high, higher qualifications needed. Work-force resentment.

11.10   (a)   A light-pen system connected to the computer can be used to read the book or borrower number. Alternatively (or supplementary) to this a VDU terminal could be used.

  (b)   (i)   Librarian records book and borrower number with light pen and stamps return date in book.

    (ii)   Librarian records returned book number using light pen; can be checked against reserved list, etc.

  (iii)   Librarian types in book number/details once a week (or according to demand) when new book arrives.

  (c)

LOANS FILE

Book number, borrower number, date issued, issue branch, renewal count, overdue status. Purpose: to record the books out on loan. The loan file will be updated as users borrow or return books. It can be used to flag overdue books so that reminder notices can be sent. Reserved books could be flagged. The popularity of each book can be found from its renewal count.

BORROWERS' FILE

Borrower number, name/address, joining date, details (age, sex, etc.), class of borrower (child, OAP, etc.). Purpose: to record the people using the library. The borrowers' file will be updated when people join or leave the library. Changes in the details about the borrowers, e.g. name or address, will also require updating of the file.

BOOKS FILE

Book number, author/title, date of purchase, price, ISBN. Purpose: to record the books held in stock. The book file will be updated as books are added or removed from stock.

(d) Two advantages for:

  (i) Customers:

- File interrogation — a book can be traced very quickly.
- A faster 'check-out' service.

  (ii) Running the library:

- Less time filling in cards and searching files.
- Lower administrative costs.

11.11 *Detectives in a murder hunt*

(a) Rapid access of accurate, up-to-date information.
Matching clues (fingerprints, stolen vehicles, descriptions, etc.) with files.

(b) Evidence: from witnesses, suspects, at the scene of the crime.
Stored in card index.

(c) Standard links into the Police National Computer (PNC) so that reference can be made to vehicle, owner, name and fingerprint databases.
NB: The Automatic Fingerprint Recognition system uses a camera to take a digitised picture of a fingerprint at the scene of the crime.

(d) For the local processing on the job itself, a microcomputer with floppy disk backing store, for direct access, and a printer would probably do, depending on the scale of the hunt. This intelligent terminal will be situated in the police station and linked to the PNC at Hendon.

For example: policemen in local station enters suspect vehicle registration number at terminal to the PNC at Hendon (Fig. 11.7).

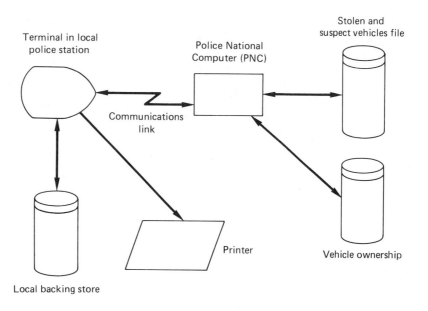

Figure 11.7 Solution 11.11(d) – system flow chart: police.

The stolen and suspect vehicle file is searched for a match or near match and a listing of vehicle descriptions are sent back to appear on the VDU screen. If these are promising, the policemen can request a search of the vehicle owner's file to establish details such as name and address. Again, the list – this time of suspects – can be displayed on the VDU. If necessary, it can be 'dumped' onto the printer for hard copy.

11.12 (a) *Real-time* systems work quickly enough to affect the outcome, i.e. input data is supplied to the computer continuously (or very often). Output is available almost immediately – to control a process or whatever. Hence monitoring water levels would be real time, tripping off the alarm if warning limits were exceeded.

(b) *Off-line* processing does not take place under the control of the CPU, i.e. devices are not directly connected to the CPU. The Kimball tag (a small ticket containing coded information) is detached from a garment on purchase, stored with others on the shop counter and sent, at the end of the day, for computer processing. The tags are used mainly for stock control.

(c) *On-line* processing takes place directly under the control of the CPU whilst the user is connected. An on-line processing system obviously includes a direct link between the user and the computer. Warehouse terminals connected directly via telephone lines to head-office computer are on-line.

12 An Introduction to Systems Analysis

12.1 What is a System?

A system consists of inputs, processes, files (storage) and outputs and is designed to fulfil some useful purpose.

Systems vary in levels of complexity, ranging from simple applications, e.g. stock control, to a complete set of systems for an organisation, known as a Management Information System. A system that has been converted to computer processing is referred to as a computer application and an integrated set of such systems is known as a computer-based management information system (CBMIS).

Development of a CBMIS is a complex process and because of this systems have been developed bit by bit. Common business applications, e.g. payroll, were designed and developed independently. However, there is now a growing acknowledgement that systems are interrelated and databases are being designed that are useful for several computer applications, e.g. the payroll would become a subsystem of the organisation's accounting system and personnel system, as payroll data is shared by both. This increase in the scope and complexity of systems has led to higher development costs and highlights the need for effective systems analysis.

(a) What is Systems Analysis?

Systems analysis is an all-embracing term for a process which covers not only the study and analysis of systems but also the design and implementation of new and better ones. An alternative phrase which is often used to describe the same function is 'systems development'. The improvement of a business system now usually implies the use of a computer in some way.

(b) Who is a Systems Analyst?

The systems analyst is a person who applies the techniques and procedures of systems analysis and, as such, plays an important role in the application of computers. He or she must maintain close contact with management and staff during systems development, not least because this may help to overcome resistance to change.

12.2 An Approach to Systems Analysis

There are obviously many ways of developing a computer-based business system. Obviously the size and complexity of the task will determine the time, money and effort to be spent on the development of a new system. Small businesses will probably not have the resources to afford outside experts or tailor-made programs but this does not devalue systems analysis as a way of thinking. For example, it can help managers to identify requirements and search for ready-made systems.

Structured systems analysis is a process which is based on several principles, as follows:

- There are a number of distinct stages which must be passed through.
- Each stage consists of a number of tasks.
- There are checkpoints at which progress is assessed.
- Special techniques are used to aid analysis.
- Accurate and detailed documentation is kept to ensure that everyone has a common set of information.
- Careful planning is an essential prerequisite.

12.3 Stages of Systems Analysis

Q. What are the stages of systems analysis, assuming that a computer system is finally introduced?

A. Structured systems analysis consists of several steps collectively known as the systems life cycle. No one standard set of stages exists, but commonly the following are used:

1. Project selection and feasibility study.
2. Systems study and analysis.
3. Systems design.
4. Programming.
5. Implementation.
6. Control and review.

Fig. 12.1 shows the stages of systems analysis together with checkpoints (the decision diamonds). The diagram implies that the steps are sequential, but in practice some of the tasks may be carried out at the same time.

Fig. 12.1 is intended to be a framework for development. The checkpoints are opportunities to review, refine or even cancel projects, although cancellation is unlikely during the later stages. For example, if the project gets as far as the programming stage and problems and delays arise, a revamp of the design work may be necessary as well as reprogramming (as the branch arrows indicate on the diagram) but a return to step 1 is unlikely, not least because of the time and money already committed.

Q. Outline the work in each of the stages of systems analysis.

A. This is as follows (a–f).

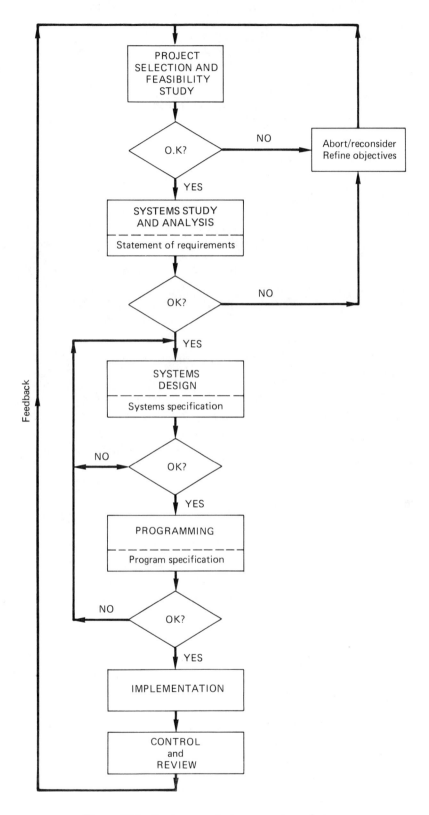

Figure 12.1 Systems analysis — overview of stages.

(a) Stage 1 – Project Selection and Feasibility Study

This stage can be subdivided into the following tasks:

- Decide the criteria for selecting a project.
- Set up and formulate a steering committee to monitor project progress.
- Involve top management and all user departments to gain their support and participation.
- Prepare an assignment brief.
  This should give a clear definition of the problem and set objectives in terms of reference for the feasibility study.
- Feasibility study –.
  This is a preliminary survey to determine whether a project should proceed (in American jargon a 'go/no-go' decision). It is usually conducted quickly and in broad terms but must be sufficiently detailed for management (the steering committee) to draw proper conclusions.
  The study will culminate in a report which should include:

  - Recommendations.
  - Options considered.
  - Economic justification for the choice (cost–benefit analysis).
  - Use of investment appraisal techniques.
  - Resource implications on staff, premises, etc.
  - Development plans and timetable for introduction.

  A feasibility study can screen out bad ideas such as a scheme which is technically possible but too expensive to implement. The project will, therefore, be rejected or the objectives redefined. If an idea is acceptable to the steering committee a written go-ahead should be given to proceed with the next stage, the systems study.

(b) Stage 2 – Systems Study and Analysis

This stage covers a review of the existing system leading to a design specification for a new system. It is a detailed study of current practices, files, documents, working methods, etc. from which can spring ideas for new systems. This is based on the notion that you can't improve a system until you understand it and what it's supposed to do.

The tasks falling within this stage are as follows:

- Define and identify the objectives of the system.
- Establish sources and types of information.
- Decide on the method and collect data. Fact-finding techniques include:
  - Interviewing.
  - Questionnaires.
  - Observations.
  - Documentation study.

- Record, store, retrieve information.
- Process, adapt and present information.
  This involves *documenting the existing system* and various charts and techniques are used to help understanding and presentation; e.g. various flow charts, decision tables, data-flow diagrams, input/output/file descriptions, procedure and organisation charts.
- Analyse information.

The techniques/charts used in the previous tasks should help in the analysis stage which is essentially concerned with interpreting information and the critical appraisal of the system. It includes the following subtasks:

- The critical assessment of performance: are the systems objectives valid; are they being met?
- The identification of key activities and interrelationships.
- The identification of strengths and weaknesses.
  What opportunities and constraints are there?
- The establishment of resource use.

In general, Kipling's six honest-serving men — who, what, why, when, where, how — should be used at the analysis stage!

- Statement of requirements (SOR).

The outcome of this stage should be a written report prepared jointly by the user(s) and analyst, submitted for management approval and, therefore, written in business terms. It should include:

- Criticisms of the existing system.
- The findings of the analysis stage and how the system can be improved.
- The objectives of the proposed system.
- A design specification, including main interfaces with other systems.
- Constraints and sample outputs.
- User responsibilities.
- An update of the cost–benefit analysis and development plan and timetable for introduction.

Again the SOR should be formally accepted in writing. It gives the steering committee a first opportunity to halt or redefine actual development work (as opposed to preliminary investigations).

(c) Stage 3 — Systems Design

The systems-design stage is essentially a process of moving from a general outline to a detailed final product. The designer usually works backwards from outputs to produce inputs (documents, files) and procedures leading to a *'systems specification'* which will be presented on standard forms. The specification should:

- Provide a basis for agreement and a source of reference between management users and analyst.
- Serve as a 'blueprint' for the specifications of computer programs, dialogues and manual procedures within the system.

The systems specification will be formally presented to the steering committee (and the programmers if accepted) and as such is often structured along the following lines:

- *Introduction* — Including aims of the system.
- *General description* — Input/output documents and explanations covering sources, purposes, frequency, volumes and an overall outline systems flow chart.
- *Detailed description* — This expands upon the last section and is designed for users. It includes outline flow charts for each part of the system and descriptions of any dialogues between man and machine and any manual procedures for data capture, processing and distribution of output. System timings and schedules for routines and jobs could also be included.

- *Input specifications* − Formal presentation of all source documents plus samples.
- *Control and Audit considerations* − Detailed information on coding systems, batching control totals, reconciliation and accuracy checks and error handling.
- *File specifications* − Print-outs, other outputs (e.g. invoices) and procedures for handling them.
- *Processing specifications* − Description of processing for each procedure from data capture to summary output, with flow charts and decision tables.
- *Development of test and conversion plans.*

Additionally, the analyst should begin to prepare user manuals and organise staff training. Both are complex and lengthy tasks and must be planned and developed as soon as is feasible.

(d) Stage 4 − Programming (See Also Chapters 9 and 10)

This stage can often be difficult and time consuming because the design has gradually to be put into practice. Programming is a logical progression from the systems specification. Indeed programmers should be involved at the design stage whenever possible. See Chapter 9 for programming tasks.

    NB: There is increasing availability and use of ready-made applications packages which, if appropriate, can save time and money on programming.

(e) Stage 5 − Implementation

This stage involves the practical work of transferring the systems design, suite of programs and database into a working system. It begins when the new system comes on stream (perhaps when the hardware contract is placed) and ends when the old system is closed down. As problems tend to be human rather than technical at this stage it must be carefully planned and is the responsibility of management.

The tasks in the implementation stage are:

- *Project management* − The planning and scheduling of resources, staff, equipment, etc. Budgeting and network analysis techniques are used to determine times and costs.
- *Staff training and education*:
  - Should not interrupt flow of work.
  - Need for good courses and manuals.
- *File conversion* − Reformating files for the new system.
- *Security*:
  - Controls.
  - Standby arrangements.
- *Documentation check*:
  - Ensuring that documents are comprehensive and up to date before accepting the system.
- *Deciding on the method of change-over*:
  - How to switch from the old to the new system (Fig. 12.2).

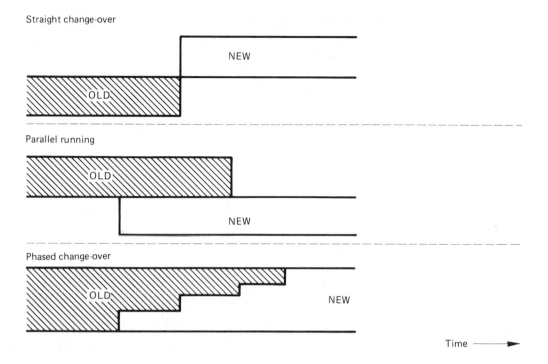

Straight change-over

NEW

OLD

Parallel running

OLD

NEW

Phased change-over

OLD

NEW

Time ⟶

Figure 12.2 Change-over methods.

(i) *Change-over*

All tests should now be complete, files converted, documents checked, training ended and all new equipment accepted. The change-over, i.e. the switch from the old to the new system, can now begin.

There are various methods of changing from the old to the new system and this depends on the nature and size of the system concerned (Fig. 12.2).

1 Straight Change-over

This is the complete replacement of the old by the new system at one go. It will usually take place during a slack period, e.g. a weekend, typically closing down the old Friday evening and opening the new Monday morning. It is a cheap, simple and clear-cut method but is risky because there is no fallback position.

It tends to be used when:

- Users have previous experience of computerisation (they are confident and well trained).
- The new system is not directly comparable with the old.
- The time-scale is tight.
- Resources are limited, e.g. no money is available to employ extra staff.
- The system is small — usually practical only in these situations.

2 Parallel Running

This is the opposite to straight change-over and includes a period when old and new run in parallel until everyone is satisfied that the new one is running success-fully and then the old can be dropped.

It is expensive to run two systems at once as this will invariably involve over-time work and the employment of extra temporary staff. It can be difficult to make direct comparisons between the results provided by both systems and even where the discrepancies are real it is not easy to persuade people that it is not the new system that is at fault. In any case more and more computer-based systems are significantly different from the manual systems they are replacing and so comparisons are not really useful.

In its favour, parallel running is a less risky method of change-over as it offers standby facilities and a useful cross-check and the opportunity for a gradual change-over.

3 Phased Change-over

This involves changing from the old to the new system in a number of stages, rather than all at once. The division may be based on:

- *Location* — e.g. for a retail shop group, one store, this month, another next month, etc.
- *Subsystem* — e.g. in a sales order processing system, order entry may be changed one period, invoicing the next.
- *Subfile* – e.g. in the Customer Account File, names beginning A–F this week, G–L the next and so on. (This method affects the approach to file conversion.)

The benefits of phased change-over are that it spreads the burden of the workload over time and presents an opportunity to learn from the problems of a previous phase.

But it is difficult to control a system working in two modes, e.g. different customers may be treated differently, getting different documents (manual or computer prepared) for the same job. Also, phased change-over has a tendency to take longer than the other methods.

4 Handover

Now that all is well (or so you hope) the system goes fully operational (it is said to 'go live') and will be formally handed over to the user.

You now have an all-singing, dancing, computer-based system!

(f) Stage 6 – Control and Review (Monitoring)

(i) *Control*

Once the system is put into action its progress will have to be monitored to see if what is actually happening matches with what should be happening. This stage involves the following tasks:

- Setting and redefining standards against which performance can be compared.
- Measuring planned against actual performances.
- Taking corrective action wherever appropriate and feasible, so that the system meets its objectives.

This stage involves regular progress meetings and is also called 'systems maintenance'.

(ii) *Review*

Periodically, usually once a year, systems are reviewed to give an overall picture of the progress made. The findings of the review can then be incorporated into subsequent systems analysis which, in theory, should be better because of the knowledge and experience gained. Review should help to provide feedback information (see feedback loop in Fig; 12.1) for the next round of decisions.

Success criteria might include whether the system produces accurate, relevant and up-to-date information at a cost-effective price.

In sum, if the objective of systems analysis is to develop a better system, is the 'right' information getting to the right person at the right time in the right place?' If so, we have the basis for better decision making and a successful organisation.

12.4 Worked Examples — Supermarket

A supermarket is considering replacing its cash registers by a point-of-sale (POS) computer-based system. Each store in the chain would purchase a minicomputer with terminals to each check-out counter, where laser-reading devices would price customers' purchases. The Stock File would be held on magnetic disk backing store and a line printer would be used to prepare management reports.

Management insists that all necessary activities for implementation of the system such as hardware selection, hardware purchase, system development and testing should be completed within 1 year. They also recommend the use of software packages wherever possible.

    (a)   Outline the potential benefits and (b) costs to the supermarket of installing such a system.

    (c)   List the stages that would be necessary to make the computer system operational within the time-scale demanded by management. Use systems charts and diagrams where applicable.

    (d)   List the possible effects on the supermarket staff of the introduction of such a system.

    (e)   List the problems that may arise once the system is operational and possible solutions to these problems.

(With acknowledgements to W. Skok.)

(a) Benefits

- *Customer service*:
  - Accuracy in pricing.
  - Itemised receipts.
  - Quicker throughout.
- *Operating improvements*:
  - Improved stock control.
  - Improved management information.
  - Improved use of shelf space.

(b) Costs

- Central computer.
- Check-out tills.
- Printer(s).
- Software.
- Personnel.
- Operating costs – reduction?

NB: Barcoding on packaging is very cheap.

(c) Implementation

Pilot store likely. Activities necessary:

- Feasibility study/hardware selection/visits to other installations.
- Ordering (and awaiting) hardware delivery.
- Employment of computer staff.
- Introduction of bar-coded labels and prices on shelves.
- Staff training – presentations, practicals.
- Installation.
- Systems development (running software, file creation).
- Systems testing.
- Publicity campaign (optional).
- Live running.

(d) Effects on staff

- Union involvement.
- Retraining.
- Cuts?
- Pay structures?
- Fear of change?
- Decline in morale?

(d) Problems and Solutions

- Dependency – what happens if system 'goes down'? Back-up facilities.
- Laser-reading device may prove faulty, causing delays at check-outs – contingency plans, revert to manual system?
- New types of fraud?
- Wrong price data – audit checks.
- Unlabelled goods – what do you do with delicatessen, fruit, etc? Separate sections in shop where goods are weighed and priced.

12.5 Choosing a Computer System

For the first-time user or when a system has to be expanded, new hardware(kit) and software may have to be selected and purchased.

(i) Which One Do I Buy?

There is a wide choice of systems available and the decision isn't made any easier by the knowledge that there are probably cheaper and better versions being developed. Remember that a system is not just a computer. It will probably include a disk drive and printer which can both be costly. The hardware, in turn, is no good without the software to run it. Some computers have a very limited range of software, so it is vital to check the software available.
Here are some guidelines to help make the choice.

- Set your budget, giving maximum/minimum prices.
- Find out which systems fall into that range and eliminate the rest.

- Write out a list of reasons as to why you are buying a computer.
- Find out which software will be most likely to satisfy your requirements (refer to your written list of reasons). NB: The manufacturer of the hardware is rarely the sole supplier of software.
- Find out which machines offer the facilities, in terms of hardware and software, that will meet your requirements.
- You should now have a shortlist of machines and the software you want to run on them.
- Find out how you will be able to get the shortlisted machines. Check on the supplier's reliability and ability to meet delivery dates. What guarantees and after-sales service (e.g. maintenance, training) are offered? This may involve contractual obligations. Ideally buy from a locally based friendly micro dealer. Next best, a shop; worst, mail order.
- Test drive the machine and read the manual. Contact local user groups, local stores — 'no hands-on experience; no hands in pocket'.
- Choose and be confident.

NB: For standard business routines e.g. word-processing and data management (filing and retrieving large amounts of information) you will almost certainly need:

- Disk storage.
- A popular computer with a standard operating system (e.g. MS-DOS) to run lots of software.
- A full-size keyboard (function or programmable keys are an asset) and a large display screen for ease of use.
- A good printer with typewriter-quality print for correspondence with suppliers and customers.

Table 13.1 is a comparison chart showing some of the factors that might influence the buying decision.

12.6 Exercises

Question 12.1

For the successful design and installation of a computerised system a systems analyst must deal with various groups of people.
Name three of these groups.

Question 12.2

A systems analyst could be responsible for the introduction of the new computerised system after the software has been written and tested and the hardware purchased. Name and describe one method of introducing this new computerised system.

Question 12.3

An organisation which has not had a computer before is having a large machine delivered in 6 months' time to help with its data processing. State four things the firm should do to prepare for the arrival of the computer. (I)

Question 12.4

What is systems analysis and design? (AEB)

Table 12.1 Comparison chart of factors influencing buying decision

Models:	1	2	3	4	5
Price (£):					
Smallest configuration					
Largest configuration					
Storage capacity:					
Floppy disc (MB)					
Hard disc (MB)					
Internal memory capacity (kb):					
Operating system					
Screen size (rows × columns)					
Business graphics					
Function keys					
Languages available:					
Basic					
Cobal					
Pascal					
Assembler					
Fortran					
PL/I					
RGP II					
Others					
Applications software:					
Timetabling					
Word Processing					
General Accounting					
School records:					
− staff					
− students					
Others					
Distribution method (e.g. mail order)					
Manufacturing base (e.g. Taiwan)					
Age of computer (since 1st prototype) (years)					
Training					
Maintenance					
Distributor					

Question 12.5

(a) List six steps in systems analysis, assuming that a computerised system is finally introduced.

(b) Describe briefly one of those steps.

Question 12.6

A school shop which sells foodstuffs, books, stationery, etc. has a manual sales systems. It is felt that it would be advantageous to computerise the system to make accounting, stock control and re-ordering more efficient.

(a) Explain each of the following steps in the design and implementation of a new system: feasibility study; system design; change-over; parallel running; pilot running; monitoring.

(b) Draw a flow chart for the daily accounting part of the system showing the steps in producing the daily statement below.

Item no.	Sold	In stock	Unit cost (£)	Total cost (£)
2341	30	150	0.25p	7.50
2349	5	50	1.25	6.25
3456	4	60	3.99	15.90
Total daily sales				55.60

(AEB)

12.7 Answers and Hints on Solutions

12.1   1, Users;
       2, managers;
       3, steering committee.

12.2   *Parallel running* — A system of change-over where the old system is run in parallel with the new for a set period of time. This is useful for comparative purposes but is costly in terms of overtime, etc.

12.3   (1) Hire and train computer staff. (2) Inform all staff of computer's impending arrival. (3) Identify applications to computerise — look for software. (4) Plan and allocate resources: room space, air conditioning, security.

12.4   Systems analysis and design (a.k.a. systems development) is the analysis of the requirements of a system. This involves a feasibility study of the potential computer involvement, a study and analysis of the existing system and the design of a new, improved one. The term can also be used to include the implementation stage as well.

12.5   (a)   1. Project selection and feasibility study.
             2. Systems study and analysis.
             3. Systems design.
             4. Programming.
             5. Implementation.
             6. Control and review (monitoring).

       (b)   See text.

12.6 (a) *Feasibility study* — A preliminary survey to see whether a scheme is economically, technically and socially justifiable, i.e. should an idea be given the go-ahead?

System design — Involves designing a new system. The systems specification will include details of inputs/files/processes/outputs/controls and should act as a 'blueprint' for writing programs, dialogues etc.

Change-over — The period of transition between the phasing out of the old system and the introduction of the new.

Parallel running — A method of change-over where the old and new systems run in parallel for a set period of time. This is useful for comparative purposes but is costly in terms of overtime, etc.

Pilot running — A method of change-over where a particular section of the organisation is chosen as a 'guinea-pig' to run the new system, e.g. a branch in a shop group.

Monitoring (a.k.a. control and review) — Is keeping a check on the performance of the computer-based system as to whether it is meeting the objectives set in terms of:

- Timing, e.g. are reports getting out on time?
- Accuracy, e.g. are the invoices correct?
- Flexibility, e.g. can the system cope with a management exception report for bad debtors?
- Cost, e.g. is the system within budget?

(b) See flow chart (Fig. 12.3).

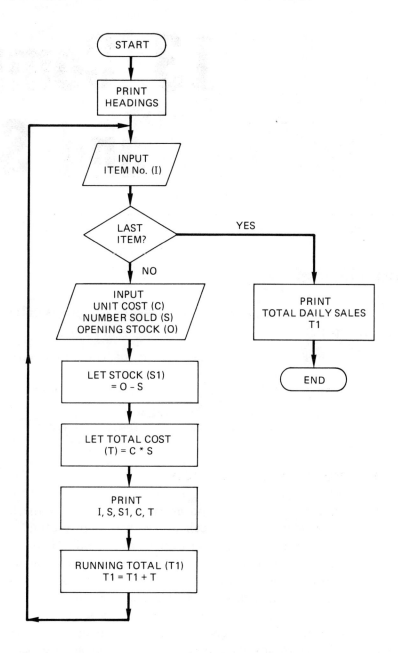

Figure 12.3 Solution 12.6(b). Flow chart to produce daily statement.

13 Computers and Society

13.1 Introduction

This chapter examines the impact of computers on people. It is divided into two parts:

- Part 1 outlines the effects of computers on employment and personal privacy.
- Part 2 looks at the types of people who work in computing.

Part 1: Computers and Society

Nothing divides opinion as much as discussing the possible long-term effects of computers and the so-called 'information revolution'.

Computing is now just about the world's largest industry and the widespread use of computers in the 'information revolution' is there for everyone to see. Information technology affects every person and organisation and the accelerating pace at which these changes are taking place has led many to question the role of computers in society: are these changes beneficial and, if so, to whom?

Fear of computers is natural; most people are frightened of the future and of change of any kind, preferring what they are used to. This fear is increased by the image of computers whose foundation is in scientific and military applications — a mysterious, sometimes evil world — which has been enhanced by books and films on 'master' computers. But computers are tools to help us; it is our choice how we use them and there is no reason why they shouldn't be 'servants', complementary to our skills and needs.

Two causes for concern are worthy of closer attention. They are:

- Effects on employment.
- Protection of privacy.

13.2 Effects on Employment

Will the microchip throw millions out of work or help create wealth which in turn will provide the spending power to generate new service, leisure and education industries in the 'post-industrial' world?

266

(a) Computers Cost Jobs

Ever since machines were first introduced someone, somewhere has opposed them. People who think that automation means lost jobs are known as *luddites*. But computers can't be the only cause of unemployment. There were many people out of work in the UK and elsewhere in the 1930s, before computers were invented.

Yet it seems apparent that not only can computers replace people but that they affect particular types of job and industry more than others. Hence the *pattern* of jobs is shifting. For example, *factory* shop-floor jobs are being replaced by robots and automated production lines (e.g. BL's Longbridge plant where the Metro is made), and *clerical* jobs are being superceded by office automation. Such jobs are usually unskilled, dull and repetitive, but do the people who lose them have alternatives? This may be largely to do with training (or re-training) for the right skills and occupations. Some countries are better at this than others and spend significantly more time and money re-training workers in the likely skills of tomorrow rather than subsidising the skills of the old declining industries. These decisions are often political.

Computing affects different industries in different ways. More than half of British manufacturers are now using micros in their products or production processes. But not every product lends itself to the incorporation of micros: whereas a car needs lots of devices to measure, monitor and control aspects of its performance, a tin of beans does not. Three industries in particular have been affected by micros in products: electrical, mechanical engineering and vehicles.

(b) Computers Create Jobs

Computers do create jobs both directly and indirectly.

Direct jobs include design, manufacture, sales and programming in the computer industry.

Indirect jobs result from the new, improved product applications of micro-electronics. Although fewer people may be needed to make these products, new or improved products should also win bigger sales.

More than 50% of the workforce is now involved in 'information occupations' compared with the declining numbers needed in manufacturing and agriculture. It seems that computer jobs often involve skilled, and therefore better-paid people, but that the jobs are fewer in number. It should be pointed out, however, that many computer jobs (e.g. data preparation, computer manufacturing) can be as boring as any other job, but many surveys have shown that people get more job satisfaction from computer-based jobs than the 'manual' equivalent (e.g. word-processor operators versus copy typists).

(c) Computers Change Jobs

Q. What happens when an organisation introduces computers?

A. Typically some new people are appointed in key posts (e.g. the information services manager) and this changes the power structure of the business (upsetting a lot of old bosses) and the methods of decision-making.

Other staff are often re-trained in 'computer skills' such as computer operators, programmers or data-preparation staff.

People leaving non-computer jobs are not always replaced (known as *natural* wastage) or they may take *voluntary redundancy* (e.g. early retirement). Either way will result in an overall decrease in the number of employees but the decrease may sometimes be offset by a growth in the company, perhaps due to the successful introduction of computers which leads to a more efficient operation and therefore increased sales and jobs.

Whichever view you take, many agree that greater unemployment would result if organisations don't seek to become more efficient and computerise and compete with other firms who are already innovating.

(i) *Trade Unions*

Trade unions' attitudes to computers vary enormously and are often quite ambivalent. They too fear that computers put people out of work, yet acknowledge that if the UK doesn't computerise, international competitors will win our markets, and therefore jobs, in any case. Indeed in the long term, computers, by contributing to improved efficiency and productivity, may actually boost the level of economic activity and therefore have a long-run benefit to jobs. Many computer personnel are trade-union members.

(ii) *Women and Computers*

One issue of concern is the fact that women tend to occupy the unskilled, badly paid jobs which, in computing, are typically data preparation or manufacturing activities. Why is it that it is predominantly men who get the interesting and well-paid jobs to design, sell and maintain computers? And why is it that more than 80% of people who sit GCSE Computer Studies are male?

13.3 Data Privacy

Q. What causes people to worry about the privacy of data stored in a computer system?

A. The issue of data privacy takes two forms:

- Fear of loss of privacy.
- Fear that data will be misused.

For every person worried about government or big business intrusion on privacy you can find another happy that his or her personal details will be locked up in a 'securable' computer rather than in the easily accessible filing cabinet of an equally anonymous official.

There is concern that personal information may be stored about you without your knowledge or control and that it may be hard, if not impossible, to check its accuracy.

Lots of personal data is already held on computers and more will follow.

13.4 Data Banks

Example 13.1

Give some examples of data banks.

Solution 13.1

A data bank is a collection of databases or large files of data.
For example, a vast amount of information is stored in government computers.

The Prison Index computer program contains the names of 300 000 people who have been in prison in the past 3 years. Many would have been on remand and subsequently acquitted in court — but ther names remain on the computer. The three biggest data banks, which would be most useful for tracing people, are the 51 million names on the social security computer (of whom 28 million are alive and living in Britain), the 32.8 million vehicle owners on both the Police National Computer and the Driver and Vehicle Licensing Centre computers, and the 18.6 million entries in the National TV Licence Records Office machine.

13.5 Data Security

Q. What controls should there be regarding data privacy?

A. There are some basic questions to answer:

- *How much* personal information should be kept?
- Who should have *access* to such information?
- How can *unauthorised access* be prevented?
- How can information given for one *purpose* be stopped from being used for another?

Much of the fear is about the amount of personal information kept irrespective of how it is stored — computer or otherwise. But most people think computers make it easier for someone to obtain confidential information about an individual illegally. At present, personal information is kept on different, unconnected computers; but would matters be worse if they were linked? In theory, all kinds of details of a person's life would then be instantly available. Certainly, information retrieval by computer is fast and efficient (this after all is one of the advantages of computers) but this doesn't mean that access should be easy for everyone, so security checks and controls can be applied.

Most countries have felt the need for laws to regulate the storage of information on computers. There should be:

- No secret personal files.
- Precautions taken against the abuse of information by governments or business agencies.

In particular:

- All information kept should be accurate. People should have the right to check and challenge any information held about them.
- Information collected and stored should be for a specific reason and no more.
- Information should be available only to legitimate people for legitimate purposes.

Q. Explain what is meant by data security.

A. Closely allied to data privacy is the notion of *data security* to prevent unauthorised access to information. Most computer systems have security checks and controls which include:

- *Physical measures* – Locks to rooms and machines, etc. Restrictions on the number of people allowed to use the computer (by using identity cards, etc.). Shredders to destroy output.
- *Access codes* – Passwords to gain access to information. These restrict the freedom of use of the machine and it is possible to have different levels of security clearance.
- *Audit trails* – To check on fraudulent activities by tracing transactions through the system.

However, 'computer-crime' – the theft or misuse of computer-based information – is a well-publicised issue. For example, employees have been known to switch funds to their own private accounts.

Part 2:   People in Computing

There are now many people involved in the design, manufacture and selling of computers and peripherals. In addition many organisations, particularly larger ones, have their own computer department.

13.6 Organisation of a Computer Department

Example 13.2

Draft the organisation chart for a typical computer department.
State any assumptions made.

Solution 13.2

See Fig. 13.1.

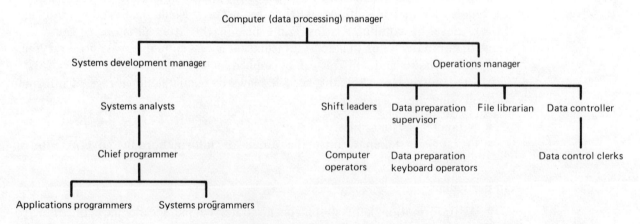

Figure 13.1 Organisation chart.

The number of people working in a computer department and what they do will depend on:

- The size of the computer and the amount of work done. Generally, larger computers are operated on a shift-work basis.
- The nature of the work.
  Complex operating systems allow both batch and on-line work together. More computer operators and data-preparation (prep) staff will be needed when there is a lot of batch work.
- How much of the software and maintenance is done 'in-house' rather than getting someone else to do them?

Assumptions: 9

- The department has about 40 staff.
- The computer is operated on a shift-work system, both on-line and there is batch work.
- The development work is based on a division of systems analysts and pro-gramming. Some software is written in-house.
- The nature and amount of work justifies having a systems and an operations manager. This is a natural split which separates the day-to-day operations from the development work. This decision is useful for security reasons also.

In smaller department it is much harder to define individual jobs as there is an overlap of duties.

13.7 Computer Managers

(a) The Computer (DP) Manager

Example 13.3

Describe briefly the work of the data processing manager in a large organisation.

Solution 13.3

The DP manager is responsible for the overall running of the department, and will usually report to the financial director of the company board. The DP manager will be in charge of:

- Data collection, preparation and control.
- Software – design and maintenance, purchase.
- Operations.
- Hardware – purchase and maintenace.

(i) *Duties*

In particular the DP manager will:

- Help to determine the long-term plans for the department. This will involve matters of policy such as equipment and software needs, etc. The manager must therefore keep up to date with new developments in computing.
- Co-ordinate with other departments to determine the computer work to be done.
- Liaise with 'outsiders', e.g. user groups, auditors.

- Set budgets and deadlines, i.e. plan, implement and control costs and times of the various jobs in the department and the department overall.
- Help to select and promote computer staff, allocate tasks and job responsibilities and chair staff meetings.

(b) The Systems Development and Operations Managers

Example 13.4

Describe briefly the work of (a) the systems development manager, and (b) the operations manager.

Solution 13.4

(a) *The systems development manager* will be in charge of the 'off-line' development, i.e. the study, analysis and design of better computer-based systems from which the organisation can benefit. The manager can also help in the implementation of any new system. He or she acts as a chief systems analyst (see below) and is responsible for co-ordinating the work of the analysts and programmers, assigning projects and tasks to them.

(b) *The operations manager* is responsible for the efficient day-to-day running of the computer operations and the operating staff.

(i) *Duties*

- Planning procedures, schedules and staff timetables, so that the various computer and programming jobs can be completed on time.
- Working out contingency plans to cope with emergencies.
- Supervising and co-ordinating:
  - Data collection, preparation and control.
  - Computer room operations.
- Liaising with the DP Manager and the systems development manager regarding:
  - Staff training or problems.
  - Improvements in work methods or equipment.

13.8 Systems Analysts and Programmers

(a) Systems Analysts

A systems analyst studies and analyses a system with a view to designing an improved computerised version. An analyst may also help to implement a new system that he or she has worked on.

This work will be carried out step-by-step. Approval to continue must be given at each step before more time and money is commited to development. This will ultimately be a board decision, although a computer steering committee (which includes the DP Manager) will monitor progress.

(i) *Duties*

- Define the objectives of a system.
- Carry out a feasibility study and write a feasibility report of a proposed new system stating:
  - Its hardware, software and personnel requirements.
  - Whether it is justifiable on economic, technical and social grounds.
- To study the existing system:
  - Seeing how it works.
  - Reading its documentation.
  - Interviewing manager and employees.
- Analyse the system to establish its strengths and weaknesses.
- Prepare a report describing the existing system:
  - Detailing existing resources — hardware, software and people.
  - Defining inputs and outputs.
  - Using flow charts and diagrams to help understanding.
- Design the new system. If the go-ahead is given the systems analyst can then design and help to implement the new system. Design includes:
  - Defining input, processing, storage and output methods.
  - Defining all manual procedures and documents.
  - Drawing up system flow charts and program specifications for the programmers to follow. This duty will be carried out with the chief programmer so that the program flow charts be prepared and the programming work allocated.
  - Providing documentation for the users of the new system.
- Help to implement the new system. The analyst may be involved in:
  - Designing test data and providing expected results.
  - Advising on the introduction of the new system:
    staff training;
    trial runs;
    change-over from the old to the new system.

(b) Computer Programmers

A programmer writes (codes) or amends programs. Usually a programmer will write a program from a program specification given by the systems analyst which states precisely what the program should do.

Sometimes programmers are involved with design and analysis work. Such people are called analyst/programmers and are to be found in smaller organisations.

Q. What are the main types of programmer?

A. There are two main types of programmer:

- A systems programmer is someone who writes the systems software. This requires a familiarity with a particular computer and its operating system. For speed and efficiency of hardware operation, systems programs are often written in low-level languages.
- Applications programmer is someone who writes program to carry out specific tasks (applications) for computer users, e.g. a sales analysis program for the marketing department of a company. This requires:
  - An understanding of the application.
  - The ability to program in high-level language.

(i) **Duties**

(See the programming task also)

- Discuss the program specification with the analyst.
- Write the source program.
- Test and debug it.
- Produce program documentation including program flow charts.
- Maintain programs by:
  - Correcting errors.
  - Making improvements.
  - Making modifications to allow for changing business methods (e.g. price increases) or new equipment.

NB: A large proportion of programmers' time is devoted to program maintenance.

Example 13.5

A data-processing department includes a programming team led by a *chief programmer*. State the activities which the chief programmer would perform which would not be performed by the rest of the team.

Solution 13.5

Many large computer departments have *chief programmers* (also known as *programming managers* or *senior programmers*).

(ii) **Duties of a chief programmer**

Their special activities include:

- Liaison with the DP and operations managers about general programming needs. For example:
  - Training for programmers.
  - Languages and equipment needed.
  - Staffing needs.
- Liaison with systems analysts about programs.
- Allocation and supervision of programming work (note top-down structured program development).

13.9 Computer Operating Staff

(a) Shift Leader (or Chief Operator)

Q. What are the special duties of a shift leader?

A. Special duties include:

- Scheduling work for the shift and telling the other operators what to do.
- Supervising the work.
- Ensuring a proper operations log is kept.
- Taking charge when problems arise.
- Liaising with the operatings manager about problems on the shift or possible improvements in work methods.

(b) Computer Operators

Q. List the jobs of a computer operator on a large system.

A. A computer operator controls and operates the hardware in the computer room.

(i) *Duties*

- Starting up equipment.
- Running programs.
- Loading peripherals with appropriate media:
  - Paper into printers.
  - Disks into disk drives.
  - Tapes into tape drives.
- Responding to messages on the operator's console, prompted by the operating system which monitors user requests and the status of the peripherals.
- Watching the progress of individual jobs and of the computer system in general.
- Dealing with faults where possible — otherwise reporting them.
- Carrying out cleaning and simple maintenance.
- Keeping a log of what happens — to supplement the log produced by the computer.

13.10 Data Preparation and Data Control Staff

(a) Data Preparation Staff

The duties of a data preparation supervisor and data preparation operators are outlined below.

(i) *Data Preparation Supervisor*

A data preparation supervisor is in charge of the data-preparation area and personnel.

1 Duties

- Allocating work to the keyboard operators.
- Checking on the quality of work produced.
- Liaising with the operations manager.
- Providing for training and assisting the operators.
- In minicomputer systems — operating the computer.

(ii) *Data Preparation Keyboard Operators*

A keyboard operator operates a key station to prepare data. The person may specialise in one type of data preparation device, e.g. key-to-disk station, or card punch.

1 Duties

- Correctly entering (keying-in) data from source documents and forms. This task is made easier by data-entry software which tells the operator what to do by a series of helpful messages.
- Keeping a record of data handled.
- Reporting problems with data or equipment to the supervisor.

(iii) *File Librarian*

A file librarian keeps all the files (e.g. tapes and disks) in a computer system organised and up to date.

1 Duties

- Keeping records of files and their use.
- Issuing files for authorised use.
- Storing files securely and preventing unauthorised use.
- Liaising with (usually) the data control supervisor or operations staff.

(b) Data Control Staff

(i) *Data Controller*

The data controller is responsible for the procedures in the collection and validation of input data.

1 Duties

- Supervising the data control clerks.
- Ensuring that the right data is processed in the right way.
- Liaising with the users to ensure that:
  - The quality of input data is acceptable for data preparation (e.g. forms are neatly and carefully filled in).
  - They are satisfied with output results.
- Keeping a record of work processed.
- Liaising with operating and preparation staff to ensure a steady flow of work.

(ii) *Data Control Clerks*

Data control clerks handle data as it enters or leaves the data production department.

1 Duties

- Accepting input data from users.
- Checking that jobs submitted are:
  - Authorised.
  - Complete.
- Ensuring that input data gets to the right place (operations or data preparation) at the right time.
- Ensuring that output is distributed correctly to users.

13.11 Computer Bureaux

Not all organisations have computers or computer departments.

Organisations may need computer facilities but for some reason cannot afford their own. Even where facilities exist, there still may be reasons for using external services, such as those provided by a bureau.

Example

Describe the range of services offered by a computer bureau.

Solution

Computer bureaux offer an independent source of computing facilities, both hardware and software, whose services may be hired to perform required jobs.

Computer bureaux vary greatly in the services that they offer, ranging from a specific service to a comprehensive set of facilities.

Such services include:

- Data preparation.
- Hiring out:
  - Computer time (time-sharing).
  - Specialist hardware, e.g. OCR devices.
- Providing program packages for common applications.
- Systems analysis, design and programming.
- Consultancy — advice and expertise.

Example 13.6

When might an organisation with its own computer facilities need the services of a bureau?

Solution 13.6

- At busy times or peak periods when the in-house facilities are over-stretched.
- For *ad-hoc* work or where specialist equipment is needed.
- To purchase applications software (custom or package).
- When there is no appropriate in-house expertise, e.g. a consultant may be called in to advise on a new computer system.

Example 13.7

List the major features which should be considered when choosing a computer bureau.

Solution 13.7

Check:

- The reputation of the bureau — who their clients are and how long they have used that bureau.
- The services provided.
- The contract terms — price, timing, etc.

13.12 Exercises

Question 13.1

State three considerations which might cause people to worry about the *privacy* of data stored in a computer system. Briefly describe two applications where either of these two considerations might be relevant. (L)

Question 13.2

State how a multi-access operating system could protect users' data from unauthorised access. (L)

Question 13.3

Distinguish between the *privacy* and *security* of information giving one example of how each may be achieved. (AEB)

Question 13.4

The introduction of a computer system by an organisation sometimes causes dissatisfaction among the staff. Some causes of this dissatisfaction are: boredom; frustration; loss of status; loss of job or career prospects; changes in patterns of work, e.g. different working hours.
- (a) Give an example of each of these causes of dissatisfaction from the computer applications which you have studied.
- (b) Describe actions by the management which could have lessened or removed some of the causes of dissatisfaction mentioned above. (L)

Question 13.5

'The increasing development of the use of *data banks* gives considerable cause for concern.'

- (a) Explain fully the term *data bank*.
- (b) Describe briefly three applications in which data banks are used.
- (c) Give three causes for concern shown about data banks, and suggest how they may be overcome. (AEB)

Question 13.6

A critic of the Police National Computer (PNC) has said, 'The Criminal Names Index contains 3.8 million names of people convicted of more serious offences. This index was based on the national Criminal Records Office files at Scotland Yard, but in the process of transferring to the PNC, these files grew from 2.2 million to 3.8 million names – the more serious offences not hitherto recorded nationally included petty thefts, wasting police time and offences under the Rent Acts. The Home Office and police whimsically call this suppressed demand information retrieval. It is known that when any car is seen in the vicinity of a casino, a suspect's house or a political demonstration, information on its owner can be easily added to the records of the PNC.'

- (a) Give three advantages to the police of having these records on a computer.
- (b) Give three advantages to the public of having these records on a computer.
- (c) Give two reasons why members of the public who are honest might be worried about some of the information recorded on the PNC. (AEB)

Question 13.7

List three duties of a: (a) systems analyst; (b) computer operator; (c) programmer.

13.13 Answers and Hints on Solutions

13.1 Three considerations.
People are worried about:

- *How much* information is kept about themselves.
- Who has *access* to this information.
- What this information is used for.

Two applications:

- Driver and Vehicle Licensing Centre (DVLC).
  This database has been used to find the most recent addresses of people avoiding tax payments.
- Prison Index.
  Contains names of people who have been in prison in the last three years. People who have been on remand and subsequently acquitted in court are on this index.

13.2 Password protection. A secret code must be given to the computer to gain access to the system or parts of it (e.g. a particular file). Different levels of access can be provided for. For further protection it is sensible to change passwords frequently.

13.3 *Privacy* of data is the recognition that certain data is private or confidential.
Security of data involves having safeguards to protect them from accidental or deliberate modification, destruction or disclosure.

13.4 (a)

- *Boredom* – Data preparation; key punching.
- *Frustration* – debugging a computer program.
- *Loss of status* – The computer manager is promoted above the office manager. Downgrading of a stock controller's job.
- *Loss of job or career prospects* – Factory automation; fewer production-line workers needed.
- *Changes in patterns of work* – Shift work; change in working hours.

13.4 (b) Overcoming dissatisfaction:

- Explain purpose of new computer system – benefits, etc.
- Involve workers in planning.
- Dispel redundancy fears – no cuts/planned voluntary redundancy/ natural wastage.
- Re-training in new skills.

13.5 (a) A data bank is a collection of databases or large files of data. A database is a collection of structured data independent of any particular application.
    (b) 1. Police National Computer – criminal records, fingerprints, stolen or suspect vehicles, vehicle owners.
    2. National TV Licence Records.
    3. Social Security (DHSS).

(c) 1. Misuse of information.
2. Who has access to it?
3. How much personal data is kept?

Controls to ensure:

1. Data stored is used for a specific purpose.
2. No unauthorised access.
3. No secret files.

13.6 (a) 1. Matching crimes to known criminals.
2. Prediction of time and place of certain crimes.
3. Planning the deployment of policemen and other resources.
(b) 1. More crimes solved and more quickly.
2. Crime deterrent.
3. Less costly operation of police service.
(c) 1. No control over holding of personal information.
2. Misuse of information (e.g. for political reasons).

13.7 (a) 1. Study the existing system and prepare a feasibility report.
2. Analyse the system and report on requirements.
3. Design a new system.
(b) 1. Running programs.
2. Responding to messages from the operating system.
3. Loading materials into peripherals (e.g. keeping printers supplied with paper.
(c) 1. Writing program.
2. Testing and debugging.
3. Writing program documentation.

14 Project Work

14.1 Introduction

All examinations in Computer Studies at the GCSE level incorporate a project (or projects).

Project work really is practical coursework and should demonstrate your ability to apply problem-solving skills with the use of a computer to the solution of practical problems.

Your project is important. It can count from 20% to 30% of the total marks (depending on the examination board) so it's work a lot of effort.

The work will usually be assessed by your teacher and moderated (i.e. checked and compared with other people's work for consistency of standards) by the examination board. Hence it is critical to keep your teacher happy.

It is worth while starting your work (or at least thinking about it) as early as possible in your course. Clearly it is good to get it out of the way so that you can concentrate on the exam itself. Holidays are a good time to research your topic.

14.2 What Project?

A project(s) need not be confined to one part of the syllabus.
Projects may include:

- Practical programming with accompanying documentation.
- Problem-solving using existing software.
- Simulation and modelling.
- Process control.
- Investigation and evaluation of computer use for a given application.

Check the details in your syllabus or with your teacher. Some boards require one major project, others three (or more) smaller ones.

As a rule-of-thumb, non-programming projects must be vigorous and analytical. It is no good writing an essay on some aspect of computer unless it includes a *critical appraisal* of the subject. Simply *describing* things will not please the examiner.

14.3 Some Hints to Help you Pass

(i) Planning for Success

- Look for project ideas in the many books and magazines available. Try to pick on a topic which you enjoy.

- Plan your work — allocate a time-slot for each week in which you will work on your project. Try to do it in blocks, e.g. in an afternoon; you will get more done.
- Work-in-progress. Arrange periodic meetings with your teacher. Be sure to keep your teacher informed at each stage. Don't pester him or her at every available opportunity. Show that you have a logical, planned workload and timetable. Any odd problems, e.g. syntax errors, can be dealt with in the meetings. If you rely *too* much on you teacher it is bound to affect your overall mark — so think the problem through for yourself before asking for help.
- Don't bite off more than you can chew. It is much better to do a relatively straightforward project which works rather than an over-ambitious one which fails because it is too complicated or you run out of time.

Good luck! Be imaginative, plan ahead and beat the deadline.

It's a great feeling to have a good piece of work (with marks that count towards the final assessment) behind you. You can enter the exam room in a more confident mood; but don't get over-confident — feeling slightly nervous will help you pass!

14.4 Programming Projects

(a) What Your Project Should Include

(i) *Project Title*

(ii) *Aims/Objectives*

- Summarise the purpose of the project, its scope and limitations.
- Write a paragraph on what your project is about, how you thought up the idea, and what you hope to achieve.

(iii) *Method(s) of Solution and Program Description*

- Say how you set about the task.
- Don't be afraid to mention the difficulties encountered and how you overcame (or avoided) them.
- Show how your solution developed in terms of, for example:
  - Outline structure charts and diagrams.
  - Flow charts.
  - Pseudocode.

These diagrams should show the logic and structure of your programs. Use correct English names and phrases, not BASIC statements in boxes.

(iv) *Program Listings*

- Include a program listing with embedded comments (REM statements) to explain each section. If helpful give notes by the side.

(v) *Data Description*

- List the use of identifiers and variables and explain the functions of each.

- Define any arrays, input strings, etc. used.
- Where files are used, explain their nature and structure, including records and fields.

(vi) *Testing*

- Show the test data used and why you picked it – aim to cover all the options (the different 'branches') of your program.
- Show your expected results (perhaps using a trace table) and compare them with the actual results of the computer run.

(vii) *Sample Runs*

Include two or three printouts of runs so that the examiner can SEE exactly what the program is doing and how the input/output data is presented. Use explanatory notes for the user and show any features of interest. Several runs should use a variety of data, including errors, to show how these are handled.

Pay particular attention to clear and easy-to-read layout.

(viii) *Documentation*

- Provides information for two types of person.
    - Another programmer who might have to amend your system.
    - The potential user who knows how to use the computer, but nothing about programming.
- A user-guide may be appropriate in some cases. This should include:
    - Title.
    - Table of contents.
    - Author.
    - Computer configuration required.
    - Input formats.
    - Data capture.
    - Output formats.
    - Operational instructions.
    It should be written in a non-technical way for the user.

In sum, the documentation should provide sufficient information for an external examiner to be able to assess the work.

(ix) *Summary*

- Assess the success of your system – did the project achieve its objectives?
- Say briefly what you think you've achieved, pointing out any shortcomings.
- Mention useful applications for your project.
- Suggest how you would improve and extend the system given more time (i.e. possible future developments).
- Thank your teacher(s), supervisor(s).
- Credit all sources, e.g. magazines, books, etc.

NB: There is nothing wrong with using an existing chunk of code – say an input/ validation routine or a sort routine – as long as you acknowledge it by noting its author and source (cf. quoting from a book). Such routines can often enhance your program and make it possible to solve realistic problems.

(b) Hints on Programming Projects

Get a friend (preferably one who isn't doing Computer Studies) to run your program:

- Was it easy to use?
- If not, why not?

It is always useful to have someone who hasn't been 'immersed' in the problem to try the program for you. For example, an instruction which was quite straightforward to you may be ambiguous or misleading to someone else. Such testing will make your system 'user-friendly'.

It is useful to develop your project in a modular fashion, i.e. break down the overall problem into a series of little problems, solve them, write the program segment and get it to work. You can join up the working bits later on. This has two benefits:

- You have at least something to show for your efforts.
- You can build on this base if you are progressing well.

This is a much nicer feeling than having to revise down your objectives on an over-ambitious program.

- Keep the program simple.
  Remember, although the examiner is a computer expert he may not be too familiar with the language (or dialect of BASIC) that you are using. So avoid clever tricks (particularly if they are machine specific) and do make your program self-documenting by including lots of explanatory comment in REM-type statements.
- Programming projects are as much about systems study, design, testing and documentation as they are about programming skills, so planning is important. Check through Chapters 9, 10 and 12 carefully.

14.5 Problem-solving Using Existing Software

Some examination boards allow you to use a package as part of your project because, after all, most people using computers use packages rather than writing programs themselves. The advantages and disadvantages of packages were outlined in Chapter 8.

What your project should include:

- A summary of the problem to be solved stating:
  - Who the user(s) is.
  - What the task(s) is.
  - What computer system you are using.
- Criteria for selection of the package:
  - How you found the package.
  - What research you did — packages investigated.
  - Why you decided on this package in particular (make sure you have your teacher's approval).
  - How data was collected.
    Include: any input forms you designed and checks on accuracy and error detection that you implemented.
- Provide hard copy evidence of output and critically assess the accuracy/ validity of the results.
- Provide, if appropriate, a user-guide. Quite often package documentation is

difficult to understand (even for the technically minded). If you can highlight any weaknesses you found in the documentation and the problems it caused, and better still, write your own user-guide, the examiner will approve. A thorough understanding of the program and clear, lucid English is all that you need!

- Finally, review the package stating its strengths and weaknesses:
  - How well did it meet the user's needs?
  - Was it entirely appropriate for your problem?
    If not, why not?

14.6 Case Studies

Some boards might require you to answer questions on a particular application, the details of which are issued prior to the examination. So it makes sense to work out *in advance*:

- The nature and need for inputs and outputs. Design carefully the format for input/output:
  - Inputs – forms design, etc.
  - Outputs – screen layouts, etc. To whom? How often? Media?
- Files:
  - Structure and content.
  - Write out a sample record.
- Decide on any coding which might be necessary.
- Hardware requirements:
  - Computer configuration.
  - Capabilities of each device – advantages and disadvantages
    (be prepared to make comparisons).
- Algorithms. It shouldn't be too difficult to spot the problems posed which arise from the system described. If you're asked to write an algorithm to solve one of the problems (or part of one):
  - Think about it.
  - Be brief (detailed code is not necessary).
  - Write in pseudocode or English unless instructed otherwise.
  - Draw a flow chart, if appropriate.

14.7 Worked Example — Case Study

A school has about 1200 pupils aged from 11 to 16 in year groups 1 to 5. Each year group is organised into eight classes each of about 30 pupils. All pupils study eight subjects and the school wishes to use its microcomputer to mark multiple choice tests in all subjects and to keep a record of the marks obtained by pupils.

The number of tests set varies from subject to subject and from year to year. The maximum number of tests for any pupil is 20 per subject per year. Tests can have any number of questions and any number of responses.

For any year group each test is marked by processing a transaction file and then merging it with the corresponding PUPIL file to produce the RESULTS LIST and an updated PUPIL file. Pupils are identified either by a six digit code or by their name depending on the nature of the processing required.

For each year group the following printouts are required:
RESULTS LISTS which give, for any particular test, a list, in descending order, of pupils and their marks;

PUPIL SUMMARIES, which contain the marks of all tests taken this academic year by any pupil or group of pupils in the same year group. A separate page of output is printed for each class. The pupil names are in alphabetical order and test results are grouped by subject description.

The school owns a microcomputer with 32 K eight bit bytes of usable RAM, keyboard, VDU and dual floppy disc drives with 256 Kbytes available on each disc. The computer's operating system allows only serial access to the disc files and it takes approximately 2 minutes to copy a disc. The VDU can display low-resolution graphics as well as characters and there is a 60cps printer for outputting results. There is a SORT program available which will sort any named file into order using any specified field as the sort key.   (L)

(a) Questions

1. For each test, the transaction file has an initial record, a variable number of answer records and a terminator record.

   The initial record has a 60-character field for a heading which will be printed at the top of the RESULTS LIST, and other fields which hold the details about the test, which are necessary to be able to update the corresponding PUPIL file.

   The answer records have a six-digit code followed by a single character for each answer. The first answer record contains the code 000000 and the correct answers for the test. The remaining records each contain a pupil's six digit code followed by the answers given by that pupil.

   The terminator record has the code 999999 and the remainder is blank.

   (a) Specify any additional fields which must be in the initial record. For each field, justify its type and length and why it is needed.   **(12 marks)**

   (b) State your reasons why the pupil code number is used as the key field rather than the pupil name.   **(8 marks)**

   (c) Design a set of PUPIL files, with a file for each year group, to support this system. Include in your answer:

      (i) details of file and record structures, justifying whether files, records, and fields are fixed or variable length;

      (ii) any coding schemes used to reduce storage requirements and any data structures needed to interpret these codes;

      (iii) a simple calculation which shows that it is unreasonable to attempt to create one PUPIL file for the whole school.   **(25 marks)**

2. (i) Describe the checks which would be used to validate the input data for a transaction file. Include in your answer an explanation of how the validation program would know how many questions there were in a particular test and how many pupils had attempted the test.   **(15 marks)**

   (ii) Describe an algorithm to update the PUPIL file records for a particular year group. Include in your answer an explanation of how the test results are assigned to the correct subject and test for each pupil.   **(15 marks)**

   (iii) Describe a detailed algorithm to produce PUPIL SUMMARIES for a batch of approximately 20 pupils in the same year group.   **(15 marks)**

3. A choice has to be made regarding the method to be used by the pupils to record their answers. The possibilities to be considered are either to write their answers on forms which will later be used as source documents for keyboard input, or to use some kind of machine-readable document, which could be a form or a card. Two available machine-readable systems are OMR and OCR. For OMR, the pupils would make marks in pre-determined and separate places for each possible answer. For the OCR system they would join up the appropriate dots in a matrix printed for each question.

   Discuss the relative merits of these three systems from:

      (i) the point of view of the pupil attempting the test,

      (ii) the person who is responsible for entering the data.

Pay particular attention to the importance of providing accurate data to the program which will mark the tests. **(10 marks)**

(b) Answers

1 (a)   File name: DISC 1 (for year 1). Additional fields in the *initial* record needed so that PUPIL file can be properly updated.

	Type – A/N	Length – No. of characters	
Subject	A	10	
Year group	N	1	1 to 5
Class	N	1	Up to 8
Date	N	6	< supplied by system?
Test number	N	2	Up to 20 tests

(b)   The key field is used to identify the record uniquely .
Pupil code numbers will be:

(i)   Unique (names can be duplicated, e.g. SMITH).
(ii)   Only six digits (some names are long and awkward to type in).
(iii)   Less prone to error (name can be easily misspelt).
(iv)   Probably used for classification.

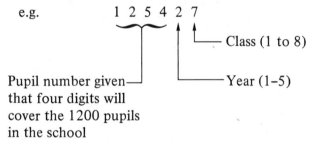

(c)   PUPIL files
(i)   Sample record:

Pupil code	N 6		1 2 3 4 5 6
Name	A 15		WILLIAMSON
First name	A 10		GRAHAM A
Subject 1 code	A 3		GEO
Test Marks	N 2		12
(1–20 tests)		Variable no. of fields	(maximum length 2 × 20 = 40 chs)
Subject 2 code	A 3		MAT
Test Marks	N 2		11
	etc.		
	;		
	;		
Subject 8	'		

Note: There may be other fields, e.g. addresses, telephone number, etc., but these are not directly needed for this problem.
(ii)   Subject codes, e.g. GEO = GEOGRAPHY (or number code).

(iii) Each PUPIL record is (approximately) 380 characters (ch) long (maximum).

- Name details + code ≃ 30
- Eight subjects: code + marks
  = 8 × (3 + 40) ≃ <u>350 ch</u>
  380 ch per record
- 380 ch × 30 pupils = 10 500 ch per class
  8 classes per year = 84 000 ch per year
  5 years = 420 000 ch for the school
  ≡ circa 420 Kbytes

(iii) According to the specification, there are only 256 Kbytes available on each floppy disk (although there are others which have bigger capacities) and so a single file for the whole school could not be held on one disk.

2 (i) *Validation checks*

Validation of the input data for a transaction file might include checks to see that the data is:

- Complete, e.g. control count on the number of pupils and the number of questions.
- Within the range of possible values, e.g. pupil code, mark total.
- The right type (e.g. numeric).
- The right format.

(ii) See Fig. 14.1.
(iii) See Fig. 14.2.

3 Relative merits of the three systems: keyboard input (from forms), OMR, OCR.

(i) From the point of view of the pupil attempting the test:

- Form-filling — easy to complete, student familiarity.
- OMR — placing marks in predetermined places, relatively straightforward but documents may be large, difficult to understand.
- OCR — may involve careful tracing — joining up the dots.

(ii) The person responsible for entering the data:

- Keyboard input will be time consuming and may lead to many transcription errors. Problems of inaccuracy.
- 'Direct' input may therefore be preferable for handling large volumes of numbers but:
  - OMR — The OMR reader will have to be programmed for each new document design (inflexible).
    Verification is difficult.
  - OCR — There are more recognition failures (i.e. a higher rejection rate). OCR readers are expensive.

14.8 Ideas for Projects

(a) Topics in the School/College

- Sports day — competitor lists and results lists.

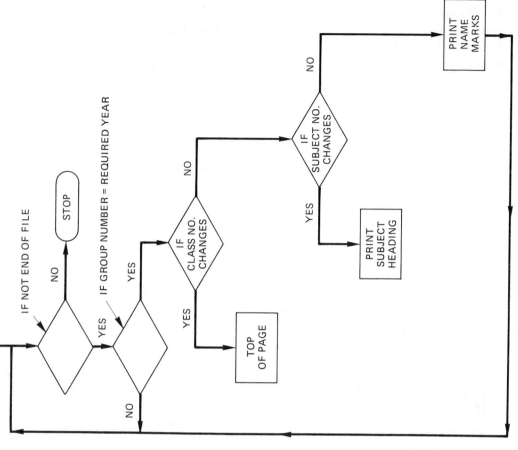

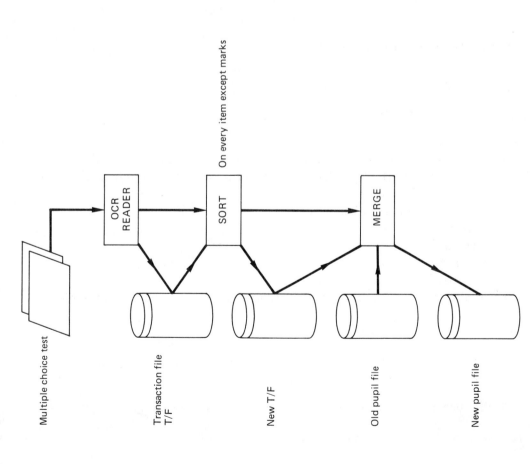

Figure 14.2 Solution 14.2(iii). Flow chart to produce PUPIL SUM-MARIES. The pupil file should be sorted by:

- Group number. Within group number sort by class number.
- Within class number sort by name.

For each pupil sort by subject number/name. Within subject number/name sort by test number.

Figure 14.1 Solution 14.2(ii). Flow chart to update PUPIL file. Record layout: 1–1200 1–5 1–8. Name, subject number, test number, marks. The merge algorithm would have tests for subject number and test number to assign the test results correctly.

289

- League tables — soccer, netball, etc.
- Timetables.
- Tuck shop — stock control, sales and invoice routines.
- Class lists and marks.
- Teaching programs — maths, spelling aids, foreign language translators.

(b) Small Business

For students interested in business studies: you may have friends/relatives who run a small business, some aspect of which (e.g. stock control, sales invoicing) you could write a program for:

- Newsagent.
- General store.
- Doctor/dentist.
- Solicitor.
- Accountant.

(c) Simulation and Modelling

For students interested in mathematics, science and engineering:

- Statistical surveys.
- Heuristic programs.
- Maths and science applications.
- Process control.

(c) More Detailed Ideas for Projects

(i) *Computerised running*

Imagine that you are organising a road race (say a marathon or half marathon) for charity.

- Design an entry form which can be used as data input to a RUNNERS file.
  NB: It is important to consider the nature of the data you wish to keep.
  Create 10–20 sample records.
  Write a program(s) which allows the user to:
  - INSERT.
  - DELETE.
  - AMEND.
  - UPDATE a runner record.
- Produce a list of runners in alphabetical and/or club order. For example:

Name	Running No.	Club	Category
Doug Taylor	1234	Humber Bridge	M60 (male over 60)
Hannah Whitehead	666	Unattached	F

- Produce a results list of runners in time order. For example:

Position	Name	Club	Time	Category
1	Reg Bridport	Ealing	1:10:07	M

Remember the importance of:

- Good documentation.
- A workable program.

(ii) *Supermarket*

A supermarket has decided that it will use point-of-sale (POS) terminals on each shop site. A bar-coded label will be attached to each item on the shelves. When a customer takes these items to the check-out, a reader will read the label on the goods and the customer's receipt will be printed at the till automatically. A further advantage is that the stock records of this item can be adjusted at the time that goods are purchased.

Your project is to take the form of a program to simulate these activities. The way in which you complete this work is left to your discretion although for guidance the following scheme is suggested:

- Your program should hold data relating to prices and stock levels in the form of DATA statements. A small representative number of items should be used.
- Your program should allow you to enter the number shown by the bar-coded label at your terminal, as if you were the reader. Produce the customer's itemised receipt at the conclusion of the entry.
- Alternative entries may be made in the program to report on current stock levels and stock usage during the period that the program is in use.

You should submit a program listing and sample run showing:

- Inputs to the bar-code reader and printout of the customer's receipt.
- A report on stock levels and stock usage in the period.

Brief comments on the use of the program should be provided which would assist the user of your system.

(With acknowledgements to Phil Jones.)

Index